MICHIGAN'S ECONOMIC FUTURE

MICHIGAN'S ECONOMIC FUTURE

A NEW LOOK

CHARLES L. BALLARD

Michigan State University Press · East Lansing

⊜ The paper used in this publication meets the minimum requirements of
ANSI/NISO Z39.48-1992 (R 1997) (Permanence of Paper).

Michigan State University Press
East Lansing, Michigan 48823-5245

Printed and bound in the United States of America.

17 16 15 14 13 12 11 10   1 2 3 4 5 6 7 8

LIBRARY OF CONGRESS CATALOGING-IN-PUBLICATION DATA

Ballard, Charles L.
    Michigan's economic future : a new look / Charles L. Ballard.
       p. cm.
    Includes bibliographical references and index.
    ISBN 978-0-87013-993-2 (pbk. : alk. paper)
    1. Michigan-Economic conditions-21st century. 2. Michigan-Economic policy-21st
century. 3. Economic forecasting-Michigan. I. Title.
    HC107.M5B347 2010
    330.9774–dc22   2010036615

Book and cover design by Charlie Sharp, Sharp Des!gns, Lansing, Mich.

g green
  press   Michigan State University Press is a member of the Green Press Initiative
  INITIATIVE and is committed to developing and encouraging ecologically responsible
publishing practices. For more information about the Green Press Initiative and the use of
recycled paper in book publishing, please visit www.greenpressinitiative.org.

Visit Michigan State University Press on the World Wide Web at:
www.msupress.msu.edu

For June

Contents

Acknowledgments

I was one of the editors of *Michigan at the Millennium: A Benchmark and Analysis of Its Fiscal and Economic Structure*, a volume of research papers on the Michigan economy.[1] About a year after *Michigan at the Millennium* was published in 2003, Michigan State University president Lou Anna Simon expressed a desire for a shorter book about Michigan's economy. The result was *Michigan's Economic Future: Challenges and Opportunities*, published in 2006. Michigan's economy has gone through momentous changes since then, and I am pleased to be able to write this new book. My first debt of gratitude is to President Simon, without whose support neither of these books would have been possible.

If I had not worked on *Michigan at the Millennium*, I would not have been in a position to write *Michigan's Economic Future: Challenges and Opportunities*. Thus I also want to thank my colleague John Goddeeris. Professor Goddeeris was chair of MSU's Department of Economics from 1996 to 2001, and it was he who asked me to be one of the editors of *Michigan at the Millennium*.

I would also like to give a very special thanks to Julie Loehr of the Michigan State University Press, who has worked with me through the development of all three of these books.

---

1. Charles L. Ballard, Paul N. Courant, Douglas C. Drake, Ronald C. Fisher, and Elisabeth R. Gerber, eds., *Michigan at the Millennium: A Benchmark and Analysis of Its Fiscal and Economic Structure* (East Lansing, MI: Michigan State University Press, 2003).

In my 2006 book, I thanked dozens of others. If I thanked you then, please accept my thanks once more.

Michigan's Economic Future: Challenges and Opportunities succeeded beyond my expectations. On many occasions, readers have asked me to speak to their organizations. This has led to more than one hundred and sixty speak ing engagements, with groups as varied as the Baker College of Flint, the Catholic Caucus of Southeast Michigan, Grand Rapids Public Schools, Jackson Citizens for Economic Growth, Lutheran Social Services of Michigan, the Michigan AFL-CIO, Michigan School Business Officials, the Midland Area Chamber of Commerce, Northern Michigan University, and the North Oakland Republican Club.

It has been fun and enlightening to share ideas with so many of Michigan's people. Space constraints do not permit me to give an individual thank you to each of the hundreds of people who have helped to sharpen my understanding of Michigan's economy and political system in the years since my earlier book was published in 2006. If you are one of the many people with whom I have had a fruitful conversation and I don't mention you specifically, I hope you will accept my thanks and my apologies. Nevertheless, I cannot refrain from offering a special thanks to the following folks, all of whom have offered valuable insights: Chris Ahlin, John Amrhein, Bill Anderson, Patrick Anderson, Chris Andrews, David Andrews, Gale Arent, Barb Arrigo, David Arsen, John Austin, Tom Baldini, Ben Baldus, Jeff Barnes, Tim Bartik, Amy Baumer, Mitch Bean, John Bebow, Frank Beckmann, Jan Beecher, Jeff Biddle, Mike Boulus, Candace Burns, Richard Burr, Dianne Byrum, Patrick Center, Dave Chapin, Chris Christoff, Nick Ciaramitaro, Tom Clay, Rob Collier, Mike Conlin, John Cote, Paul Courant, Darren Cunningham, John Czarnecki, Bob Daddow, Tim Daman, Scott Darragh, Rob Davidek, Scott Davis, Susan Demas, Stacy Dickert-Conlin, Jennifer Dowling, Doug Drake, Ron Dzwonkowski, Jack Ebling, Peter Eckstein, Jamie Edmonds, Todd Elder, Ann Emmerich, George Erickcek, Andrew Farmer, Dale Fickle, Mark Fisk, Mike Flanagan, Rob Fowler, George Fulton, Nicole Funari, Mark Gaffney, John Gallagher, Liz Gerber, Lou Glazer, John Goddeeris, Allen Goodman, Tom Goodwin, Paul Graveline, Don Grimes, Jeff Guilfoyle, Mark Haas, Rick Haglund, Steven Haider, Pat Harrington, David Haynes, Neal Hegarty, Howard Heideman, Steve Henderson, Alison Himelhoch, Jim Hines, Kathy Barks Hoffman, Karen Holcomb-Merrill, Dave Hollister, Ray Holman, Mark Hornbeck, Jan Hudson, Bob Hughes, Sarah Hulett, Saul Hymans, Azlan

Ibrahim, Tom Ivacko, Brian Jacob, Lynn Jondahl, Jack Jordan, Dale Kildee, Dan Kildee, Tricia Kinley, Stephanie Kolp, Cindy Kyle, Claire Layman, Jack Lessenberry, John Lindstrom, Scott Loveridge, Peter Luke, Brian Lund, Terance Lunger, Eric Lupher, David Martell, Larry Martin, Tim Martin, Sean McAlinden, Jack McHugh, Derek Melot, Benita Melton, Paul Menchik, Steve Miller, Jack Minore, Larry Molnar, David Morris, Mark Murray, Charity Nebbe, Meghan Norman, Gary Olson, Leslie Papke, Sharon Parks, Doug Paterson, Cynthia Paul, Rick Pluta, Bernie Porn, Phil Power, Doug Pratt, Peter Pratt, Deb Price, Judy Putnam, Doug Roberts, Rich Robinson, Alex Rosaen, Peter Ross, Doug Rothwell, Craig Ruff, Bill Rustem, Gary Sands, Kurt Schindler, Andrea Schroeder, Patrick Schuh, Eric Scorsone, Tom Scott, Joan Sergent, Michael Patrick Shiels, Nancy Short, Scott Shrager, the late Mike Simpson, Mark Skidmore, Tim Skubick, Joel Slemrod, Paul W. Smith, Walt Sorg, Don Sovey, David Sowerby, Amanda Stitt, Chuck Stokes, Rich Studley, Kathryn Summers, Bob Swanson, Craig Thiel, Phil Thompson, Susan Tompor, Jan Urban-Lurain, Bob Van Dellen, Dave Waymire, Steve Webster, Arnold Weinfeld, Bill White, Tom White, Cynthia Wilbanks, Jeff Williams, Jeff Wooldridge, Jay Wortley, Mark Wyckoff, Jennifer Youssef, Lauren Zakalis, Jane Zehnder-Merrell, and David Zin.

About a year after my earlier book was published, I met with Doug Roberts, the former treasurer of the State of Michigan who currently serves as director of Michigan State University's Institute for Public Policy and Social Research (IPPSR). Dr. Roberts asked me to become the director of the State of the State Survey (SOSS), a quarterly public-opinion survey of Michigan residents. I am grateful to Dr. Roberts for providing me with this opportunity. As the director of SOSS, I have gained a better understanding of the opinions and attitudes of Michigan's people at a critical time in the economic life of the state. The things I have learned from them are reflected in the findings from SOSS that are reported here. I am grateful to all the members of the IPPSR staff whose hard work has helped to make SOSS a success. My thanks go to Larry Hembroff, director of IPPSR's Office for Survey Research (OSR) and one of the founders of SOSS. Karen Clark, Senior Project Manager and Web Survey Coordinator for OSR, deserves a very special thanks for her work as a SOSS project manager. My thanks also go to Jill Hardy, another project manager who has often lent her expertise to SOSS. I also thank Linda Stork, director of survey operations for OSR; Cindy Kyle, who handles communications and publicity for IPPSR; AnnMarie Schneider, who directs the Michigan

Applied Public Policy Research Grants program and the IPPSR forums; and John Schwarz, who provides hardware and software support. Finally, I thank IPPSR staffers Katherine Cusick, Debra Rusz, Milly Shiraev, and Iris Taylor.

I am very grateful to the many current and former students at Michigan State University who have provided valuable research assistance. Thanks to Adam Cogswell, Deborah Foster, Michael Gallagher, Alyssa Hazelwood, Tim Hodge, Michael Leonard, Krish Mehta, Monthien Satimanon, Colin Tolmie, and Haogen Yao.

All of these people deserve some of the credit for this book. Any errors are my responsibility alone.

And finally, I would like to thank the most special people of all: Anne, Mark, and Scott; Mary Fran and Don; Andy, and June, with all my love.

Introduction

In 2003, the Michigan State University Press published *Michigan at the Millennium: A Benchmark and Analysis of Its Fiscal and Economic Structure.*[1] It was an honor for me to serve as one of the editors of this landmark work, which was sponsored by Michigan State University, the University of Michigan, and Wayne State University, with additional financial support from the Charles Stewart Mott Foundation. It includes thirty-three chapters covering nearly every aspect of economic life in Michigan. Because of its exhaustive coverage, *Michigan at the Millennium* is an essential reference work for anyone who wants to gain a highly detailed, in-depth understanding of the Michigan economy.

However, there is a downside to this level of detail: *Michigan at the Millennium* is more than seven-hundred pages long. In an attempt to provide a shorter and more accessible discussion of the critical economic issues facing us in Michigan, I wrote *Michigan's Economic Future: Challenges and Opportunities*, which was published in 2006. The subsequent four years have been among the most turbulent in the history of the Michigan economy. Thus the time has come for this new book, to amplify the themes of the first edition and analyze the momentous changes that have taken place in the last few years.

Some Key Themes of This Book

This introduction will set the stage by briefly discussing a few issues and ideas of central importance in this work.

The Decline of Manufacturing

In the late nineteenth century, much of Michigan's economy was agricultural, but massive changes were under way. There was an opportunity to create a more prosperous future in an economy based on manufacturing. Visionaries like Henry Ford, Herbert Dow, W. K. Kellogg, R. E. Olds, and W. E. Upjohn helped to turn that opportunity into reality for Michigan. By the middle of the twentieth century, Michigan was an industrial powerhouse whose economy was the envy of the world. Millions flocked to Michigan to work in the automobile plants and other manufacturing facilities.

However, manufacturing's share of the economy has been shrinking for more than half a century both in Michigan and in the rest of the United States. This long transition has been more painful for Michigan than for most states because manufacturing was (and still is) a much larger portion of the economy in Michigan than in the average state. In a sense, Michigan has become a victim of its own success. Few regions, if any, were more successful than Michigan in riding the wave of manufacturing, and this made the transition out of manufacturing more difficult for Michigan than for most other states.

For the foreseeable future, manufacturing will certainly continue to be an important part of Michigan's economy. But all the evidence suggests that a more diversified economy is crucial if Michigan is to achieve a more prosperous future. If we in Michigan are to realize our economic potential in the coming decades, we will need to focus more on the skill-intensive, knowledge-driven sectors of the economy.

When I wrote my earlier book in 2005 and 2006, the U.S. economy was expanding, but Michigan's economy was basically flat. We in Michigan weren't losing a lot of ground, but we weren't gaining much either. By December 2007, however, the U.S. economy had sunk into a recession.[2] For the first eight months of 2008, the national recession was fairly mild, but then in September 2008, the Lehman Brothers investment bank collapsed. Credit markets froze up to a degree not seen since the Great Depression of the 1930s. From then until the summer of 2009, the national economy was in free fall, and

Michigan's manufacturing economy was hit especially hard. As a result, the unthinkable became a reality: both General Motors and Chrysler went into bankruptcy in 2009.

In the pages to come, I will describe this devastating recession in more detail, and I will offer some thoughts about what we can learn from it. In addition, I will take a more detailed look at the decline of manufacturing, with particular emphasis on the struggles of the automotive industry. And I will identify some of the sectors of the Michigan economy that can propel future economic growth.

The Widening Gap between Rich and Poor

The American economy enjoyed tremendous success from the end of the Second World War to the mid-1970s, and Michigan's economy was an important part of that success. The economy grew rapidly, and the gains were shared throughout the population. Incomes grew for those at the bottom and middle of the economic ladder, as well as for those at the top.

Since about 1975, however, the distribution of income has become increasingly unequal.[3] The top 20 percent of households have done very well, and the top 5 percent have done even better. At the very top of the scale, the incomes of the top one-hundredth of a percent have grown with astonishing speed, to levels never before seen in human history.[4] On the other hand, incomes have grown much more slowly, if at all, for those in the middle and at the bottom of the economic scale. The labor-market earnings of college-educated workers have surged ahead, while the earnings of those with only a high school diploma have stagnated, and the earnings of high school dropouts have plummeted.

There are many reasons for the widening gap between those at the top and those at the bottom. However, it appears that a very important cause is an increase in employers' demand for highly skilled and highly educated workers. Changes in technology have tended to favor workers who have high levels of education and training.

The Crucial Role of Highly Skilled Workers

It was once perfectly sensible for young Michigan residents to say, "I'll get one of those high-paying factory jobs, so I don't need a college education." However, for the vast majority of today's young people, the old days are gone and they are not coming back. If today's young people are to compete effectively in the global marketplace, they must have strong skills. Unfortunately, Michigan lags behind the rest of the country in its percentage of the population with a college education, and Michigan is also below the national average in other indicators of educational attainment.

It is especially unfortunate that much of the Michigan public appears to be in denial about the problem. Michigan's public policies toward education would seem to indicate that the general public is becoming *less* interested in providing people with the skills that will be required in the economy of the future. Michigan's budget for higher education has been slashed repeatedly in recent years. The State of Michigan supports fifteen four-year universities, and budget cuts have been spread across all fifteen. The total size of the budget cuts (after adjusting for inflation) is equivalent to the *complete elimination* of state support for Eastern Michigan, Ferris State, Grand Valley State, Lake Superior State, Michigan Tech, Northern Michigan, Oakland University, Saginaw Valley State, University of Michigan–Dearborn, and University of Michigan–Flint, along with a major reduction in support for Central Michigan.[5] I am *not* advocating that we close two-thirds of Michigan's universities. I am merely trying to dramatize the magnitude of the reduction in support for education.[6]

Fortunately, however, many of Michigan's citizens do recognize the importance of higher education. These issues are discussed eloquently in the report of the Lieutenant Governor's Commission on Higher Education and Economic Growth (also known as the Cherry Commission), which was issued in December 2004.[7] These ideas will be discussed in more detail in Chapter 2. For now, I quote a key passage from the Cherry Commission Report: "Michigan's residents, businesses, and governments can either move forward to a future of prosperity and growth fueled by the knowledge and skills of the nation's best-educated population, or they can drift backward to a future characterized by ever-diminishing economic opportunity, decaying cities, and population flight—a stagnant backwater in a dynamic world economy."

In this book, I will make the case for an enhanced commitment to education. The details of this argument are mostly in Chapter 2. I would like to emphasize that I am *not* referring only to four-year universities. I have been on the faculty at Michigan State University for twenty-seven years, so *of course* I believe in higher education. But higher education is only one part of the picture. In Michigan, we are underinvested in education from preschool to PhD, from cradle to career.

We need to start at the very beginning, with prenatal care, early-childhood education, and solid instruction in elementary school. We need to decrease the number of high school dropouts. We need to make sure that those who receive a high school diploma have truly received a high school education. And we need to increase the number of students who go on to some sort of additional education or training, which could take the form of job-skills training, community college, or study at a four-year college or university.

How Do We Pay for Increased Investments in Education?

The case for increasing the skills of the Michigan population is absolutely compelling. If we are to make progress in strengthening our skills, it will take more resources. We will need more and better classrooms, more and better laboratories, more and better computers, more and better teachers, and so on.

If we are to increase our investment in education, how will we pay for it? One option is to increase the efficiency with which we provide education. Indeed, a lot of savings have already been realized: Many school districts have saved money by reducing, sharing, privatizing, or eliminating services. Universities have also reduced or eliminated programs. These cost-cutting trends are likely to continue. However, I honestly do not see how we can provide the kind of education that our children deserve unless we devote more money to education. This, in turn, will necessitate some changes in the state budget. We can either reduce spending on the noneducational activities of government, or we can increase the total amount of resources available for public services.

It may be possible to make some spending cuts elsewhere in the budget. However, unless we make truly massive reductions in the rest of the budget, they are unlikely to be large enough to make room for the necessary amount of educational investment. Note that many of the services provided by state and local governments in Michigan have already gone through very large reductions in recent years. Thus it will be very difficult to provide the educational system that our children deserve, unless we provide some increased tax revenues.

A few years ago, I was discussing some of these issues in an undergraduate classroom. I explained that I could not see any way to do what needs to be done without additional resources. One of my students asked, "So you're saying we should spend more on education, and we should raise taxes to pay for it?" The answer is yes. The student then said that such a strategy would be political suicide.

I have thought a lot about that conversation, especially about "political suicide." Undoubtedly, there is fierce political opposition to devoting additional resources to education and other public services. But if it really is political suicide to do what needs to be done for the future of Michigan's economy, then we are dead already.

The Weaknesses of Michigan's Tax System

I will discuss Michigan's state and local tax systems in detail in Chapter 6. For now, here are a few basic points about taxes in Michigan.

The tax system in Michigan is slowly being eaten away, like a house full of termites. Because of structural flaws in the taxes used in Michigan, the system is losing more and more revenue every day, even when there are no changes in the tax laws. As we shall see in Chapter 6, the termites are at work in *all* the major taxes in Michigan, including the sales tax; the income tax; the property tax; and the taxes on beer, wine, tobacco products, and motor fuels. One example of such a flaw involves the Michigan sales tax. Most services and entertainments are not subject to Michigan's sales tax, even though services and entertainments have been growing more rapidly than the things that are subject to the sales tax. In other words, the sales tax applies to an ever-shrinking portion of the economy. Thus recent revenue losses are *not* just the result of the recession. The Michigan economy is slightly smaller than it was a few years ago, but tax revenues have shrunk *far* more rapidly than the economy.

As a result of these flaws, the overall level of tax revenues has decreased substantially in recent years. If we take all state and local taxes paid in Michigan and express them as a percentage of the total income received by Michigan's people, the percentage is now at its lowest level in decades. If that percentage were to return to the levels of only a few years ago, *billions* of dollars per year in additional revenues would be available for schools, roads, and other public services. Revenues have fallen so rapidly that it is difficult to give a precise estimate of how much revenue has been lost. The most complete data on state and local revenues are from the U.S. Census Bureau's Census of Governments.[8] The Census of Governments has only been updated through 2007, since it takes time for the Census Bureau to collect revenue data from all the counties, cities, townships, villages, school districts, and special districts. However, the State of Michigan estimates that state revenues as a percentage of the state economy have fallen by more than $9 *billion per year* when compared with their levels in the year 2000.

Thus when I say we need more revenues, I am *not* calling for taxes in Michigan to rise to unprecedented levels. Instead, I am calling for an end to the drastic decreases of recent years and a return to something closer to a level of taxation under which Michigan residents have prospered in the past. In a sense, I am not calling for tax increases at all. I am calling for a reversal of some of the massive tax cuts that have shriveled public services in Michigan in recent decades.

Michigan has a regressive tax system. A regressive tax system is one that takes a higher percentage from low-income residents than from those with high incomes. There are several reasons for this, including the fact that Michigan's income tax has a single flat rate on all taxable income, in contrast to the graduated-rate systems that are used in most other states.

Thus we are faced with a great irony. As mentioned earlier, the distribution of income has become more and more unequal during the last thirty-five years. Many of those with the highest incomes have become even more affluent, while many of those with the lowest incomes have suffered a declining standard of living. At the same time, the fortunate folks at the top pay a relatively small share of the taxes in Michigan. The ability to pay taxes has become increasingly concentrated at the top of the income scale, but those at the bottom are forced to bear a disproportionate share of the tax burden.

For these reasons, I say that the *income tax* should play a prominent role in fixing the structural budget deficits that have plagued the State of Michigan in recent years. Of course, the income tax does not have to be the only solution to the budgetary problems. (In Chapter 6, I will discuss reforms to a wide variety of additional revenue sources, including the dilapidated sales tax.) But unlike other taxes, the income tax is the only source of revenue that is deliberately designed with the idea of taxing people according to their ability to pay. In view of the increased level of inequality, it is common sense and common decency to ask those at the top of the income scale to pay their share.

I do not make this recommendation lightly. First of all, let's face it: *nobody* enjoys paying taxes, myself included. Also, much of my research career has been devoted to thinking about the negative effects of taxes on the economy.[9]

Taxes can cause people to reduce their work effort, reduce their savings and investment, or make other undesirable changes in their behavior. These changes in behavior impose real costs on society. However, it is important to keep these costs in perspective. The goal of fiscal policy is not to eliminate taxes. Rather, the goal is to find the correct balance between the benefits of public services and the costs of the taxes that are used to finance them. In the Michigan economy of today, the benefits of educational investments are enormous. The people of Michigan also reap tremendous benefits from many other public services, including transportation infrastructure, police and fire protection, and many more. In my judgment, these benefits are large enough to justify an increased investment in education and other public services, even though it will be necessary to pay for them.

A Perspective on Policy Analysis and Values

Much of this book is devoted to setting out the facts about the Michigan economy. Much of the information concerning the economic reality of Michigan is misunderstood by the general public and elected officials, which sometimes causes policy decisions to be based on misinformation and myth. I try to set out these facts in a way that is as objective as possible. In addition to the facts, I also offer a number of personal opinions and policy recommendations. These are my own views, and they do not necessarily represent the views of Michigan State University, the MSU Department of Economics, the Institute for Public Policy and Social Research, or any of my coauthors, coeditors, or other collaborators.

Even though I strive to be objective, my *values* (or, if you prefer, my morals or ethics) will inevitably come through. Thus from the very beginning, let me be clear about my perspective. My approach to public policies can be summarized by the title of a book by the Princeton University economist Alan Blinder. The book is called *Hard Heads, Soft Hearts*.[10] Most economists (including me) are fairly hard-headed. We spend a lot of our time dealing with hard economic realities, and we do not like wasteful or inefficient policies. On the other hand, many economists (myself included) are soft-hearted, in that we care about the less fortunate among us. The distribution of income has become dramatically more unequal in the last third of a century, and this trend is very troublesome to me. For a generation, incomes have stagnated for those in the middle and at the bottom. I believe we should adopt policies to ease the plight of these people, and not just to help those at the top. I believe we should have a social safety net that protects children; people who are elderly, disabled, or sick; and others who need help.

In this book, I will be both hard-headed and soft-hearted. In so doing, I will say some things that are controversial. In particular, I expect that some of my statements will be more hard-headed than some readers would like, and I also expect that some of my statements will be more soft-hearted than other readers would like. But in the end, I hope to challenge people from all across the political spectrum to take a fresh look at where Michigan is going.

In writing this book, one of my goals has been to make it accessible to a wide audience. Thus I have tried to keep the book reasonably short. In so doing, I have had to make choices about what to emphasize and what not to emphasize. All of these choices are affected by my values. Inevitably, it has been necessary to devote relatively little space to some important topics. That's why I have included many references to other sources of information about the Michigan economy. Even with these references, I acknowledge that this book is only a starting point, and not a complete encyclopedia.

What's to Come?

Half a century ago, the world was knocking on Michigan's door. The 1950s were a great time for the Michigan economy, and we should all be proud of that success. But yesterday is gone, and it is not coming back. If the people of Michigan are to achieve a brighter economic future, we will need to develop new ways of thinking and new ways of engaging with the rapidly changing global economy.

Policy discussions in Michigan often have a tinge of nostalgia for the economy of the 1950s and 1960s. It is time to shed those attitudes and replace them with a new set of attitudes—creative, highly skilled, flexible, and entrepreneurial. If we can make the transition to a new mind-set, we really can achieve a vibrant future for Michigan. With these ideas in mind, the following is the plan for the rest of this book.

Chapter 1. In this chapter, I describe the overall structure of the Michigan economy. I take a longer look at the growth and shrinkage of various industries as well as the trends in employment and income. I also stress the importance of Michigan's economic connections with the rest of the United States.

Chapter 2. In this chapter, I focus on human resources. In particular, I look at Michigan's population, workforce, and educational system. I have already stressed the importance of education and training, and I elaborate on those ideas in Chapter 2. This chapter is the longest in this book for good reason. Nothing is more important to Michigan's future than our human resources.

Chapter 3. In this chapter, I examine Michigan's physical resources with special emphasis on environment, land use, and transportation. Much of Michigan's road system is in bad shape, and there is evidence that we could do a much better job of providing for surface transportation than we do now. One of the biggest issues facing Michigan is how to preserve open space, and I will discuss this in Chapter 3. Chapter 3 also includes a discussion of Michigan's water resources.

Chapter 4. In this chapter, I discuss Michigan's role in the world economy. I will cover international trade, international investment, and immigration. America's top trading partner is Canada, and the top gateway to Canada is Michigan. Consequently, this discussion focuses more on Canada than on any other country. However, since the entire world economy is becoming more and more intertwined, I will also discuss Michigan's relationships with other countries.

Chapter 5. In Chapter 5, I consider some issues of public expenditure and public policy that have not been emphasized in the earlier chapters. These include corrections, health care, and income-maintenance programs.

Chapter 6. In this chapter, I discuss the tax system in Michigan. I have already argued that the income tax has an especially important role to play in our economic future, but I also discuss reforms of the sales tax and several other revenue sources. The Michigan Business Tax (MBT) is a perennial source of controversy, and I discuss the possibilities for reform or elimination of the MBT.

Chapter 7. In this concluding chapter, I ask what the Michigan economy will look like in twenty years. I firmly believe that we can have a much brighter future, both in terms of the economy and in other ways. We have so many assets, including hard-working people, great colleges and universities, one-fifth of the world's fresh water, and a beautiful landscape. However, to get to that brighter future, we will have to do things differently. Many of the most important changes need to occur in our political system. In recent years, Michigan politics have become more bitter, polarized, and dysfunctional. I will present some reforms for our political institutions, including reforms of our highly restrictive legislative term limits, reforms of the ways in which legislative districts are drawn, and reforms of our campaign-finance laws.

These are exciting times for anyone interested in the economic issues that will shape Michigan's future. I invite you to read on.

NOTES

1. Charles L. Ballard, Paul N. Courant, Douglas C. Drake, Ronald C. Fisher, and Elisabeth R. Gerber, eds., *Michigan at the Millennium: A Benchmark and Analysis of Its Fiscal and Economic Structure* (East Lansing, MI: Michigan State University Press, 2003).

2. The authoritative analysis of the beginning and ending of recessions is performed by the Business Cycle Dating Committee of the National Bureau of Economic Research. For the history of U.S. recessions, see the National Bureau of Economic Research, "Business Cycles Expansions and Contractions," http://www.nber.org/cycles.html. As of the middle of 2010, the committee has decided on the beginning date for this most recent recession, but they have not picked the ending date. The committee only makes its decisions after lengthy deliberations. As a result, they often do not call the beginning of a recession until it is well under way, and they often do not call the end of a recession until long after it is over. Many economists believe that the most recent recession probably ended in the summer of 2009. When economists say that the recession has ended, they mean that the economy has hit bottom and begun to move upward. However, that does not mean that all is well. It will take a long time to make up the ground that has been lost. In particular, the job market recovers slowly in most economic cycles, which means that unemployment is likely to remain high for a considerable length of time. We will take a deeper look at employment and unemployment in the Chapter 1.

3. Paul Menchik and I discuss the widening inequality in our article "Changes in the Income Distribution in Michigan, 1976–2006, with Comparisons to Other States," available at the Web site of MSU's Institute for Public Policy and Social Research, http://ippsr.msu .edu/Publications/BEBallard.pdf. Rebecca Blank also compares the trends in Michigan's income distribution with the trends for the nation as a whole, in her chapter "The Less Skilled Labor Market in Michigan," in *Michigan at the Millennium*.

4. See Thomas Piketty and Emmanuel Saez, "Income Inequality in the United States, 1913–1998," *Quarterly Journal of Economics* 118 (2003): 1–39. Updated information is available at Saez's Web site, http://www.econ.berkeley.edu/~saez.

5. The data for these funding levels were taken from the executive budget for selected years. The executive budgets for previous years are available at the State of Michigan Web site. See the Michigan Department of Technology, Management, and Budget, "Prior Year Budgets," http://www.michigan.gov/budget/0,1607,7-157-11460_18526---,00.html. In order

to adjust for inflation, I used the Personal Consumption Expenditures deflator from the Bureau of Economic Analysis. See the U.S. Department of Commerce Bureau of Economic Analysis, "Table 1.1.4. Price Indexes for Gross Domestic Product," http://www.bea .gov/national/nipaweb/SelectTable.asp?Selected=N.

6. For a time, the reductions in funding for the universities were offset somewhat by the Michigan Promise Scholarship program, which provided funds directly to students. However, in 2009 the Promise Scholarship program became a broken promise. Governor Granholm has proposed to reinstate the program, but it faces an uncertain future in the legislature.

7. See the Lieutenant Governor's Commission on Higher Education and Economic Growth, "Final Report," http://www.cherrycommission.org/docs/finalReport/CherryReportFULL.pdf.

8. U.S. Census Bureau, "State and Local Government Finance," http://www.census.gov/govs/ estimate.

9. For example, see Charles Ballard, John Shoven, and John Whalley, "General Equilibrium Computations of the Marginal Welfare Costs of Taxation in the United States," *American Economic Review* 75 (1985): 128–38; Charles Ballard and Jaimin Lee, "Internet Purchases, Cross-Border Shopping, and Sales Taxes," *National Tax Journal* 60 (2007): 711–25; and Mark Skidmore, Charles Ballard, and Timothy Hodge, "Property Value Assessment Growth Limits and Redistribution of Property-Tax Payments: Evidence from Michigan," *National Tax Journal* 63 (2010): 509-38.

10. Alan S. Blinder, *Hard Heads, Soft Hearts: Tough-Minded Economics for a Just Society* (Cambridge, MA: Perseus Books, 1987).

An Overview of the Michigan Economy

This book is concerned with the economic policy issues facing Michigan. However, before we can dive into policy discussions, we need a basic understanding of the facts of the economy. What's big? What's little? What's growing? What's shrinking? The purpose of this chapter is to provide some of those basic facts, in four areas:

- First, we look at the industrial composition of Michigan's economy and compare it with the economy of the United States as a whole. We pay special attention to the long-term decline of the manufacturing sector and the automobile industry in particular. Michigan has been involved in manufacturing to a greater degree than most other states. Thus the decrease in the relative importance of manufacturing is at the center of many of Michigan's economic problems. On a much more positive note, we will discuss the industries that have greatest potential to lead the Michigan economy in the future.
- Second, we look at the trends in employment and unemployment. Overall, the Michigan labor market has been extremely poor in the last decade. More than one out of every six jobs in Michigan has been lost since 2000. However, different regions of Michigan have very different employment

situations, and some sectors have done much better than others. We will discuss these regional and sectoral differences.

- Third, we look at incomes. After adjusting for inflation, per capita income in Michigan grew very substantially in the twentieth century. Today, income per person is twice as high as it was in 1965, even after adjusting for inflation. However, the rate of growth has been less rapid in Michigan than in the rest of the United States, especially since 2000. Until the early 1980s, per capita income in Michigan was consistently above the U.S. average. For most of the last thirty years, however, Michigan incomes have been below the national average. By 2008, per capita income in Michigan was 13 percent below the national average, and Michigan ranked thirty-seventh among the fifty states. We also look at the trend toward greater income inequality. In the last thirty-five years, those at the top of the income scale have experienced rapid income growth, while many middle-income and low-income Michigan residents have seen their incomes stagnate or decline.

- Fourth, we look at the economic connections between Michigan and the rest of the United States. (We will look at international connections in Chapter 4.) Michigan's economy is very closely interconnected with the economies of the other states. This makes the people of Michigan much more prosperous than we would be if we were cut off from the other forty-nine states. However, this also means that Michigan's economic performance depends a great deal on economic developments in the rest of the country, far beyond Michigan's borders.

The Industrial Structure of the Michigan Economy

We begin our tour of Michigan's economy by looking at the relative sizes of various industries in 2008.[1] Table 1.1 provides a list of various industries in Michigan. The second column shows each industry's percentage of the Michigan economy. To calculate this percentage, we take the number of dollars that originate in a particular sector and divide it by the total number of dollars generated in the economy, and express the result as a percentage. The third column of Table 1.1 gives the comparable percentage for the United States as a whole. The industries are shown in order of their importance in Michigan.

TABLE 1.1. Value of production in selected industries as a percentage of total value of production for Michigan and the United States, 2008

INDUSTRY	MICHIGAN	UNITED STATES
Services	29.39	27.02
Manufacturing	16.14	11.56
Wholesale and retail trade	12.81	12.03
Government	11.64	12.29
Real estate, rental, and leasing	11.50	12.59
Finance and insurance	6.03	7.52
Construction	3.40	4.11
Information	2.76	4.39
Transportation and warehousing	2.63	2.93
Utilities	2.55	2.16
Agriculture, forestry, fishing, and hunting	0.75	1.11
Mining	0.39	2.30

Source: U.S. Department of Commerce, Bureau of Economic Analysis, "Gross Domestic Product by State," http://www.bea.gov/bea/regional/gsp.

The first row of Table 1.1 shows that the service sector is the largest sector of the Michigan economy. The service sector encompasses a wide range of activities, including legal, medical, management, and accounting services; computer-systems design; performing arts and museums; food services; and many more. In 2008, the service sector accounted for about 29.4 percent of Michigan's economy and about 27.0 percent of the economy of the entire United States.

Table 1.1 also shows that more than 16 percent of Michigan's economy was in manufacturing in 2008, while manufacturing accounted for less than 12 percent of the U.S. economy as a whole. In other words, manufacturing is substantially more important for Michigan than for most states. The data shown in Table 1.1 are highly aggregated. More detailed data (not shown here) indicate that Michigan's heavy reliance on manufacturing is concentrated in durable-goods manufacturing and especially in the automobile industry. In recent years, the automobile industry has accounted for less than 1 percent of the U.S. economy but more than 6 percent of Michigan's economy.

Table 1.1 shows that agriculture, forestry, fishing, and hunting made up three-fourths of a percent of the Michigan economy in 2008. This compares with a bit more than 1 percent of the national economy. I have often heard it said that agriculture is the "second largest industry in Michigan." However, if we define agriculture as growing crops and raising livestock, it is not one of the larger sectors of the economy either in Michigan or in the entire United States. On the other hand, it should be noted that the agriculture sector shown in Table 1.1 does not include agricultural equipment, food processing, food distribution, food retailing, or restaurants and bars, which are included in other sectors. If we were to combine all these activities into a "food-related" industry, it would be substantially larger. (For example, food-product manu-facturing in Michigan is larger than agriculture, and restaurants and bars are more than twice as large as agriculture.)

When I say that agriculture is not one of the largest sectors of the econ-omy, I am *not* saying that agriculture is unimportant. Without agriculture, we would starve to death. My point is not to demean or belittle agriculture; I am merely trying to provide some perspective on the relative sizes of the varied activities that make up the Michigan economy.[2]

One sector where Michigan lags behind the national average is the infor-mation industry, which includes publishing, software, broadcasting, and telecommunications. These industries tend to be strongest on the east and west coasts.

Mining is also relatively small in Michigan. Table 1.1 shows that mining was about 2.3 percent of the national economy in 2008 but less than one-half of a percent of the economy in Michigan. This is partly due to the relatively small size of the oil and gas industry in Michigan. Oil and gas extraction accounted for less than one-tenth of a percent of the Michigan economy. This compares with a national average of about 1.2 percent.[3]

The Relative Decline of Manufacturing

Table 1.1 has provided a "snapshot" of the Michigan economy in 2008. Figure 1.1 is like a "motion picture" of manufacturing's share of the economy,

FIGURE 1.1. Manufacturing as percent of gross state product
for Michigan and for the United States, 1963–2008

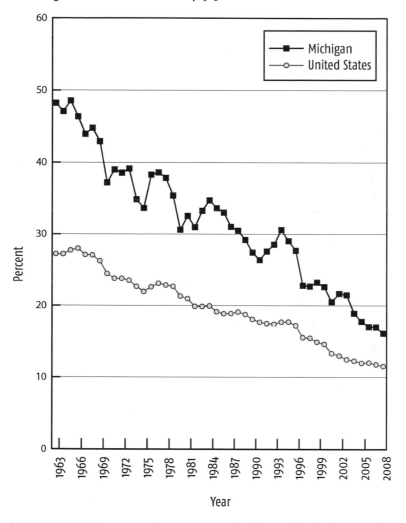

Source: U.S. Department of Commerce, Bureau of Economic Analysis, "Gross Domestic Product by State," http ://www.bea.gov/bea/regional/gsp.

dating back to 1963, the first year for which this information is available for the
fifty states. Throughout this entire period, manufacturing has been a larger
part of Michigan's economy than of the overall U.S. economy. All across the
country, the trend has been for manufacturing to decline as a percentage of the

economy. Manufacturing actually shrank in some years. However, in many of the years shown in Figure 1.1, the manufacturing sector grew, but other things grew faster. Both for Michigan and for the entire United States, manufacturing's share of the economy was less than half as great in 2008 as it had been in 1963.[4] In fact, in Michigan, manufacturing's share of the economy is now only about one-third as large as it was in 1963.

Figure 1.1 begins in 1963 because, as previously stated, it is the first year for which relevant, high-quality economic data are readily available in a convenient format. However, other data sources indicate that manufacturing has probably been declining (as a percentage of the economy) since the early to mid-1950s. Thus Michigan is heavily involved in a sector of the economy that has been in relative decline for more than half a century. That simple fact is the source of many of the challenges facing Michigan's economy.

Figure 1.1 shows that the relative decline of manufacturing is a very long-term phenomenon. Long-term structural changes to the economy will not easily be changed by short-term gimmicks. It will take much time and effort to reinvent Michigan's economy.

Figure 1.1 also reveals something that is important to understand in today's highly partisan political environment, where some Democrats are tempted to blame everything on Republicans and vice versa. Manufacturing's share of the Michigan economy was 48.2 percent in 1963, the year in which George Romney (a Republican) took office as governor of Michigan. By 1969, when Bill Milliken (another Republican) took office, manufacturing's share had fallen to 42.9 percent. When Jim Blanchard (a Democrat) took office in 1983, it was 33.3 percent. In 1991, the first year in office for John Engler (a Republican), it was 26.4 percent. In 2003, when Jennifer Granholm (a Democrat) became governor, it was 21.5 percent. In 2008, the latest year for which we have data, it was 16.1 percent. In other words, the relative decline of manufacturing in Michigan has continued at a fairly steady pace throughout the administrations of the last five governors, spanning nearly fifty years. Neither political party has been immune from the trend.

This is *not* to say that elections and public policies don't make any difference. In fact, much of this book is devoted to discussing public policies that will help to secure a better economic future for Michigan. It's just that we need to understand that Michigan's economy has been sailing into a gale-force headwind for half a century. When you're sailing into a headwind with that much strength, it is hard to make fast progress, no matter who is at the helm. If we had adopted different policies twenty or thirty or forty years ago, I truly believe that we could be in substantially better shape now. But there are limits to how much better off we could be because of the tremendous pressures on the manufacturing sector.

Painful Changes in the Automobile Industry

The automobile industry is at the head of the list of manufacturing industries in Michigan. As with so many manufacturing industries, the automobile industry has accounted for a shrinking percentage of output and employment in the United States. However, the automobile industry has fared worse in Michigan than in the United States as a whole. This is largely because the automobile industry in Michigan is dominated by the U.S. automakers, General Motors, Ford, and Chrysler. In the middle of the twentieth century, these companies enjoyed a cozy situation. They did not usually compete vigorously with each other, and they faced very little competition from abroad.[5] As a result, they were able to raise prices to higher levels than could be sustained in a competitive market. The industry was very profitable, and the members of the United Auto Workers union (UAW) were able to capture a portion of the profits. Eventually, however, companies from Japan and other countries brought increased competition to the American market, and the American companies steadily lost market share in the U.S. market for passenger cars. The foreign-owned companies have expanded their production facilities into the United States, but these facilities have tended to be located in other states, such as Alabama, Kentucky, South Carolina, and Tennessee.[6]

Increased competition in the automobile industry has been great for consumers, who have benefited from lower prices and a wider variety of products. But competition cut deeply into the profits of the Michigan-based auto companies, who found themselves with a cost structure that could not be sustained in the face of such strong competition.

In 2007, the three U.S. automakers reached a series of landmark agreements with the UAW. The UAW made major concessions in wages and benefits. If the volume of automobile sales had maintained itself, these agreements might have been enough to stabilize the companies for the long haul. However, the recession led to a devastating decrease in sales. For most of the time from

1999 to 2006, annual light vehicle sales were a little above sixteen million. By December 2008, on an annualized basis, sales were below ten million.

As of 2010, auto sales are slowly rebounding, but sales are still far below their levels from a few years ago. In fact, it now seems likely that it may be a long time before auto sales return to their old levels. During the years when annual light vehicle sales stayed above 16 million, a substantial fraction of those sales were probably the result of an unsustainable trend in consumer spending. A speculative bubble in the housing market allowed many Americans to borrow against the inflated value of their homes. This borrowing financed a spending binge that temporarily boosted sales of many things, including cars. However, when the housing bubble came crashing down, the debt-fueled spending binge could not be sustained.

Thus for the moment, I am not expecting the automobile sector to be a major source of growth in the Michigan economy. However, for Michigan's economy to start growing again, we don't need the auto sector to grow. We just need it to stop shrinking. Indeed in some ways, it is simply impossible for the auto sector to shrink as fast in the future as it shrank in the first decade of the twenty-first century. Michigan has lost well over two-hundred thousand automobile industry jobs in the last decade. That can't happen again, because only about one-hundred thousand of those jobs remain in Michigan.

It would be good if automobile industry employment in Michigan could grow. For now, however, it would also be a big improvement if automobile sector employment in Michigan could just stabilize at or near its current level. Obviously, if the number of automobile-related jobs in Michigan is to stabilize, GM, Ford, and Chrysler have to sell cars. For many years, some of the cars produced by these companies were perceived as having lower quality than some of the cars produced by rival companies. The American companies have made tremendous strides in quality (as I can attest when I drive my 2008 Chevrolet Malibu, which is a terrific car). Also, in early 2010 Toyota's reputation was tarnished by a series of well-publicized safety problems. Thus there are good reasons to believe that the worst days are over for the automobile industry in Michigan, but it remains difficult to make any iron-clad predictions about the future.

Even when the automobile sector stabilizes, it is unlikely to become a major source of employment growth in Michigan, because of continuing gains in productivity that make it possible to build cars with fewer workers.

The Transitions in Agriculture and Manufacturing

In many ways, the long-term changes being experienced in manufacturing are similar to earlier changes that occurred in agriculture. In much of the nineteenth century, the Michigan economy was dominated by agriculture. In those days, the average farm worker could only produce enough to feed a few people. The only way for the population to feed itself was for a large fraction of the labor force to be employed in agriculture.

However, as a result of unprecedented improvements in agricultural productivity (some of which were developed at Michigan Agricultural College and its successors), the average farm worker in America today can produce enough food for several dozen people. This increase in agricultural productivity was essential for the economic development of the United States, because it allowed us to feed ourselves while freeing resources for pursuits other than agriculture. (Around the world today, the most prosperous countries have the smallest percentages of their labor forces in agriculture. On the other hand, the poorest countries have large percentages of their labor involved in agriculture because these countries have low agricultural productivity.)

The improvements in agricultural productivity were crucial for economic growth, but they were not painless. As agricultural productivity increased, fewer workers were needed in the farming sector. (That is the nature of a productivity increase—it allows us to produce more with fewer people.)[7] Millions of Americans left the farm during the twentieth century. Many found manufacturing jobs and quickly achieved a new prosperity. But some farm workers encountered a difficult transition in the search for new occupations.

For better or for worse, the long transition out of agriculture has already run most of its course.[8] But the transition out of manufacturing is still under way. The two transitions are very similar in both positive and negative ways. Improvements in agricultural productivity paved the way to a higher standard of living, and improvements in manufacturing productivity have had the same beneficial effect. But just as some farm workers were left stranded by the changes in agriculture, some factory workers have also been left stranded by the changes in manufacturing. And since Michigan's economy is so deeply involved in manufacturing, the transition continues to be more difficult for Michigan than for most of the rest of the country.

One of the biggest challenges facing Michigan is how to handle the ongoing transition out of manufacturing. One possibility is to do nothing, other than hope for the good old days to return. But that would be very unwise. To see why, we only need to recall the history of the transition out of agriculture. One hundred years ago, it would have been unwise to do nothing while merely hoping that the dominance of agriculture would somehow reestablish itself. Instead of hoping for a return of the past, Michigan embraced the future (which, at that time, was in manufacturing). Similarly, today it would be unwise to do nothing while merely hoping that the dominance of manufacturing will reestablish itself. Instead of hoping for a return of the past, Michigan would be smart to embrace the future. Increasingly, future prosperity lies in a more highly skilled work force and more advanced technologies.

Perhaps the most important challenge facing Michigan today is a psychological one. It will be difficult for our economy to move ahead unless we are mentally prepared to do so. As long as some of Michigan's people hold onto the false hope that yesterday is coming back, it will hinder our progress toward tomorrow. For too long, too many people in Michigan have cast their gaze toward the rearview mirror. It is time to focus relentlessly on the road ahead.

Potential Sources of Future Growth

Some people have asked, "What's the one thing that will replace the automobile industry in Michigan?" My answer is that I don't want us to replace the automobile industry with just *one* thing. We have seen the problems that can arise from an undiversified economy. My hope is that the Michigan economy of the future will have *many* sources of strength. In this section, I discuss a few of the possibilities.

Of course, there is no need to abandon the manufacturing industries that have played such a large role in Michigan's economy in the past. Manufacturing will continue to be an important part of the Michigan economy. In fact, one of the bright spots of the Michigan economy in recent years has been the growth of automotive high-technology research. Michigan has become the world center for automotive engineering, research, and design.[9]

Where else might Michigan find opportunities for growth? First of all, Michigan's economy will be greatly strengthened if we can continue to be a center for industrial high technology, while increasing our share of biotechnology and information technology. The "Life Sciences Corridor" has already begun to reap benefits, and it has tremendous potential for the future.

In 2008, the National Superconducting Cyclotron Laboratory at Michigan State University won a half-billion dollar contract to build the "Facility for Rare Isotope Beams." This high-technology physics project has the potential to create a wealth of scientific discoveries, including new cancer treatments.[10] More generally, this kind of high-tech project can create high-paying jobs for scientists, engineers, and technicians.

Alternative energy is another area that is almost certain to grow. Michigan will benefit by increasing its role as a center of alternative-energy research, development, and production. It is hard to say exactly what America's energy system will look like in twenty years. Hydrogen, solar power, wind power, and even fusion are among the energy sources that may become much more important than they are now. In 2008, Michigan adopted a set of "renewable portfolio standards." The renewable portfolio standards mandate that 10 percent of the state's energy come from renewable sources by 2015, and they include a requirement that utilities meet an additional 5.5 percent of Michigan's annual electricity demands through energy efficiency by 2015. The Obama Administration is devoting unprecedented amounts of attention and resources to green energy. Companies and universities in Michigan can leverage these federal resources in a way that will have long-term benefits for the Michigan economy.

If we glance again at Table 1.1, we can see some other sectors that would make good candidates for future economic growth. The service sector has been growing rapidly for decades, both in Michigan and in the rest of the country. Many people have an unfavorable impression of services, because some service-sector jobs pay low wages. (The stereotypical service-sector job involves saying, Do you want fries with that?) However, we should remember that doctors, lawyers, accountants, and other highly paid professionals are also in the service sector. Services are likely to continue to grow. If Michigan can capture an increased share of the more highly skilled service jobs, it will be to our benefit.

One service industry that deserves special mention is health-care services. During the first decade of the twenty-first century, when so many parts of the Michigan economy were flat or shrinking, health care experienced strong growth. Moreover, the health-care sector is likely to grow very rapidly in the next few decades. One reason for this is the aging of the population. The oldest members of the baby boom generation are now nearly 65 years old. As this group gets older, the demand for health-care services is likely to keep growing. It is well known that doctors are among the most highly paid workers in the economy. Many nurses, medical technicians, and other health-services providers arc also well paid. If Michigan's medical centers can succeed in expanding their role as regional and national centers of excellence, it will be a boon for our economy.

The expansion of the health-care sector also provides opportunities for growth in health-related manufacturing, as well as in services. The coming decades are likely to see substantial growth in the production of medical equipment, devices, and supplies. Michigan's economy will be stronger if we can gain a larger share of that booming sector.[11]

Another sector with growth potential is tourism. The Great Lakes and many smaller lakes provide Michigan with some of the most picturesque shorelines in the world. For now, Michigan may not rival Las Vegas or parts of Florida as a vacation spot, but Michigan has excellent potential for growth as a tourism center. Of course this will only happen if people are aware of Michigan's attractions. More aggressive marketing is necessary to unlock the potential. That's why I am a big supporter of the "Pure Michigan" advertising campaign.[12]

We should also remember the important role that can be played by finance and insurance. The public image of the financial-services industry has been damaged by the actions of firms such as Lehman Brothers and AIG, which contributed heavily to the financial crisis. Nevertheless, a well-functioning financial sector is crucial to the success of a modern economy. If we can grow a larger and more vibrant finance and insurance sector in Michigan, it will have positive ripple effects throughout our economy as more funds become available for investing. Many of Michigan's banks, credit unions, and insurance companies provide good jobs, and also contribute to their local communities in many other ways. Also, the finance and insurance sector is one of the "greenest" sectors around—these companies don't create much pollution and industrial waste.

In this section, I have listed some of the sectors that might help to revitalize Michigan's economy in the years to come. However, I have to admit that I do not know for certain which sectors will have the strongest growth. If I knew the future for certain, I would be a billionaire many times over, and (sad to say) I'm not a billionaire.

To illustrate how difficult it is to predict the future, it is only necessary to look at the growth of the Internet. When I began my career at Michigan State University in 1983, no one in the Department of Economics had a personal computer in his or her office. If you had asked me at that time about how the Internet would affect people's lives, I would not have been able to answer the question, because I had not yet heard of the Internet. (The beginnings of the Internet had been developed by then, but they had not yet had much effect on the lives of most Americans.) Today, Web browsers, Web pages, and e-mail are a regular part of my daily life and the daily lives of millions of others.

Thus, in today's rapidly changing world, it is very difficult to know exactly what the "next big things" will be. Our children and grandchildren may have careers that we haven't even dreamed of. However, I am confident that those who have the most education, training, and skill will have the greatest ability to take advantage of opportunities when they arise.

Realizing the Potential for Future Economic Growth

We have identified several sectors that have the potential to contribute greatly to the future growth of Michigan's economy. However, that growth potential will not be realized automatically. In order to unlock its potential for future economic growth, Michigan has to provide an environment in which businesses will decide to establish new operations in Michigan, or to expand existing operations. The process of providing that kind of environment is called *economic development*. Michigan, like other states, has a very wide range of activities in this area. These include tax reductions, infrastructure development, assistance to businesses in dealing with regulations, and job training, among other things.[13] All around Michigan, I have met people who are working hard to develop our economy. Organizations like Lansing's Prima Civitas, Ann Arbor SPARK, Detroit's Tech Town, the regional offices of Michigan Works, and many other state and local economic-development authorities are hard at work, strengthening existing employers and luring new ones.

The business pages of Michigan newspapers reveal that these efforts have generated many successes. That may be hard for some folks to believe because they have heard so much bad news in recent years. However, the success stories are there. It's just that the shrinkage of some parts of manufacturing has been so large that it has outweighed the growth in other sectors of the economy. I firmly believe that our economic-development efforts will bear fruit over time.

Before leaving this topic, I need to comment on the role of taxes in economic development. Some folks make it sound as if low taxes are the only thing that a business cares about. In fact, businesses take a host of considerations into account when they make their decisions about where to locate and where to expand. The most important consideration of all is that businesses need a labor force with the appropriate skills. If a business owner cannot find workers to do the jobs that need to be done, the business will fail, regardless of whether taxes are high, low, or zero.

In addition to skilled workers, businesses also need good labor–management relations, and they need access to natural resources and a customer base. They need transportation and communications infrastructure. They need communities that provide a decent quality of life, with recreational, cultural, and educational opportunities. All of these things are at least as important as taxes. If low taxes were the only consideration in business-location decisions, the entire U.S. economy would be located in Alabama. (Actually, if low taxes were the only consideration in business-location decisions, there would not be any U.S. economy at all, because everything would have moved to the Bahamas, Liechtenstein, and other tax-haven countries.)

Still, some folks insist that if we just slash taxes far enough, businesses will flock to Michigan. It hasn't worked thus far, and it won't work in the future, either. The problem is that slashing taxes also means that we slash public services. In the last decade, we have reduced our educational investments, and we have allowed our infrastructure to deteriorate. Business owners do want low taxes, all else equal. However, business owners also want to be able to hire skilled workers, and they want to send their children to good schools, and they want to ship their merchandise over roads and bridges that aren't crumbling. A blind reliance on slashing taxes will not get us where we need to go. The way to a brighter future is to achieve a better balance between the costs of taxes and the benefits of public services.

Although I have said that low taxes are not the only priority (or even the most important priority) for businesses, I am *not* saying that taxes are irrelevant. In fact, for reasons that I will outline in Chapter 6, I believe that the Michigan Business Tax (MBT) is an absolute mess. I am in favor of reducing or even eliminating the MBT, *but only if we replace the revenues fully*. If we do not replace the revenues, we will have to make even more cuts to educational programs and other public services that have been slashed in recent years. That would be a huge step in the wrong direction.

Employment and Unemployment in Michigan

In April 2010, about 4.88 million Michigan residents were in the labor force. About 4.2 million were employed, while about 681,000 were unemployed.[14] That works out to an unemployment rate of 14 percent. At the same time, the national unemployment rate was 9.9 percent. This means that in early 2010, the Michigan economy would have needed more than 200,000 additional jobs to bring Michigan's unemployment rate into line with the national average. Michigan's unemployment rate was the highest among the fifty states in April 2010. At the other end of the spectrum, North Dakota had the lowest unemployment rate in the United States, at 3.8 percent. Between these two extremes, there is a great deal of variation. In April 2010, the unemployment rate was 12.6 percent in California, 13.7 percent in Nevada, 8.4 percent in New York, 10.9 percent in Ohio, and 8.3 percent in Texas.

Just as there is variation among the unemployment rates of the fifty states, there is also variation among the regions within each state. The Labor Department regularly calculates unemployment rates for fourteen metropolitan areas in Michigan. For example, in March 2010 Ann Arbor had the lowest unemployment rate at 9.6 percent, while Flint's unemployment rate stood at 16.3 percent.[15] This disparity is not too surprising, Because of the University of Michigan, the region of Ann Arbor and Washtenaw County has a highly skilled labor force. On the other hand, Flint and Genesee County have suffered disproportionately from the shrinkage of the automobile industry. In a sense, Flint is one of the poster children for the manufacturing economy that was so successful in the middle of the twentieth century, while Ann Arbor is one of the poster children for the highly skilled Michigan economy of the future.[16]

Trends in Employment and Unemployment

In Figure 1.2, we compare the trends in the official unemployment rate for Michigan with those for the United States as a whole. However, before we delve

FIGURE 1.2. Unemployment rates in Michigan and the
United States, 1970–2009 (annual averages)

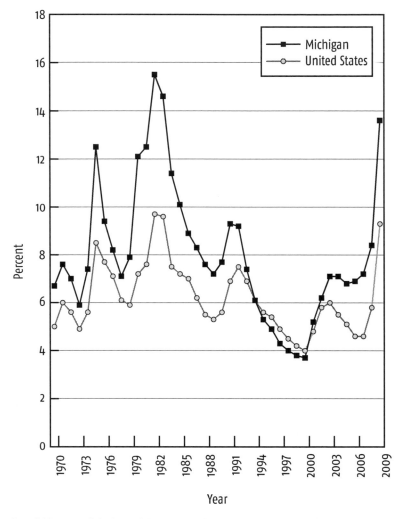

Source: U.S. Department of Labor, Bureau of Labor Statistics, "Local Area Unemployment Statistics," http://stats.bls.gov/lau.

into the details of Figure 1.2, we should be clear about what the official unemployment rate tells us and what it doesn't tell us. The unemployment rate is the number of unemployed people as a percentage of the labor force. The labor force only includes those who are actively looking for work. Thus children and retired people aren't in the labor force, and neither are "discouraged workers," who have given up looking for work.[17] If we include discouraged workers, the unemployment rate rises. If we include those who are working part time even though they would prefer to work full time, the rate of unemployment and underemployment rises even higher. For example, the U.S. Department of Labor estimates that the annual average unemployment rate in Michigan for the year 2009 was 13.3 percent, but if we include discouraged workers and those who can only find part-time jobs, the rate was 21.5 percent.[18]

In the next few paragraphs, we will focus on the standard unemployment rate. However, it should be clear that these data (like any given set of data) only provide a part of the picture. If we were to include discouraged workers and those who have settled for part-time employment, the overall picture of unemployment and underemployment would be worse.

With these qualifications in mind, it is still true that Figure 1.2 has several important stories to tell. First, Figure 1.2 provides some perspective on the current situation in Michigan. Even though the Michigan unemployment rate is much higher today than anyone would wish, it is actually somewhat lower than it was in 1982. In November 1982, the U.S. unemployment rate reached its highest level since the Great Depression, at 10.8 percent, and the unemployment rate in Michigan also reached its highest level since the Great Depression, at 16.7 percent. I do not mean to suggest that the people of Michigan should be happy with today's employment situation. However, it should be clear that we have weathered tough times before.

Figure 1.2 also illustrates that the unemployment rate in Michigan has often had a strong tendency to move in the same direction as the unemployment rate in the rest of the country. Good times for the rest of the United States tend to be good for Michigan. But when a recession leads to higher unemployment in the nation as a whole, Michigan tends to suffer. This reminds us that Michigan's economy is intimately connected to the economy of the rest of the country. For better or worse, it is difficult to separate Michigan's fortunes from those of the United States.

Figure 1.2 also reveals that for much of the period shown, the Michigan economy was more volatile than the national economy. For example, from 1973 to 1975, a recession pushed the national unemployment rate up by 3.6 percentage points, from 4.9 percent to 8.5 percent. At the same time, Michigan's unemployment rate rose by 6.6 percentage points, from 5.9 percent to 12.5 percent. Why has the roller coaster of the business cycle had steeper ups and downs for Michigan than for many other parts of the country? A big part of the answer lies in Michigan's heavy dependence on durable-goods manufacturing. The durable-goods sector produces "big-ticket items," such as automobiles and appliances. Consumers tend to postpone purchases of durable goods during hard times. Thus the durable-goods industries are often hit hard during recessions. On the other hand, there is often a surge in the demand for durable goods during an economic recovery. Consequently, durable-goods manufacturing tends to have larger cycles than most other sectors of the economy. However, because of the decrease in the relative importance of durable-goods manufacturing, it now appears that Michigan may not be as cyclically sensitive as it once was.

Finally, Figure 1.2 indicates that, as the national economic boom of the 1990s took hold, the Michigan economy experienced strong growth. From 1994 to 2000, the unemployment rate in Michigan was *lower* than the national unemployment rate.

Unfortunately, the boom of the 1990s gave way to a new decade in which global economic forces have been very unkind to Michigan. The United States as a whole endured a mild recession in 2001, and then had a very sluggish recovery. (Nationally, employment continued to slip for two years after the recession was officially over.) Employment in Michigan began to sink in the summer of 2000. But then, even when the rest of the country began to see employment growth, Michigan did not. The Michigan economy lost jobs in the second half of 2000, and it has lost jobs in every year since then. The staggering magnitude of the job losses is shown in Table 1.2. During this period of nine and a half years, Michigan has lost more than eight-hundred thousand jobs, which is more than 18 percent of the jobs that were in Michigan at the beginning of the period. Most of the job losses are in the manufacturing sector, where there are only about half as many jobs as there were ten years ago.

If jobs are lost for a year, or even two or three years, the losses can usually be explained as part of the ordinary workings of the business cycle. However, Michigan has now had nearly ten years of job losses. That's why this trend is more than a normal business cycle; it is *a fundamental structural transformation.*

During the recession of the middle 1970s, some people in Michigan said that it was time to diversify our economy. But then the recession ended, and we went back to business as usual. The same thing happened during and after the recession of the early 1980s and the recession of the early 1990s. But the most recent decade has seen a much more prolonged downturn.

TABLE 1.2. Employment losses during Michigan's structural transformation

June 2000–December 2000	29,000
2001	171,700
2002	20,900
2003	64,100
2004	4,300
2005	28,800
2006	79,700
2007	50,900
2008	203,900
2009	207,100
Total for the period	**860,400**

Source: U.S. Department of Labor, Bureau of Labor Statistics, "State and Metro Area Employment, Hours, and Earnings," http://stats
.bls.gov/sae.

If there is a silver lining in the cloud, it is this: The structural transformation of the last decade has been so profound that more and more of Michigan's people have come to understand that we are now in a different world. When our economy bounced back quickly from earlier recessions, it was too easy to ignore the warning signs and revert to our old ways of doing things. If the recent struggles convince enough of the people in Michigan of the need for change, then they will help lay the foundation for future growth.

It currently appears that the long decline in employment in Michigan is very nearly at an end. After the horrendous free fall of late 2008 and early 2009, the number of jobs in Michigan has basically remained the same since June 2009. There is reason to hope that 2010 may be the first year in a decade with job growth in Michigan.

Incomes in Michigan: Levels and Trends

Figure 1.3 shows the growth of per capita personal income in Michigan from 1929 to 2008. This graph shows "real" (inflation-adjusted) income; all the values in Figure 1.3 have been converted to 2008 dollars.[19] Figure 1.3 shows an

FIGURE 1.3. Inflation-adjusted per capita personal income in Michigan, 1929–2008

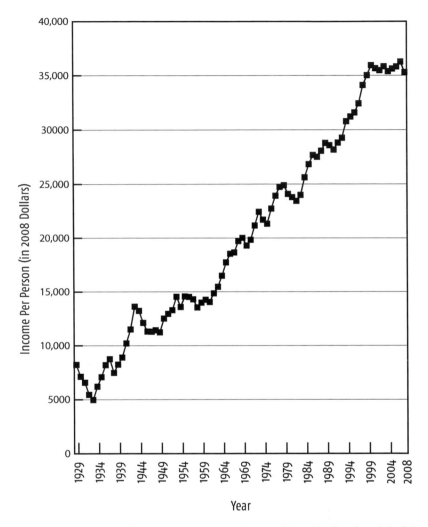

Source: U.S. Department of Commerce, Bureau of Economic Analysis, "State Annual Personal Income," http ://www.bea.gov/regional/spi.

overall pattern of remarkably strong income growth, although the growth rate has not been smooth over time. Not surprisingly, income per person decreased dramatically from 1929 to 1933, during the worst part of the Great Depression. However, after the worst of the Depression was behind us, Michigan incomes enjoyed sixty years of nearly uninterrupted growth.

In Michigan, income per person was about twice as large in 2008 as it had been in 1965, even after adjusting for inflation. Looking further back, per capita income in 2008 was about four times as high as it had been in 1940, and more than seven times as high as it had been at the depths of the Great Depression in 1933. The rising affluence shown in Figure 1.3 may come as a surprise to some people, since we in Michigan have heard a lot of bad news about the economy in recent years. However, while Michigan's economy has not done nearly as well as we would have liked in recent years, it is still true that Michigan is not poor. This is Michigan, not Malawi, Mongolia, Mozambique, or Myanmar. There are poor people in Michigan, but Michigan is not a poor place overall.

There are two reasons for emphasizing the fact that we are not poor. The first reason is that we need to hold our heads high. It is psychologically important to remind ourselves of some of the good things about Michigan. If we succumb to the negative news, it would be easy to sink into a psychological paralysis of gloom and doom. If that were to occur, it would be all the more difficult to do the work that needs to be done.

The second reason for emphasizing that we are not poor has to do with public policy. Again and again in recent years, some politicians have used the poor performance of the economy as an excuse to slash our investments in education and other public services. We have been told that we are being "forced" to make deep cuts, and that we "can't afford" to maintain our investments. The real truth is that if we want to educate our children and provide for other public services, we have the resources to do so. The political will to provide adequately for education and other public services is often lacking, but the resources are there. In fact, when I look at the phenomenal importance of highly skilled workers in today's economy, it seems to me that we can't afford *not* to maintain our investments.

Even though I stress that Michigan is not a poor place, it is still clear that the Michigan economy has done relatively less well in the last few decades than it did in the middle of the twentieth century. The rate of income growth was much slower in the second half of the period shown in Figure 1.3. After adjusting for inflation, per capita incomes in Michigan grew by about 140 percent in the thirty-nine-year period from 1929 to 1968, but only by about 76 percent in the thirty-nine-year period from 1969 to 2008. In fact, inflation-adjusted per capita incomes in Michigan were approximately flat from 2000 to 2008, with small increases in some years and small decreases in others and an overall loss of about 2 percent. As of the middle of 2010, the income data for 2009 are not yet available. When they do become available, however, they are likely to show a further decline of a few percent. The total decline in inflation-adjusted income from 2000 to 2009 is probably 4 or 5 percent.[20]

Comparing Incomes in Michigan with Incomes in the Rest of the United States

Table 1.3 shows per capita personal income for the fifty states and the District of Columbia for 2008. In that year, incomes in Michigan ranked thirty-seventh among the fifty states or thirty-eighth if we include the District of Columbia. Michigan's per capita income was about 13.1 percent below the national average. Many economists are predicting that when the data for 2009 become available, Michigan will have fallen a few more spots in the rankings, possibly as far as forty-first among the fifty states.

The book I wrote in 2006 had a similar table, with data for 2004. In that year, Michigan ranked twenty-first among the fifty states, with per capita income that was about 3 percent below the national average. Thus Michigan's relative standing has slipped substantially in only a few years.

Figure 1.4 shows the trend over time in the relationship between per capita personal incomes in Michigan and those in the United States as a whole, from 1950 to 2008. In this figure, the income level in Michigan is shown as a percentage of the U.S. average. Thus if we were at 100 percent in Figure 1.4, we would be exactly at the national average level of income.

Figure 1.4 shows that income per person was consistently higher in Michigan than in the rest of the country until the early 1980s. For several years in the 1950s and 1960s, Michigan incomes were more than 10 percent above the national average.[21] However, the deep recession of the early 1980s was especially hard for Michigan. Incomes in the state fell below the national average for the first time since the 1930s. Since the early 1980s, the level of income in Michigan has most often been below the national average.

It is useful to compare Figure 1.4 with Figure 1.3. Figure 1.3 reveals the good news that, until recently, incomes in Michigan have grown a great deal. But Figure 1.4 shows the bad news that income growth has been slower in Michigan than in the rest of the country for more than half a century.

Figure 1.4 includes a trend line that provides the best fit for the data. The trend line shows that, relative to the national average level of income, Michigan has lost about 2 percentage points every five years. If this trend were to continue

TABLE 1.3. Per capita personal income (in dollars) in the fifty states and the District of Columbia, 2008

RANK	JURISDICTION	INCOME	RANK	JURISDICTION	INCOME
1	District of Columbia	66,119	27	Texas	37,774
2	Connecticut	56,272	28	Wisconsin	37,767
3	New Jersey	51,358	29	Iowa	37,402
4	Massachusetts	51,254	30	Missouri	36,631
5	New York	48,753	31	Maine	36,457
6	Wyoming	48,608	32	Louisiana	36,424
7	Maryland	48,378	33	Oregon	36,297
8	Virginia	44,224	34	Ohio	36,021
9	Alaska	44,039	35	Oklahoma	35,985
10	California	43,641	36	North Carolina	35,344
11	New Hampshire	43,623	37	Tennessee	34,976
12	Minnesota	43,037	**38**	**Michigan**	**34,949**
13	Colorado	42,985	39	Georgia	34,893
14	Washington	42,857	40	Montana	34,644
15	Illinois	42,347	41	Indiana	34,605
16	Hawaii	42,055	42	Arizona	34,335
17	Rhode Island	41,368	43	Alabama	33,768
18	Nevada	41,182	44	New Mexico	33,430
19	Delaware	40,519	45	Idaho	33,074
20	Pennsylvania	40,140	46	South Carolina	32,666
21	North Dakota	39,870	47	Arkansas	32,397
22	Florida	39,267	48	Kentucky	32,076
23	Nebraska	39,150	49	Utah	31,944
24	Kansas	38,820	50	West Virginia	31,641
25	Vermont	38,686	51	Mississippi	30,399
26	South Dakota	38,661		**U.S. average**	**40,208**

Source: U.S. Department of Commerce, Bureau of Economic Analysis, "State Annual Personal Income," http://www.bea.gov/regional/spi.

for another few decades, Michigan's relative standing would be similar to that currently occupied by Mississippi, which has the lowest per capita income in the United States today. If we were to continue the relative decline at the rapid pace of the last few years, we would get to Mississippi's level by 2017.

FIGURE 1.4. Per capita personal income: Michigan as a percentage of the United States, 1950–2008

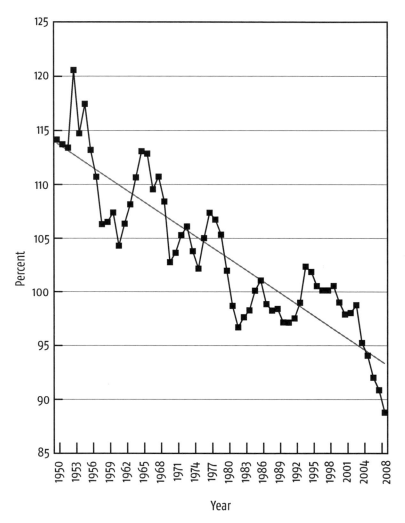

Year

Source: U.S. Department of Commerce, Bureau of Economic Analysis, "State Annual Personal Income," http://www.bea.gov/regional/spi.

Incomes in Michigan have been declining relative to the U.S. average for a very long time. In the chapters to come, I will offer some more thoughts about how we can turn this trend around. For now, I must emphasize again that long-term problems require long-term solutions. Of course, policies focused on the short term can sometimes make a difference. (For example, if we build a new bridge over the Detroit River, it will provide a short-term boost to the economy, in addition to positioning Michigan to take better advantage of trade with Canada for years to come.) However, there are no quick fixes to most of the fundamental economic problems facing the people of Michigan. If we habitually think in terms of quick fixes rather than long-run strategies, the results are likely to be disappointing. At a recent public forum, Mitchell Bean of the House Fiscal Agency put it nicely, "If someone offers you a silver bullet, the first thing you should do with that bullet is shoot 'em."[22]

The Rise in Income Inequality

In the previous section, we saw that per capita income in Michigan has grown substantially since the middle of the twentieth century (although the growth has been at a slower pace than in the rest of the country, and per capita income has declined slightly in the last decade). However, growth in per capita income or *average* income does not necessarily translate into income growth for *everyone*. In fact, the degree of inequality in the United States has increased tremendously since about 1975. In 1975, the most affluent 20 percent of U.S. households received about 43.6 percent of the income in the country, according to census data. By 2008, the income share of the top 20 percent of households had risen to 50 percent.[23] Over the same time period, the income share of the top 5 percent of households rose from 16.5 percent to 21.5 percent. In the United States, income inequality has now risen to levels that have not been seen since the early part of the twentieth century.

This massive change is probably the most important economic story of our time. Here is one way to get a sense of the size of the change: if income had been distributed across the income classes in 2008 in the same way that it was distributed in 1975, the 5 percent of American households with the highest incomes would be receiving about $600 *billion less* per year, and the poorest 95 percent would be receiving about $600 *billion more* per year. Shortly, we will see that the trend toward greater inequality in Michigan is similar to the trend in the United States as a whole.

There are several reasons for the increasing concentration of income in the hands of the most affluent. One of the most important reasons has to do with the increase in the wage premium for workers with higher levels of skill. The wages of college-educated workers have increased strongly in recent decades, while the wages of other groups have stagnated or even shrunk. In *Michigan at the Millennium*, these trends are discussed by Rebecca Blank of the University of Michigan, in a chapter titled "The Less-Skilled Labor Market in Michigan." She shows that the median weekly wage of Michigan workers with at least a bachelor's degree increased by nearly 30 percent from 1979 to 2000, after adjusting for inflation. For those with only a high school diploma, inflation-adjusted wages fell by 8.5 percent. The wages of workers without a high school diploma fell by an astonishing 25 percent.

The increase in the earnings of those with high levels of education is one important explanation for the trend toward greater inequality. It explains much of the growth in the incomes of those who might be called "upper middle class." However, there is also another part of the story that cannot be explained merely by looking at educational levels. In the last thirty years, the most phenomenal income growth has been at the very top of the income scale. The economists Thomas Piketty and Emmanuel Saez have used tax-return data to document the phenomenal growth in the income shares of the most affluent one-hundredth of a percent.[24]

The top one-hundredth of a percent of American households is an extraordinarily elite group, numbering only about 15,000 households. By way of comparison, this group has fewer people than East Lansing, Michigan. Back in 1975, the top one-hundredth of a percent received a little more than one-half of a percent of all the income in the United States (if we exclude the capital gains on their stock-market portfolios), and almost 1 percent of all income if we include capital gains. By 2007, this group had more than 3.6 percent of all the income in the country (without capital gains), and more than 6 percent when capital gains are included. The amazing increase in the share of income going to those at the very top is shown in Figure 1.5.

Jon Bakija and Bradley Heim have used these data to investigate the occupations of those at the very top.[25] Many are Chief Executive Officers (CEOs), and many work on Wall Street. (In 2006, the top twenty-five hedge-fund managers made an average of about $560 million each. In 2009, the top twenty-five made an average of more than $1 *billion* apiece. One fellow made $4 billion in one year.[26])

Bakija and Heim studied similar data for France and Japan, and they did not find the same sort of trend. Thus the astonishing success of the folks at the very top appears to be a uniquely American phenomenon. This leads to the question of why America is so different from other countries in this respect. Economists prefer to explain things in economic terms, but the amazing

FIGURE 1.5. Percentage of income in the United States received by the top one-hundredth of one percent, 1975–2007

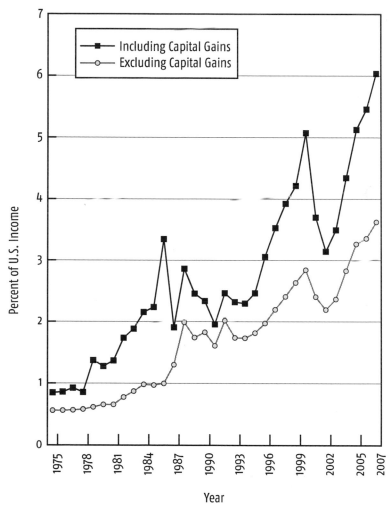

Source: Author's calculations based on Thomas Piketty and Emmanuel Saez, http://elsa.berkeley.edu/~saez.

surge in compensation for the folks on Wall Street is difficult to understand without turning to sociological and anthropological explanations. It appears that "social norms" may have changed. In other words, it may be that there has been a weakening in the informal social rules that used to discourage CEOs and Wall Street financiers from exploiting their power to fullest.

The data in Figure 1.5 are for the entire United States. We don't have a comparable breakdown for Michigan. However, in research conducted with my MSU colleague Paul Menchik, I have found a pattern of increasing inequality in Michigan that is very similar to what we see in the rest of the country.[27] From 1976 to 2006, the top 20 percent of Michigan households increased their share of Michigan income from about 40.9 percent to about 47.4 percent.

In its June 22, 2009 issue, *Crain's Detroit Business* published the 2008 compensation for the fifty top-compensated CEOs in the metro Detroit area.[28] Thirty-four of these fifty men had annual compensation in excess of $1 million apiece.[29] Each of the top twelve received annual compensation in excess of $5 million.

Thus it is important to qualify the statements that one hears about the poor performance of the Michigan economy. The economy has been mediocre overall, but it has not been mediocre for everyone. The recent economic situation has been fabulous for the most affluent people in Michigan and across the country. For those at the top, there has been unprecedented prosperity. For those in the upper-middle income group, times have been very good. For those in the middle, the Michigan economy of recent decades has been lackluster at best. For many of those at the bottom, it has been an economic disaster.

The increase in inequality has two very important implications. First, the rising wage premium for a college education tells us that the future belongs to the educated, now more than ever. Unfortunately, as we shall see in the next chapter, Michigan lags behind the national average in terms of educational attainment. The second implication of the increase in inequality has to do with how taxes should be distributed among Michigan's people. Now more than ever, those at the top have greater ability to pay taxes. In Chapter 6 of this book, I will discuss tax policy in considerable detail. I will argue in favor of a graduated income tax, which would shift more of Michigan's taxes toward the affluent. These folks, who have been extraordinarily fortunate in recent years, have the greatest ability to pay taxes.

Michigan's Economic Connections with the Rest of the United States

During the first few years after America won its independence from Great Britain, the thirteen former colonies had the authority to use tariffs to interfere with trade across state lines. The leaders who wrote the U.S. Constitution in

1787 recognized that these tariffs were harming the national economy. In article I, sections 8 and 10, the Constitution enshrined the principle that Congress (rather than the individual states) has the responsibility to regulate interstate commerce. Thus today a Michigan company does not have to pay tariffs when it sells to customers in Colorado, Georgia, or Ohio. In effect, the Constitution created a nation that would eventually become the world's largest free-trade zone. This has contributed tremendously to American economic growth.

Michigan's economy is closely intertwined with the economy of the rest of the United States. (Michigan's economy also shares important connections with other countries, especially Canada. We will discuss Michigan's role in the global economy in Chapter 4.) The positive aspect of these close connections is that we, the people of Michigan, are much more affluent than we would be if we were completely on our own. If Michigan were "self-sufficient," Michigan residents would be restricted to consuming things that are made in Michigan. There would be few fresh vegetables in winter and few citrus fruits at any time of year. There would be very little gasoline. And, if the state were cut off from the rest of the country, Michigan residents would not be able to sell cars, chemicals, office furniture, or breakfast cereal to people in other states.

Overall, Michigan gains a great deal from being able to trade freely with the rest of the country. However, since the Michigan economy depends so much on connections with the rest of the United States, there are limits on the ability of the people of Michigan to control their own economy. Most people probably yearn to be the masters of their own destiny, but the fact is that Michigan's economic situation is greatly affected by things that happen beyond Michigan's borders.

The U.S. Economy: Prospects for Recovery

Since Michigan's economy is so closely connected with the rest of the United States, economic decisions made in Washington and on Wall Street can have a profound effect on Michigan. In my 2006 book, I did not say much about the overall macroeconomic performance of the U.S. economy. However, in the autumn of 2008, we experienced the scariest financial crisis in seventy-five years. This turned a relatively mild recession into the worst economic downturn since the Great Depression.[30] It is necessary to discuss these issues here, since they have had such a huge effect on the Michigan economy.

Some of Michigan's economic problems can be blamed on the inability of Michigan-based automobile companies to maintain their market share. However, very little of the blame for the financial meltdown of September 2008 can be placed on mistakes made in Michigan. All over the country, banks made mortgage loans that should not have been made. All over the country, individuals and families borrowed money that they should not have borrowed. Mortgages were bundled into exotic derivative securities that most people did not understand. Bond rating agencies turned a blind eye to the possible problems with these securities, and gave high ratings to stuff that turned out to be toxic. Wall Street firms pumped up their balance sheets with dangerous assets. Regulatory agencies, such as the Securities and Exchange Commission, were asleep at the wheel. Last but certainly not least, Congress facilitated all of this by loosening the system of financial regulations.

Very few people were able to see that the gathering storm would be so enormous and so damaging. (For example, by the summer of 2007, I was fairly sure that we were on the brink of a recession, but I did not foresee that it would eventually become a once-in-a-lifetime crisis.) Regardless of whether the crisis was foreseen, it did happen, and we can learn from it if we are willing to take the right lessons from the experience.

To illustrate the crisis and its aftermath, and to point the way to the lessons we can learn for the future, I will use an extended metaphor. In this metaphor, I compare the U.S. economy to a person with heart disease. For much of the first decade of the twenty-first century, we gorged ourselves on the economic equivalent of cheeseburgers, pizza, and fries. We did not realize that this would lead to an economic heart attack, but it did. The heart attack struck in the early-morning hours of Monday, September 15, 2008, with the collapse of Lehman Brothers, the Wall Street investment banking firm. By the middle of that week, the credit markets had nearly ceased to function. The patient was barely conscious.

It would have been much better if we had not wolfed down all of those burgers, pizzas, and fries. Thus I give poor marks to the Clinton and Bush administrations, Congress, and the Federal Reserve for policies that contributed to the heart attack. However, once a heart attack occurs, the first priority is to revive the patient, and that is exactly what the authorities did. Presidents Bush and Obama, Federal Reserve Chairman Bernanke, and many others deserve high marks for acting boldly to avert a total collapse of the economy.

Some critics say that the Federal Reserve should not have moved so aggressively to inject capital into the ailing financial system. Some say that the Bush administration and the Obama administration should not have undertaken expansionary fiscal policies. That is like saying, "That person has had a massive heart attack, but don't perform CPR and don't get the person to the hospital. The body's natural processes will take care of everything." I vehemently disagree. Our economy does have some very good self-regulatory characteristics, but they are imperfect, and they are exceptionally inadequate in a financial crisis like this one.

How sick was the patient? Henry Paulson, who was President Bush's Treasury Secretary at the time of the Lehman Brothers collapse, suggests that the national unemployment rate might have risen to 25 percent by late 2009 if dramatic action had not been taken in late 2008. I think Secretary Paulson is probably right about that. And if the national unemployment rate were 25 percent, then Michigan's unemployment rate might be 35 percent. When a patient is that sick, it's crazy not to do CPR.

The authorities *did* perform CPR, and the patient *did* survive. However, when a patient has had a massive heart attack, he or she is not going to be running the high hurdles any time soon. In other words, as a result of the tremendous damage that was inflicted on the economy and financial system, a long and difficult recession was inevitable. In my view, President Obama's economic team made a major error by suggesting that it might be possible to keep the national unemployment rate below 8 percent. This financial crisis was so severe that we are lucky that the national unemployment rate only rose to about 10 percent, and the Michigan unemployment rate only rose to about 15 percent.

It is particularly annoying to hear some pundits and politicians say things like "the unemployment rate is still high; therefore, the stimulus programs must not be working." That kind of talk shows a sad lack of understanding of the pace at which the economy can recover from a damaging recession. It also shows a lack of understanding of how the labor market works. In fact, without various monetary and fiscal stimulus programs, the unemployment rate would be far higher now.

As of this writing, it is a little more than two years since the onset of the national recession. When we were at this same point in the last three business cycles (i.e., the recessions of 1982, 1991, and 2001), the number of jobs in the U.S. economy was 1 or 2 percent lower than it had been at the beginning of the recession. This time, however, the number of jobs in the national economy is about *6 percent* below where it had been. Therefore if this latest recession had unfolded similarly to the previous three recessions, employment in the U.S. economy would be greater than it is now, by about *6 million jobs.*

Although I am hopeful that the U.S. economy will rebound quickly, it seems more realistic that the recovery will be slow. And since the U.S. economy has such a tremendous effect on the Michigan economy, it is likely that our economy in Michigan will also take time to recover. Thus we will need to be patient. I know this is difficult for the people of Michigan to hear, because they feel (quite correctly) that they have already shown plenty of patience. But while we all hope for a quick recovery, we should be emotionally prepared for the recovery to be slow.

So far, we have established three things about this financial crisis. First, it would have been better not to clog our arteries with burgers, pizza, and fries. (In other words, we got our economy into a big mess with a lot of bad decisions.) Second, once the heart attack came, it was best to perform CPR. (In other words, the authorities are to be applauded for moving aggressively to ward off a systemic collapse of the economy.) Third, when there is a severe heart attack, even if CPR is successful, it will take time before the patient is back at full strength. (In other words, the recovery from this crisis is likely to be slow.) This metaphor still has one more very important lesson to teach us: when a patient is recovering from a heart attack, it's best to get on an exercise program and a low-fat diet. In other words, we need to take steps to avoid a repeat of the financial crisis.

In some ways, we are heading in the right direction. Many banks are avoiding the kind of silly loans they made a few years ago, and many individuals and families are being more prudent with their finances. However, unless we make some further policy changes, our economy is in danger of finding itself back in the emergency room. In particular, a big part of the problem was that several financial companies were "too big to fail." They could behave in an extraordinarily risky fashion, comfortably knowing that the authorities would be forced to ride to their rescue if things went wrong.[31] Both houses of Congress have been working on a package of reforms to provide financial managers with a better set of incentives and to provide better protections for consumers. If these reforms become law, they will be a big positive step. However, it remains to be seen whether these reforms will ultimately be enough. If we are to avoid another financial meltdown, it will require continual vigilance on the part of the press, the public, Congress, and the regulatory authorities.

Looking to the longer term, it is crucial for the U.S. economy to wean itself from its excessive dependence on debt. Borrowing is fine, up to a point. But households, businesses, and governments have all increased their borrowing in an unsustainable fashion. Unless the private sector begins to save more and borrow less, the U.S. economy will ultimately be in a great deal of trouble. In addition, although large government budget deficits were inevitable in the recent recession, the federal government simply cannot continue to borrow at this rate indefinitely. The long-term solution lies in a combination of reductions in Social Security, Medicare, and other programs, as well as increased tax revenues.[32]

Michigan's Geographic Isolation

I have emphasized that connections with the rest of the U.S. economy are vitally important for Michigan's prosperity. However, Michigan is not as connected to the rest of the country as it might be, because of accidents of geography. The Great Lakes are a wonderful asset for Michigan, but they place physical barriers between Michigan and the rest of the country. Whereas states like Missouri and Tennessee are completely surrounded by other states, much of the outline of Michigan does not have a direct land connection to other states. Only Alaska, Hawaii, and Maine have a smaller percentage of their borders connected to other states.

This relative isolation has an important effect on the distribution of economic activity in Michigan. It means that an economic advantage is enjoyed by the parts of Michigan that are closer to the rest of the country. This is one of the reasons why more than 90 percent of Michigan's population and more than 92 percent of its economy are in the southern half of the Lower Peninsula (south of a line from Oceana County, just south of Ludington, to Bay County, at the southwestern end of Saginaw Bay).[33]

Regional Income Differences in Michigan

As suggested in the previous paragraph, there are big differences in the level of economic activity among the regions of Michigan. Table 1.4 reveals striking regional disparities in the level of per capita income for Michigan counties in 2008. The per capita incomes for individual counties range from more than $53,000 in Oakland County (just north of Detroit) to about $22,000 in Luce County (in the Upper Peninsula). Thus the most affluent parts of Michigan are

TABLE 1.4. Per capita incomes (in dollars) in 2008 for Michigan's eighty-three counties

RANK	COUNTY	INCOME	RANK	COUNTY	INCOME
1	Oakland	53,650	31	Antrim	30,727
2	Midland	41,990	32	Lenawee	30,594
3	Leelanau	40,656	33	Iron	30,277
4	Washtenaw	39,107	34	Saginaw	30,143
5	Livingston	39,039	35	Sanilac	30,143
6	Emmet	37,935	36	Keweenaw	30,048
7	Macomb	36,462	37	Benzie	29,763
8	Grand Traverse	36,129	38	Delta	29,760
9	Charlevoix	36,120	39	Jackson	29,610
10	Huron	36,024	40	Ontonagon	29,592
11	Clinton	35,913	41	Schoolcraft	29,571
12	Kalamazoo	35,190	42	Mason	29,515
13	Kent	35,099	43	Genesee	29,488
14	Dickinson	34,209	44	Otsego	29,152
15	Ingham	33,685	45	Van Buren	28,934
16	Berrien	33,669	46	Menominee	28,736
17	Monroe	33,397	47	Manistee	28,079
18	Ottawa	33,009	48	Muskegon	28,062
19	Cass	32,983	49	St. Joseph	28,058
20	Mackinac	32,957	50	Cheboygan	28,018
21	Eaton	32,906	51	Gogebic	27,717
22	Barry	32,743	52	Isabella	27,639
23	Wayne	32,094	53	Arenac	27,273
24	St. Clair	31,956	54	Shiawassee	27,163
25	Allegan	31,837	55	Gratiot	27,047
26	Calhoun	31,652	56	Wexford	27,010
27	Alpena	31,340	57	Hillsdale	26,923
28	Bay	30,971	58	Roscommon	26,768
29	Marquette	30,838	59	Presque Isle	26,657
30	Lapeer	30,829	60	Oceana	26,585

(continued on next page)

TABLE 1.4. Per capita incomes (in dollars) in 2008 for Michigan's eighty-three counties (*continued*)

RANK	COUNTY	INCOME	RANK	COUNTY	INCOME
61	Newaygo	26,577	73	Mecosta	24,747
62	Clare	26,392	74	Crawford	24,743
63	Houghton	26,107	75	Gladwin	24,643
64	Iosco	26,005	76	Kalkaska	24,632
65	Branch	25,901	77	Chippewa	24,586
66	Tuscola	25,818	78	Missaukee	24,541
67	Baraga	25,767	79	Montmorency	24,481
68	Ionia	25,371	80	Oscoda	24,064
69	Ogemaw	25,314	81	Alger	23,728
70	Alcona	25,293	82	Montcalm	22,755
71	Osceola	25,218	83	Luce	22,158
72	Lake	24,926		**Median county**	**29,515**
				Statewide average	**34,188**

Source: U.S. Department of Commerce, Bureau of Economic Analysis, "Local Area Personal Income," http://www.bea.gov/regional/reis.

very affluent indeed. However, the poorest Michigan counties have income levels that are similar to those in countries like Greece, South Korea, or Spain.

Table 1.4 shows that Oakland County is by far the most affluent county in Michigan. The table also reveals that the affluence of Oakland County is part of a broader pattern. The regions with the highest incomes in Michigan are mostly in the southern Lower Peninsula. Four of the seven counties with the highest per capita incomes are in the region served by the Southeast Michigan Council of Governments (SEMCOG).[34] All seven of the SEMCOG counties rank among the twenty-four counties with the highest incomes, out of the eighty-three counties in Michigan. As a result, the SEMCOG counties have about 55 percent of the personal income in Michigan, even though they include only about 48 percent of the population. Fourteen of the twenty highest-income counties in Michigan are in the southern Lower Peninsula.

All of the major metropolitan areas in Michigan are in the southern half of the Lower Peninsula. Thus when we say that the most affluent counties in

Michigan tend to be in the southern Lower Peninsula, it is almost the same as saying that the most affluent counties tend to be in metropolitan areas. However, a handful of nonmetropolitan counties are among the most affluent in Michigan. Four of the other six counties in the top twenty for per capita personal income are in parts of the northern Lower Peninsula that thrive on recreation, tourism, and affluent retirees. Specifically, these are Charlevoix, Emmet, Grand Traverse, and Leelanau Counties.[35]

In this chapter, I have used the phrase "the Michigan economy" on dozens of occasions. However, I hope it is clear that this phrase should be interpreted with caution. When I say "the Michigan economy," I am usually referring to averages. But averages can be deceiving. When we focus on averages, it would be easy to slip into thinking that "the Michigan economy" is all one shade of gray. In fact, it is a mosaic of many pieces. Some pieces are very bright, some are gloomy, and there are lots of shades in between. In other words, some of Michigan's people, regions, and industries are doing very well and others are not.

Conclusion

In this chapter, we have taken a brief tour of the Michigan economy. Here are some of the highlights:

- Manufacturing accounts for a larger share of the economy in Michigan than in most of the rest of the United States. In 2008, manufacturing was more than 16 percent of the Michigan economy, but less than 12 percent of the overall U.S. economy. Manufacturing has been declining as a percentage of the economy for several decades, both in Michigan and in the rest of the United States. Many of the challenges facing Michigan today are due to the fact that the Michigan economy is heavily involved in a sector that has been in relative decline.
- Because of the shrinkage of manufacturing (and especially the automobile industry), Michigan never really emerged from the 2001 recession. This had devastating consequences for the job market in Michigan. By the end of 2009, employment in Michigan had fallen by more than 18 percent from its peak in the summer of 2000. The number of people employed in Michigan in 2009 was about the same as it had been nineteen years earlier.

- Unemployment in Michigan tends to rise when national unemployment is rising and fall when national unemployment is falling. In addition, heavy dependence on durable-goods manufacturing has historically made the economy more cyclical in Michigan than in the rest of the United States, with larger upward and downward swings in the unemployment rate. Today, however, Michigan's economy is probably not as volatile as it once was.

- Even after adjusting for inflation, per capita income in Michigan is twice as high as it was in 1965 and four times as high as it was in 1940. However, income growth has been slower in Michigan than in the United States as a whole. Until the early 1980s, per capita incomes in Michigan were higher than the national average. Since then, however, Michigan's incomes have been below the national average in most years. By 2008, per capita income in Michigan was 13 percent below the national average, and Michigan ranked thirty-seventh among the fifty states.

- In Michigan, as in most of the rest of the United States, the distribution of income has become starkly more unequal since the 1970s. The households at the top of the income distribution have received most of the income gains. The earnings of college-educated workers have risen rapidly when compared with the earnings of those with a high school education or less. Many people in the middle and at the bottom of the income distribution have suffered a decrease in their standard of living.

- The Great Lakes are a magnificent natural resource. However, in this era when land-based transportation is far more prevalent than lake-based transportation, much of Michigan is geographically isolated. The major land connections with the rest of the United States are concentrated in the southern Lower Peninsula. The population and the economy of Michigan are both dominated by southern Lower Michigan. Per capita incomes tend to be substantially higher in the southern part of the state. The southern half of the Lower Peninsula accounts for more than 90 percent of Michigan's population and income.

This chapter analyzes some of the central facts and trends of Michigan's economy. In the next chapter, we take a closer look at Michigan's human resources. The skills of our people have played a huge role in the past, and they will be even more crucial in the knowledge-driven economy of the future.

NOTES

1. The Bureau of Economic Analysis (a branch of the U.S. Commerce Department) provides statistics for the value of production in various industries for the fifty states and the District of Columbia. See the U.S. Department of Commerce, Bureau of Economic Analysis, "Gross Domestic Product by State," http://www.bea.gov/bea/regional/gsp.

2. In fact, I work for a university that began as an agricultural college. Thus I have many friends in Michigan's agriculture sector, and in MSU's College of Agriculture and Natural Resources and the MSU Extension. The farmers and others involved in the food chain play a very important role in the Michigan economy, and MSU researchers help to keep Michigan agriculture on the cutting edge of technological changes.

3. In 2007, oil and gas extraction accounted for about 7.5 percent of the economy in Texas, about 7.8 percent in Oklahoma, about 10.1 percent in Louisiana, and about 23.9 percent in Alaska. Thus in 2007, Michigan's oil and gas sector was *very* small in comparison with the oil and gas sector in these other states.

4. For the United States as a whole, the trend for manufacturing is almost continuously downward. For Michigan, the overall trend is downward, but there are some noticeable short-term upturns. In fact, it is common for regional economies to be more volatile than the national economy. By definition, the U.S. economy is the weighted average of the economies of all of the states; the fluctuations in the individual states tend to even out when we combine them into a national average.

5. When competition from abroad finally did have an effect on the American auto industry, the competition came mainly from Germany, Japan, and Korea. Germany and Japan were both devastated by the Second World War, which ended in 1945. Korea was devastated by the Korean War, which ended in 1953. Thus the lack of foreign competition in the auto industry in the 1950s resulted more from historical circumstances than from economic fundamentals.

6. For a discussion of the southward trend in automobile production in the United States, see Kim Hill and Emilio Brahmst, "The Auto Industry Moving South: An Examination of Trends," Center for Automotive Research, http://www.cargroup.org/pdfs/North-South Paper.pdf. The Center for Automotive Research is an excellent source for information on a very wide range of topics regarding the automobile industry.

7. In addition to requiring fewer workers, agriculture now requires less land. At one time, about 19 million acres of land in Michigan were used for agricultural purposes, out of about 35 million acres total in the state. However, agriculture currently uses only about

10 million acres in Michigan. In other words, about one-fourth of the land in Michigan is land that was once involved in agriculture but is no longer cultivated. Much of this is land that is only marginally productive in agriculture, in the northern Lower Peninsula and Upper Peninsula. A lot of the land in those regions has now returned to forest. For a discussion, see Arlen Leholm, Raymond Vlasin, and John Ferris, "Michigan's Agricultural, Forestry, and Mining Industries," in *Michigan at the Millennium: A Benchmark and Analysis of Its Fiscal and Economic Structure*, ed. Charles L. Ballard, Paul N. Courant, Douglas C. Drake, Ronald C. Fisher, and Elisabeth R. Gerber (East Lansing, MI: Michigan State University Press, 2003).

8. The transition out of agriculture is not the first major transition for the Michigan economy. For thousands of years, the economy of this region was dominated by hunting and subsistence agriculture. For the first two-hundred years after Europeans came to this part of the world, the region's economy was dominated by the fur trade. By the 1830s, fur trapping was very much in decline and was rapidly being replaced by agriculture. The Michigan economy has also seen temporary surges in timber and copper. Thus major transitions are nothing new for Michigan's economy. For a detailed discussion, see Willis F. Dunbar and George F. May, *Michigan: A History of the Wolverine State*, 3rd ed. (Grand Rapids, MI: William B. Eerdmans Publishing Company, 1995).

9. See "High Technology in Michigan's Economy," by Abel Feinstein (an independent consultant) and George Fulton and Donald Grimes (both of the University of Michigan), in *Michigan at the Millennium*.

10. For an entertaining, non-technical introduction, see http://www.youtube.com/watch?v =677ZmPEFIXE (or just Google "frib rap").

11. For a detailed discussion of health care in Michigan, see "Health Care in Michigan" by John Goddeeris of Michigan State University, in *Michigan at the Millennium*.

12. I recently heard a story about some Californians visiting the Grand Traverse Resort. The Californians told their Michigan host that they did not have any idea there was anything so beautiful in Michigan. They thought Michigan was abandoned factories and warehouses, from one end of the state to the other. We need to do a lot more to remind the rest of the world (and ourselves) that Michigan is a great place, despite its recent difficulties.

13. For more discussion of Michigan's economic-development efforts, see "Economic Development Policy in Michigan," by Timothy Bartik and George Erickcek of the Upjohn Institute and Peter Eisinger of Wayne State University, in *Michigan at the Millennium*.

14. For data on employment and unemployment for states and metropolitan areas, see the Bureau of Labor Statistics, "Local Area Unemployment Statistics," http://stats.bls.gov/lau.

15. As of May 2010, preliminary unemployment estimates for the entire state have been released through April 2010, whereas estimates for the metropolitan areas have only been released through March. Although the Ann Arbor unemployment rate was 9.6 percent in March 2010, it was only 4.6 percent in March 2007. Similarly, although the Flint unemployment rate was 16.3 percent in March 2010, it was 8.4 percent in March 2007. These two comparisons illustrate how the last few years have wreaked havoc throughout the state's job market.

16. In "Automotive and Other Manufacturing Industries in Michigan: Output, Employment, Earnings, and Collective Bargaining, 1980-2001," in *Michigan at the Millennium*, Richard Block and Dale Belman provide a fascinating discussion of one of the reasons why Flint bore such a large portion of the decline. The degree of tension between labor and management appears to have been higher in Flint than in other places. When General Motors had to close some plants, the place with the most contentious labor–management relations was a prime candidate.

17. The unemployment rate is *not* based on eligibility for unemployment insurance. As of the spring of 2010, fewer than half of the unemployed are eligible to receive unemployment benefits. This has led to discussions about whether the unemployment insurance system is performing adequately in today's economic environment.

18. Bureau of Labor Statistics. "Alternative Measures of Labor Underutilization for States, 2009 Annual Averages." http://stats.bls.gov/lau/stalt.htm.

19. The income data for states are from the Bureau of Economic Analysis of the U.S. Department of Commerce. See the Bureau of Economic Analysis, "State Annual Personal Income," http://www.bea.gov/bea/regional/spi. The adjustment for inflation is based on the Personal Consumption Expenditures deflator, which is also calculated by the Bureau of Economic Analysis. See the Bureau of Economic Analysis, "Table 1.1.4. Price Indexes for Gross Domestic Product," http://www.bea.gov/bea/dn/nipaweb/SelectTable.asp?Selected=N.

20. In this chapter, we have seen that average incomes have dropped by a few percent, even though the decrease in the number of jobs has been more than 18 percent. This suggests that some of those who still have a job have done fairly well. Later in this chapter, we will see some information regarding the increase in income inequality.

21. From the 1950s to the 1970s, per capita personal income in Michigan often ranked about eleventh or twelfth among the fifty states.

22. Mitchell Bean's presentation was part of "Michigan's Economic Turnaround: State Budgets of the Past, Present, and Proposals for Change," Forum sponsored by Michigan State University's Institute for Public Policy and Social Research, February 17, 2010.

23. See Carmen DeNavas-Walt, Bernadette D. Proctor, and Jessica C. Smith, *U.S. Census Bureau Current Population Reports: P60–236, Income, Poverty, and Health Insurance Coverage in the United States: 2008*. (Washington, DC: U.S. Government Printing Office, 2009). This report is available at http://www.census.gov/prod/2009pubs/p60–236.pdf. For the income share of the top 20 percent of households, see "Table A.3: Selected Measures of Household Income Dispersion: 1967 to 2008."

24. See Thomas Piketty and Emmanuel Saez, "Income Inequality in the United States, 1913–1998," *Quarterly Journal of Economics* 118 (2003): 1–39. The data used in their paper have been updated through 2007 and are available at Saez's Web site, http://elsa.berkeley.edu/~saez.

25. Jon Bakija and Bradley Heim, "Jobs and Income Growth of Top Earners and the Causes of Changing Income Inequality: Evidence from U.S. Tax Return Data," http://www.williams.edu/Economics/bakija/BakijaHeimJobsIncomeGrowthTopEarners.pdf.

26. If one were to make millions or billions in other industries, the marginal tax rate in the federal income tax is 35 percent. However, the hedge-fund millionaires and billionaires are taxed at a rate of 15 percent, which is the same as the rate applied to non-hedge-fund married couples with incomes below $68,000.

27. This unpublished paper, "The State(s) of Inequality: Changes in Income Distribution in the 50 States and the District of Columbia, 1976-2006," is available on request.

28. Ryan Beene, "Recession drags down CEO pay; Full impact may not have played out", Crain's Detroit Business, June 22, 2009.

29. All fifty of the most highly compensated executives in the Detroit metro area are men. In Chapter 2, we will see that women have made great strides in the labor market in recent decades. However, while the earnings of the *average* woman have increased relative to the earnings of the *average* man, the executive suite is still largely a male preserve. Despite some cracks, the "glass ceiling" is still largely intact.

30. Earlier in this chapter, it was noted that the unemployment rate was actually higher in 1982 than it has been in the latest downturn. However, the unemployment rate is only one of several measures that economists use to judge the severity of an economic contraction. By several measures, the recession of 2008–2009 has been by far the most severe since the 1930s.

31. For a thought-provoking discussion of the rise of concentrated financial power and the threats it poses, see Simon Johnson and James Kwak, *Thirteen Bankers: The Wall Street Take-over and the Next Financial Meltdown* (New York: Pantheon, 2010).

32. One of the leading voices for restoring fiscal balance to the federal government is David M. Walker, who was Comptroller General of the United States and head of the Government Accountability Office in the Clinton and Bush administrations. Walker explains his ideas

in his book, *Comeback America: Turning the Country Around and Restoring Fiscal Responsibility* (New York: Random House, 2010).

33. Of course, the Great Lakes offer opportunities for *waterborne* commerce, even though they form a barrier to *land* connections. However, in today's economy, the vast majority of commercial transportation is by land. See Kenneth Boyer, "Michigan's Transportation System and Transportation Policy," in *Michigan at the Millennium*, Boyer reports that more than three-fourths of the value of Michigan freight originations are in shipments that are transported by truck. It is possible that there could be a resurgence of shipping on the Great Lakes at some point in the future. For now, however, the land highways are king, and this provides a major economic advantage for the southern Lower Peninsula, relative to the rest of Michigan.

34. SEMCOG includes the following counties: Livingston, Macomb, Monroe, Oakland, St. Clair, Washtenaw, and Wayne.

35. For a discussion of tourism, see Donald Holecek, "Travel, Tourism, and Recreation in Michigan," in *Michigan at the Millennium*.

Michigan's Human Resources

M ichigan's greatest asset is its people. In this chapter, we consider the population, labor force, and educational system in Michigan. We begin with a brief look at the trends in population.[1]

Population Trends in Michigan

In 2009, Michigan had a population of about 9.97 million. This makes Michigan the eighth-most populous state. Table 2.1 provides some perspective by showing the twenty states with the largest populations in 2009.[2]

Michigan entered the union in 1837. The first census after statehood was in 1840, when Michigan had about 212,000 people. Michigan's population passed the one million mark at about the time of the Civil War. By 1900, the population of Michigan had grown to about 2.4 million. Thus Michigan has had a long history of very substantial population growth. However, the rate of growth has been uneven over time. Figure 2.1 shows that Michigan's population grew very rapidly from 1910 to 1930. The growth slowed down in the Great Depression decade of the 1930s, both for Michigan and for the rest of the United States. Michigan once again experienced rapid population growth from 1940 to 1970. Michigan's manufacturing-based economy was booming in the middle decades of the twentieth century, and this was associated with rapid population growth.

TABLE 2.1. Populations of the twenty largest states, 2009

RANK	STATE	POPULATION (IN MILLIONS)
1	California	36.96
2	Texas	24.78
3	New York	19.54
4	Florida	18.54
5	Illinois	12.91
6	Pennsylvania	12.60
7	Ohio	11.54
8	**Michigan**	**9.97**
9	Georgia	9.83
10	North Carolina	9.38
11	New Jersey	8.71
12	Virginia	7.88
13	Washington	6.66
14	Arizona	6.60
15	Massachusetts	6.59
16	Indiana	6.42
17	Tennessee	6.30
18	Missouri	5.99
19	Maryland	5.70
20	Wisconsin	5.65
	United States	**307.01**

Source: U.S. Census Bureau, "Population Estimates," http://www.census.gov/popest/states/states.html.

Since 1970, however, the growth rate of Michigan's population has fallen dramatically. In the thirty-year period from 1940 to 1970, the state's population grew by about 69 percent. In the next 30 years, from 1970 to 2000, the population grew by only 12 percent. If the population had grown as rapidly after 1970 as it grew in the thirty years before 1970, it would be more than seventeen million, instead of the approximately ten million who actually live in the state today!

FIGURE 2.1. Population in Michigan, 1840–2009

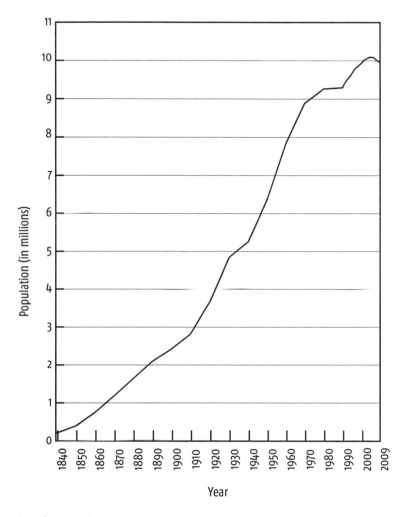

Year

Sources: Before 1900: U.S. Census Bureau, "Statistical Abstract of the United States: 1900," http://www2.census.gov/prod2/statcomp/
documents/1900-02.pdf; 1900 to 1990: U.S. Census Bureau, "The 2010 Statistical Abstract: Historical Statistics," http://www.census.gov/
statab/hist/HS-04.pdf; 1991 to 1999: U.S. Census Bureau, "Population Estimates: Intercensal Estimates," http://www.census.gov/popest/
archives/2000s/vintage_2001/CO-EST2001-12/CO-EST2001-12-26.html; 2000 to 2009: U.S. Census Bureau, "Population Estimates: Vintage 2009,"
http://www.census.gov/popest/states/states.html.

The population of Michigan peaked at about 10.09 million in 2005. Michigan has lost population in every year since then. The total population loss
since 2005 is about 121,000. This means that Michigan's population in 2009
was about 1.2 percent smaller than in 2005.

As a result of slower population growth in the last forty years, Michigan's share of the U.S. population has decreased from 4.4 percent in 1970 to 3.2 percent in 2009. This slower growth is partly a reflection of Michigan's sluggish economic performance in recent decades, which we have already discussed in Chapter 1. It is also a reflection of the general movement of the U.S. population toward the south and west.[3]

There is one silver lining in the cloud of slower population growth. All else equal, a smaller population means less pressure on the environment. Michigan (especially the southern Lower Peninsula) has much more open space than it would have had if the rapid population growth of the mid-twentieth century had continued. We will return to issues of land use and the environment in Chapter 3.

The Aging of the Michigan Population

In 1900, about 5 percent of Michigan's people were 65 years of age or older. By 2008, the elderly population had increased to about 13 percent of the state's total population.[4] In Michigan, as in the rest of the United States, that percentage is expected to continue to increase. The Census Bureau has estimated that the 65-and-over age group will rise to 16 percent of the Michigan population by 2020 and to 19.5 percent by 2030.[5] Thus the percentage of the population who are elderly is projected to grow by almost as much in the next twenty years as it grew in the previous century. As we shall see, the aging of the population has important implications for health care policy, pension policy, and tax policy.

Population Growth in Different Regions in Michigan

Just as the population has grown unevenly over time, it has also grown unevenly across the regions of Michigan. As a result, the geographical distribution of Michigan's population has been changing. In recent decades, the northern Lower Peninsula has had the most rapid growth in percentage terms, and the counties on the fringes of metropolitan areas (such as Livingston County) have had the greatest absolute amounts of growth. At the other end of the spectrum, the Upper Peninsula's population is smaller now than it was in 1910. The population of the Upper Peninsula has changed very little in the last century, while the rest of Michigan has (until recently) experienced substantial population growth. As a result, the Upper Peninsula has claimed a shrinking percentage of Michigan's residents. In 1910, about 11.6 percent of Michigan residents lived in the Upper Peninsula, but the Upper Peninsula's share of the Michigan population is now only about 3.1 percent.

Population Decline and Racial Isolation in Central Cities

The meteoric rise and dizzying fall of Detroit's population are much more dramatic than the population trends for the entire state. Between 1900 and 1930, Detroit's population grew with astonishing speed, from fewer than 300,000 to more than 1.5 million. In 1930, more than 32 percent of Michigan residents were Detroiters. The city's highest population reading came with the 1950 Census, when Detroit had about 1.85 million people. Since then, however, the city has lost more than half its population.[6]

The racial composition of Detroit's population has changed in equally dramatic fashion. In 1960, black residents accounted for about 29 percent of Detroit's population. Since then, the number of white residents in Detroit has decreased by more than one million. In 2000, 81.6 percent of Detroit's people were African American and fewer than 13 percent were white.

Figure 2.2 shows the astonishing degree of racial segregation in the Detroit metropolitan area.[7] This figure shows Wayne, Oakland, and Macomb counties as a mosaic. Each piece of the mosaic is a "census tract," which is roughly a neighborhood. The tracts are color-coded on the basis of their racial and ethnic composition. If a neighborhood is less than 20 percent nonwhite or Hispanic, it is shown in white. If a neighborhood is more than 80 percent nonwhite or Hispanic, it is shown in black. There are three shades of gray in between. The figure shows an amazingly sharp division at the border between Detroit and its northern suburbs: virtually every census tract south of Eight Mile Road is more than 80 percent nonwhite, whereas virtually every tract north of Eight Mile Road is more than 80 percent white. I refer to Eight Mile Road as "Michigan's Berlin Wall."

In discussions of policy and politics in Michigan, race is often the elephant in the room. No one wants to talk about it, but it is there. If we are to bridge the divide between city and suburb, we must confront racial issues, just as we must confront other issues.

FIGURE 2.2. Minority population of census tracts in the Detroit area (Macomb, Oakland, and Wayne Counties), 2000

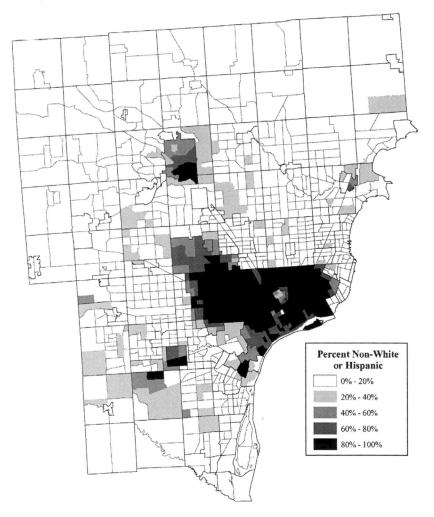

Source: Figure 3.22 in Kenneth J. Darga, "Population Trends in Michigan" in *Michigan at the Millennium*, eds. Charles L. Ballard, Paul N. Courant, Douglas C. Drake, Ronald C. Fisher, and Elisabeth R. Gerber (East Lansing, MI: Michigan State University Press, 2003). Darga's figure, in turn, is based on U.S. Census Bureau, "Census 2000, Summary File 1, Table P4."

On one occasion in the 1980s, I was visiting in Royal Oak with a group of affluent, elderly white women. One said she had not been to downtown Detroit in fifteen years. Others competed for bragging rights by saying they had not been downtown for twenty-five or even thirty years. It is hard to imagine that there could be a comparable group of ladies from Short Hills, New Jersey, who have not been to Manhattan for decades or a group from Wilmette, Illinois, who have not been to downtown Chicago for decades. It is difficult for me to gauge the extent to which these ladies' statements were driven by race, but at the same time, it is also difficult for me to imagine that race was not at least a part of the picture. In any event, as long as it is a badge of honor for some Detroit-area suburbanites to avoid downtown Detroit, it is a problem for all of Michigan, not just for our largest city.

The preceding paragraph does *not* say that suburban whites bear all the responsibility for the racial divisions in the Detroit metropolitan area and elsewhere in Michigan. People of all races can suffer from attitudes that inhibit communication and cooperation across racial lines. For example, in December 2007, I was speaking with an African American gentleman from Detroit. He explained that while he would like to see Barack Obama elected as president of the United States, he felt certain that white America was far too racist ever to allow a black man to achieve the nation's highest office. The suspicions on both sides of the racial divide are very substantial. The divide will only be bridged with sustained effort on both sides.

So far, I have singled out Detroit, which deserves special attention because of its size. However, Detroit is not the only city that faces severe difficulties. Benton Harbor, Flint, Pontiac, Saginaw, and other cities struggle with racial isolation and high rates of poverty. Michigan can never achieve its full potential while many of its largest cities are racially isolated and economically depressed. For one thing, in the future the economy will increasingly be driven by talent and creativity. Creative people often congregate in vibrant cities. Right now when a talented young person looks for a vibrant city, he or she is much more likely to think of Chicago than Detroit. In recent years, Michigan's economy has suffered from the loss of tens of thousands of young people. Revitalized cities and especially a revitalized Detroit will help Michigan to retain these valuable human resources.

Our efforts to deal with the problems of our metropolitan areas cannot succeed unless both cities and suburbs are involved. Regional problems require regional solutions. This is highlighted by David Crary, George Erickcek, and Allen Goodman in *Michigan at the Millennium*. They emphasize that strong cities are also in the interest of suburban residents. A successful metropolitan area "has both a healthy central city and a healthy suburban ring. . . . Suburban residents can benefit from quality entertainment and cultural events that a thriving central city can provide, and better conditions in the city mean fewer negative spillover effects, such as crime, from the central city."[8]

The Michigan Labor Force

In this section, we take a brief look at some key characteristics of the labor force in Michigan. In the next section, we consider the educational attainment of the labor force, which is the most important characteristic of all.[9]

Women in the Michigan Labor Force

Throughout the United States, the labor-force participation rate of women has been increasing for decades. The trend in Michigan is fairly similar to the trend in the United States as a whole. In 1976, about 39.5 percent of the workers in Michigan were female, compared with about 40.5 percent of the national labor force. By 2008, the female proportion was about 47.1 percent in Michigan and about 46.5 percent nationally.[10] Since the 1970s, the wage gap between men and women has decreased substantially. As shown in George Johnson's chapter in *Michigan at the Millennium,* the average forty-year-old female worker with a high school diploma earned about 57.4 percent as much as her male counterpart in 1973. By 2000, this ratio had risen to about 71 percent. Women with college degrees showed similar improvements relative to men with college degrees.[11] As we shall see later in this chapter, the educational attainments of women are increasing much more rapidly than those of men. Also, there is some evidence that the amount of labor-market discrimination against women has decreased. Thus there are good reasons to believe that the trend toward a smaller gender-earnings gap will continue.

Minorities in the Michigan Labor Force

In 1910, about 99 percent of Michigan's people were non-Hispanic whites, compared with about 89 percent of the population of the United States as a whole. Over the last century, however, both Michigan and the United States have experienced a major increase in racial and ethnic diversity. By 2008, more than 14 percent of Michigan's people were African American. This was slightly higher than the national average of 12.8 percent. By 2008, about 4.1 percent of Michigan residents were Hispanic. This is a substantial increase since Hispanics were virtually nonexistent in Michigan before 1930. However, the Hispanic proportion of the Michigan population is still relatively small in comparison to the national average of 15.4 percent.[12]

As their shares of the population have grown, African Americans and Hispanics have also accounted for larger portions of the labor force. However, unemployment rates tend to be higher among minorities than among non-Hispanic whites. Thus the minority percentage of *workers* is slightly smaller than the minority percentage of the *population*.[13]

In the United States overall, the wage gap between blacks and whites is smaller than it was in the middle of the twentieth century, although the relative progress of blacks has been uneven over time and across different regions of the country. Michigan State University's Paul Menchik and I have compared the earnings of black and white full-time year-round male workers. We found that blacks have made substantial relative progress in the Deep South since the 1970s. However, Michigan is one of several states in which the wage gap has actually *increased* since the 1970s. In other words, in Michigan in recent decades, black men have *lost ground* relative to white men. This is probably because black men have suffered disproportionately from the shrinkage of the manufacturing sector.[14]

Unions in the Michigan Labor Force

Union membership grew rapidly after the passage of the National Labor Relations Act in 1935. American labor unions reached their peak in the 1950s, when about one out of every three U.S. workers was a union member. Since then the number of union members has not changed a great deal, while the labor force has grown tremendously. As a result, union members have accounted for a shrinking percentage of the work force. By 2009, only 12.3 percent of U.S. workers were members of labor unions. The unionized percentage of the Michigan work force has also been falling for decades, although unions have consistently represented a larger fraction of the labor force in Michigan than in most of the rest of the country. In 2009, 18.8 percent of the workers in Michigan were union members. This was the fifth-highest percentage among the fifty states.[15]

Different sectors of the economy have widely varying degrees of unionization. In particular, public-sector employees are much more heavily unionized than those who work for private employers. Michigan's unionization rates are higher than the national average both in the public sector and in the private sector. In 2009, 12.2 percent of private-sector workers in Michigan were members of unions, versus 7.2 percent of private-sector workers in the United States as a whole. At the same time, 57.1 percent of public-sector workers in Michigan were union members, whereas only 37.4 percent of public-sector workers in the entire United States were union members.

Labor unions are complex organizations, and they serve social and political functions as well as economic ones. Thus any brief discussion about labor unions is bound to be incomplete. However, it is clear that unions typically desire to increase the wages and benefits of their members. There is ample evidence that unions have succeeded in raising their workers' wages and benefits to higher levels than what otherwise would have been obtained in a fully competitive labor market. In *Michigan at the Millennium*, George Johnson of the University of Michigan presents evidence that the wage premium for union membership is around 10 percent for workers with less than a college education.[16] However, once a union has succeeded in pushing the *wages and benefits* above their equilibrium levels, the union typically has much greater difficulty in maintaining *employment levels*, because of competition from nonunionized firms.[17] This has been especially important in the automobile industry in Michigan.

My research indicates that unions have generally exerted an equalizing influence.[18] In other words, the distribution of income is more equal than it would have been in the absence of unions. Thus the decline in the relative importance of unions has contributed to the increase in income inequality.

It is sometimes suggested that Michigan would benefit from becoming a "Right to Work" state, which means that the laws would be changed to make it more difficult for unions to organize. It seems to me that this is unlikely to have a very large effect, because unions have been weakened to such an extent that Michigan is not far from a "Right to Work" state already. A Right to Work law might succeed in getting or keeping some low-wage jobs in Michigan, but it would put further downward pressure on the wages of workers with relatively low skills. It is not clear that this would be a beneficial outcome for Michigan's people.

In any event, in the long run the most important influence that will determine the wages and benefits for Michigan's workers is their level of education and training and skill. We now turn our attention to educational attainment and educational policies.

Educational Attainment in Michigan

Educational attainment is the single most important factor in determining success in the labor market. In this section, we present some measures of educational attainment for Michigan with comparisons to other states.

Completion of High School and College

Table 2.2 shows the percentage of the population aged 25 and over with at least a high school education for the fifty states and the District of Columbia, averaged over the years 2005 to 2007.[19] This table shows that about 87 percent of Michigan adults have a high school credential. Michigan's percentage was above the national average of about 84 percent, and Michigan ranked twenty second among the fifty states.

Many of the states with the lowest levels of high school attainment have large numbers of Hispanic immigrants, who have less education on average. One reason that Michigan ranks as highly as it does in this category is that Michigan has relatively few Hispanic immigrants. Nevertheless, when it comes to educational achievement for racial and ethnic minorities, Michigan has many of the same problems that are faced by the rest of the country. Some high schools in Michigan have graduation rates close to 100 percent, but the Detroit public schools, with a student body that is overwhelmingly black, have a graduation rate of only 58 percent.[20] (It should be noted that some individual high schools in Detroit have excellent graduation rates, while others have graduation rates well below 50 percent.)

Table 2.3 is similar to Table 2.2, except that Table 2.3 shows the percentage of the population with at least a bachelor's degree. Michigan's position among the states is much lower in terms of college education than high school education. Among Michigan residents who are at least 25 years old, only 24.7 percent have a college degree. This is below the national average of 27 percent,

TABLE 2.2. Percentage of population age 25 and older with at least a high school education, for the fifty states and the District of Columbia, 2005–2007

RANK	STATE	PERCENTAGE	RANK	STATE	PERCENTAGE
1	Minnesota	90.7	27	Delaware	85.5
2	Vermont	90.5	28	Illinois	85.3
3	Wyoming	90.5	29	Indiana	85.3
4	Alaska	90.5	30	Virginia	85.3
5	Utah	90.3	31	Missouri	85.0
6	Montana	89.9	32	Florida	84.5
7	New Hampshire	89.7	33	Oklahoma	84.1
8	Nebraska	89.6	34	District of Columbia	84.0
9	Iowa	89.1	35	New York	83.8
10	Washington	89.0	36	Arizona	83.4
11	Maine	88.9	37	Nevada	83.4
12	Hawaii	88.8	38	Rhode Island	82.5
13	Kansas	88.6	39	North Carolina	82.2
14	Wisconsin	88.5	40	Georgia	82.2
15	Colorado	88.3	41	New Mexico	81.9
16	North Dakota	88.0	42	South Carolina	81.5
17	Massachusetts	88.0	43	West Virginia	81.0
18	Connecticut	87.8	44	Tennessee	80.9
19	South Dakota	87.6	45	Arkansas	80.7
20	Oregon	87.6	46	California	80.0
21	Idaho	87.3	47	Alabama	80.0
22	**Michigan**	**87.1**	48	Kentucky	79.6
23	Maryland	86.9	49	Louisiana	79.2
24	Pennsylvania	86.3	50	Texas	78.6
25	Ohio	86.3	51	Mississippi	78.0
26	New Jersey	86.3		**U.S. average**	**84.1**

Source: U.S. Census Bureau, "Table 13: Educational Attainment of Persons 25 Years Old and Over by Sex and State, 2005–2007," http://nces.ed.gov/programs/digest/d09/tables/dt09_013.asp.

TABLE 2.3. Percentage of population age 25 and older with at least a bachelor's degree, for the fifty states and the District of Columbia, 2005–2007

Rank	State	Percentage	Rank	State	Percentage
1	District of Columbia	45.3	27	Pennsylvania	25.6
2	Massachusetts	37.0	28	Wisconsin	25.5
3	Maryland	34.8	29	Arizona	25.3
4	Colorado	34.7	30	Florida	25.2
5	Connecticut	34.2	31	North Carolina	25.1
6	New Jersey	33.6	32	New Mexico	24.8
7	Vermont	32.9	33	Texas	24.8
8	Virginia	32.9	**34**	**Michigan**	**24.7**
9	New Hampshire	31.4	35	South Dakota	24.4
10	New York	31.2	36	Missouri	24.1
11	Minnesota	30.4	37	Iowa	23.9
12	Washington	30.0	38	Idaho	23.8
13	Rhode Island	29.1	39	Ohio	23.4
14	California	29.1	40	South Carolina	23.0
15	Illinois	29.0	41	Wyoming	22.7
16	Hawaii	28.5	42	Oklahoma	22.2
17	Kansas	28.5	43	Tennessee	21.8
18	Utah	28.3	44	Indiana	21.7
19	Oregon	27.5	45	Alabama	21.0
20	Delaware	26.8	46	Nevada	20.9
21	Nebraska	26.6	47	Louisiana	20.0
22	Georgia	26.4	48	Kentucky	19.7
23	Montana	26.4	49	Arkansas	18.7
24	North Dakota	26.3	50	Mississippi	18.6
25	Alaska	26.2	51	West Virginia	17.0
26	Maine	25.9		**U.S. average**	**27.0**

Source: U.S. Census Bureau, "Table 13: Educational Attainment of Persons 25 Years Old and Over by Sex and State, 2005–2007," http://nces .ed.gov/programs/digest/d09/tables/dt09_013.asp.

and it puts Michigan in thirty-fourth place (or thirty-third if we exclude the District of Columbia).

This relatively poor standing in terms of college attainment is not a recent development. For decades, Michigan has consistently had a smaller percentage of college graduates than the national average. On the bright side, the percentage of people with a college education has been increasing in Michigan. However, Michigan has often been more than 3 percentage points below the national average in recent decades. Thus we find ourselves perpetually behind in terms of the post high school educational attainment of our population.

Educational Achievement

The completion rates in the previous section are important, but they do not tell the entire story. Ultimately, an individual's *level of skill* can be just as important as a diploma or other credential.

Of course, "skill" has many dimensions, and therefore any simple measure of skill is bound to be imperfect. However, one measure of skill that has some merit is the National Assessment of Educational Progress (NAEP), available at http://nces.ed.gov/nationsreportcard. The NAEP allows us to make comparisons among the states in terms of student achievement on tests in reading, mathematics, and other subjects. (The most recent data are for 2009 for mathematics and 2007 for reading.)

Table 2.4 shows the percentage of students who achieve a "basic" level of achievement on math and reading tests in the fourth and eighth grades. On the basis of these data, the only reasonable conclusion is that Michigan is doing a mediocre job of preparing its children for the future.

Michigan's children are slightly below the national average in each of the categories shown in Table 2.4. If the national average were impressive, then perhaps we could celebrate the fact that Michigan is not far below the national average. But the national average is not at all impressive. Neither Michigan nor the United States as a whole is anywhere near where it needs to be. In each of the four categories, at least 22 percent of Michigan children are not even achieving a "basic" level.

The percentage of students achieving at a "proficient" level is much lower than the percentage achieving at the "basic" level. Only 28 percent of Michigan eighth graders were deemed "proficient" in reading and only 31 percent in mathematics. To put things bluntly, more than two out of every three Michigan eighth

TABLE 2.4. Percentage of students achieving a "basic" level of achievement, as reported in the National Assessment of Educational Progress

FOURTH GRADE READING*	PERCENTAGE OF STUDENTS AT A BASIC LEVEL
U.S. average	67
Highest state (Massachusetts)	81
Michigan	**66**
Lowest state (Mississippi)	51
District of Columbia	39

Michigan ranks thirty first among the fifty states (tied with Texas).

FOURTH GRADE MATHEMATICS†	PERCENTAGE OF STUDENTS AT A BASIC LEVEL
U.S. average	82
Highest state (Massachusetts)	92
Michigan	**78**
Lowest state (Mississippi)	69
District of Columbia	56

Michigan ranks thirty eighth among the fifty states (tied with Alaska, Georgia, and South Carolina).

EIGHTH GRADE READING	PERCENTAGE OF STUDENTS AT A BASIC LEVEL
U.S. average	74
Highest state (Montana)	85
Michigan	**72**
Lowest state (Mississippi)	60
District of Columbia	48

Michigan ranks thirty second among the fifty states (tied with Oklahoma).

EIGHTH GRADE MATHEMATICS	PERCENTAGE OF STUDENTS AT A BASIC LEVEL
U.S. Average	73
Highest state (North Dakota)	86
Michigan	**68**
Lowest state (Mississippi)	54
District of Columbia	40

Michigan ranks thirty sixth among the fifty states (tied with Oklahoma and Rhode Island).

* Data for reading from 2007.
† Data for mathematics from 2009.
Source: National Center for Education Statistics, "State Profiles," http://nces.ed.gov/nationsreportcard/states.

graders are *not* proficient in either of these categories. Each of these figures is close to the national average, but once again the national average is a disgrace. If we were to prepare adequately for the future, virtually all students would achieve a "basic" competency, and a strong majority would be "proficient."

Table 2.4 shows that the District of Columbia does less well than any of the fifty states in all four of these categories of educational achievement. It is also true that minorities make up a higher percentage of the school population in DC than in any of the fifty states. This is no coincidence. In many cases, the states with the lowest percentages achieving the "basic" or "proficient" level have relatively large minority populations. America continues to do a poor job of achieving strong educational outcomes for minority children. This is true in Michigan, just as in the rest of the country. Whereas 77 percent of all Michigan eighth graders achieved the "basic" level in math, only 32 percent of black Michigan eighth graders achieved at that level. Some 37 percent of all Michigan eighth graders achieved the "proficient" level in math, but only 5 percent of black Michigan eighth graders did so.

One way to describe the problem is that many of Michigan's young people reach the age of 18 with only a sixth-grade, eighth-grade, or tenth-grade education (even though they may have a diploma from a Michigan high school). This is an unconscionable waste of human resources, and it is also a waste of financial resources. At today's level of spending, Michigan taxpayers spend well over $100,000 on every student who goes from kindergarten through twelfth grade in Michigan public schools. To say the least, it is disappointing for us to spend $100,000 to produce students who do not know how to use fractions or how to write a paragraph that is clear and grammatically correct. Anyone who spends $100,000 on a house has a right to expect that the foundation will be solid and that the wiring will be in order. And if we spend $100,000 on a child, we have a right to expect the child to have a twelfth-grade education.[21]

Later in this chapter, I will offer some thoughts on how to improve educational outcomes for Michigan's children.

The Beneficial Effects of Education

We have seen that Michigan's population is above the U.S. average in attainment of a high school education but below the U.S. average in attainment of a college degree. What effects do these educational differences have on incomes? The answer is that in today's economy, a high level of college attainment has *far* more impact on the incomes of a state's people than a high level of high school attainment.

Effects of Education on Incomes and Employment

Table 2.5 shows the extent to which labor-market earnings increased with education for the United States as a whole in 2008. The data in Table 2.5 are for men, ages 45 to 54, who worked full time for the entire year. (A similar pattern would emerge if we were to look at the numbers for women or for other age groups.) On average, the men in this age group with only a grade school education earned a little more than $30,000 in 2008. High school graduates earned an average of nearly $40,000. Men with a bachelor's degree averaged about $95,000, and those with a professional degree earned about $190,000, on average.[22]

In addition to having higher earnings, people with more education are more likely to be employed. In April 2010, the national unemployment rate

TABLE 2.5. Average earnings in 2008 by level of education for men age 45 to 54 who worked full time year round

Level of education	Average earnings from employment (in dollars)
Professional degree	190,909
Master's degree	116,129
Bachelor's degree	94,642
Associate's degree	60,788
Some college (no degree)	58,439
High school graduate	49,003
Some high school (no diploma)	34,707
Less than ninth grade	30,166

Source: U.S. Census Bureau, "Educational Attainment—People 25 Years Old and Over, by Total Money Earnings in 2008, Work Experience in 2008, Age, Race, Hispanic Origin, and Sex," http://www.census.gov/hhes/www/cpstables/032009/perinc/new03_208.htm.

was 4.9 percent for workers with a bachelor's degree or higher, 8.3 percent for those with some college or an associate's degree, 10.6 percent for high school graduates with no college, and 14.7 percent for those with less than a high school education.[23]

Figure 1.4 showed that per capita incomes in Michigan have been growing less rapidly than the national average for several decades. We used to be well above the national average, and we are now well below it. It's a trend that everyone in Michigan would like to reverse. Thus it makes sense to look at other states that have fared better and to ask what's different about those other states.

In fact, there are not many states for which we can make a very meaningful comparison. We would not learn much from comparing incomes in Michigan with those in North Dakota, because North Dakota's economy is so different from ours. We also would not learn much from comparing incomes in Michigan with those in Delaware, because Delaware is such a small state. However, it is instructive to compare incomes in Michigan with those in Massachusetts. The population of Massachusetts is about two-thirds as large as the population in Michigan, and both states are industrial states. Figure 2.3 shows such a comparison. Figure 2.3 repeats the information in Figure 1.4 by showing per capita incomes in Michigan as a percentage of the U.S. average. Figure 2.3 then compares these data to the information for Massachusetts.

In the 1950s, 1960s, and 1970s, Michigan was ahead of Massachusetts in some years, and Massachusetts was ahead of Michigan in other years. If we take the average for those three decades, Michigan's income level was about 1 percent higher than the income level in Massachusetts. However, in the late 1970s and early 1980s, Massachusetts took off in one direction, and Michigan took off in the other. By 2008, per capita income was about 47 percent higher in Massachusetts than in Michigan.

What does Massachusetts have that Michigan doesn't have? The answer is simple. Massachusetts has the most highly educated population in the country. As we saw in Table 2.3, the percentage of the adult population with a bachelor's degree or more is higher in Massachusetts than in any other state. Forty years ago, a person's level of education did not make as much difference as it makes now. Since that time, however, there has been a phenomenal increase in the financial payoff associated with a college education. Thus the states with more highly educated populations have fared very well in the last thirty or thirty-five years. States with lower levels of education haven't done so well.

FIGURE 2.3. Per-capita personal income in Michigan and
Massachusetts as a percentage of the U.S. average, 1950–2008

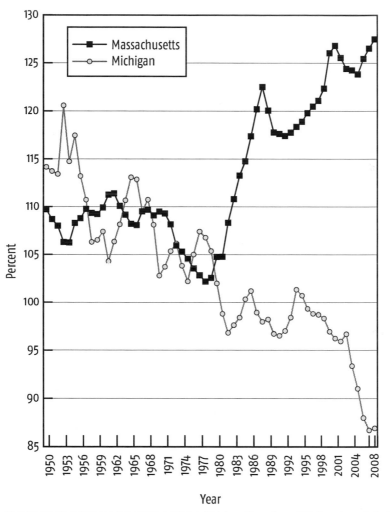

Source: U.S. Department of Commerce, Bureau of Economic Analysis, "State Annual Personal Income," http://www.bea.gov/regional/spi.

In Table 1.3, we saw the ranking of the fifty states according to per capita personal income. The four states with the highest income levels were Connecticut, Massachusetts, New Jersey, and New York. All four of these states are in the top ten for college attainment, while they all rank quite a bit lower in terms of high school attainment. This suggests that in today's economy college education has the greater influence on income levels in the states.

Figure 2.4 shows the level of college attainment and the level of per capita income for each of the fifty states in 2006. This figure includes a marker for each of the fifty states. The diagram does not have enough room to label each state individually, but almost half of the states are labeled. The five states with the highest incomes in 2006 (Connecticut [CT], Maryland [MD], Massachusetts [MA], New Jersey [NJ], and New York [NY]) all have high levels of college attainment. The three states with the lowest incomes (Arkansas [AR], Mississippi [MS], and West Virginia [WV]) all have low levels of college attainment. Between these extremes, most states are fairly close to the line that shows the best statistical fit to the data in Figure 2.4. The trend line slopes steeply upward, which indicates the strong effect of college attainment on per capita incomes. Michigan (MI) is below average in both college attainment and per capita income.

The Equalizing Effect of Education

An individual is more likely to be employed and is more likely to earn a great deal more if he or she has more education. An increase in the educational level of the labor force can also lead to important benefits, even for those with lower levels of education.

This may seem surprising. How can an individual with less education be helped when *someone else* gets more education? For one thing, an increase in a community's educational level can improve the overall productivity of the local economy. Some recent evidence along these lines is presented in a paper by Timothy Bartik of Kalamazoo's Upjohn Institute for Employment Research.[24]

There is also a second reason why increased education has positive spillover effects for those with less education. This has to do with the interaction of supply and demand in labor markets. When there is an increase in the number of college-educated workers, more people will be competing for the top jobs, and fewer will be competing for the jobs at the bottom of the ladder. All else equal, this will lead to an increase in the wages of workers with less education, compared to those with more education. (Workers with more education will still be earning more than those with less education, but the gap will be smaller than it would be otherwise.)

FIGURE 2.4. Income and college attainment for the fifty states, 2006

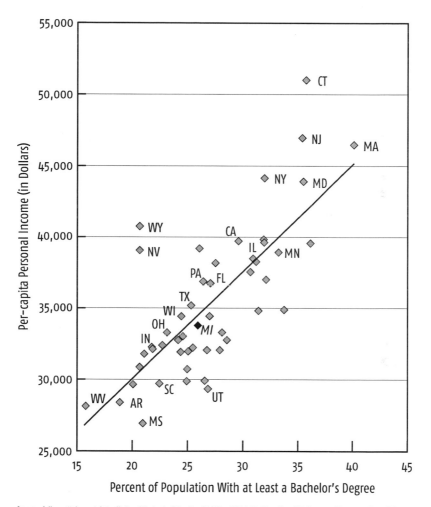

Sources: College attainment data : National Center for Education Statistics, "Table 11 : Educational Attainment of Persons 18 Years Old and Over By State, 2000 and 2006," http://nces.ed.gov/programs/digest/d08/tables/dt08_011.asp. Income data : U.S. Department of Commerce, Bureau of Economic Analysis, "State Annual Personal Income," http://www.bea.gov/regional/spi.

A dramatic example of this occurred in the United States in the early part of the twentieth century. In 1910, only about 10 percent of young Americans were getting a high school diploma. Then the state legislatures passed laws requiring school districts to provide high school education. If a district did not have a high school of its own, it had to pay to send its children to the nearest high school. (This was greatly facilitated by the growing availability of school buses.) By 1940, about 60 percent of students were finishing high school. By 1960, that number had increased to more than 80 percent.

This was a revolutionary change. As a result of this tremendous expansion of educational opportunity, there was a huge increase in the number of workers who could compete for the better jobs. (Nowadays, a "highly skilled" worker is usually one with a college degree, but a hundred years ago the mark of a "highly skilled" worker was a high school diploma.) At the same time, fewer workers were competing for jobs as laborers, and the wages of laborers rose rapidly. This is one of the reasons that the distribution of income in the United States became dramatically more equal in the first half of the twentieth century.[25]

Thus, in general, education does more than make the economy more productive. It also leads to greater equality. Yet within the last thirty-five years, the distribution of income has become starkly more unequal in the United States, even though educational opportunity has continued to expand. This is because the *demand* for highly skilled labor has increased even more rapidly than the *supply* of highly skilled labor. If educational attainment had not continued to expand during the last thirty-five years, the widening of the income gap between workers with high skills and those with low skills would have been even more severe. All else equal, however, when more workers become highly skilled, some benefits accrue even to those who do *not* acquire more skill.

The Benefits of Education beyond the Labor Market

So far our discussion of education has focused on the effects on wages and employment levels. Although these effects are very important, they are only a part of the story. People with higher levels of education do better in many aspects of life. For one thing, those with more education are able to make smarter purchases.[26] More highly educated folks statistically have better health outcomes, live longer, engage in less criminal behavior, and generally provide a better environment in which their children can grow and learn. Robert Haveman and Barbara Wolfe survey these effects and suggest that we greatly understate the value of education if we merely concentrate on education's effect on incomes and employment levels.[27]

These facts suggest that gains can be made by increasing the quality of education *throughout the entire spectrum of educational attainments from kindergarten through college.* It is especially important to increase the percentage of the population with a bachelor's degree because the payoff for a bachelor's degree is substantially larger than it was a few decades ago. However, bachelor's degrees are not the only game in town. For one thing, if a young person is to have any hope of getting a college education, he or she must first complete an elementary and secondary education. Just because the payoff for a bachelor's degree is higher than it used to be, we absolutely cannot neglect our children at earlier stages in their studies.

Michigan is underinvested in education from cradle to career, from preschool to PhD. We need to increase our investments in early-childhood education. Michigan's economy will also be strengthened by increasing the percentage of students who obtain high school diplomas, college degrees, and graduate degrees. Moreover, at every step along the way, it is essential to make sure that students are really developing their skills and not merely getting a credential.

The Critical Importance of Early Childhood

In the upcoming sections, I will highlight two parts of the educational process that are extremely important: early-childhood and college education. In the next section, I will continue the discussion of college education, which is more important than ever before. However, to get to college, it is necessary to finish high school. To succeed in high school, it is necessary to get a strong foundation in elementary and middle school. And to succeed in elementary and middle school, it is necessary to get a strong foundation in the first few years of life. This section focuses on the importance of early-childhood education.

Increased funding for early-childhood education programs can play an extremely important role in helping children to prepare for school. *In fact, early-childhood education earns a higher rate of return than any other investment our society can make.* Investments early in life are extremely valuable because skill leads to more skill, and motivation leads to more motivation. If a child gets motivation and stimulation early in life, he or she is more likely to go from one success to another. On the other hand, if motivation and stimulation are lacking early in life, the child is more likely to experience social and economic failure as an adult.

How early should we begin? *Very* early. In fact, prenatal care is extremely important. After birth, the first three years are the most important years for the child's cognitive, social, and emotional development.

The huge payoff to early-childhood programs has been demonstrated again and again by researchers. One of the most famous studies of early-childhood programs was the Perry preschool project, conducted in Ypsilanti, Michigan.[28] The children who were in the program were much more likely to finish high school and much less likely to be involved in crime. They had higher earnings in the labor market. The list of benefits goes on and on.

Timothy Bartik of the Upjohn Institute in Kalamazoo wrote an outstanding research paper about the effects of early-childhood programs on economic development.[29] Bartik suggests that early-childhood programs can be more effective than business subsidies, as a tool of economic development. Bartik is in good company. James Heckman, the Nobel Prize–winning economist at the University of Chicago, has done a great deal of work in this area. Heckman is one of the most vocal advocates of the viewpoint that early development leads to improved development in later life stages, both in terms of cognitive development and in terms of social and emotional development. Ability gaps between advantaged children and disadvantaged children begin to emerge before the age of two, but if society intervenes early enough, it can raise the abilities and the health of disadvantaged children.[30]

The longer we wait, the more difficult it becomes to help disadvantaged children. Early interventions have much higher rates of return than later interventions such as reduced pupil–teacher ratios, public job training, convict rehabilitation programs, adult literacy programs, tuition subsidies, or expenditure on police.

Studies have shown that early-childhood investments can pay for themselves many times over. If we invest early on, we will end up with adults who earn more money and commit fewer crimes.

In light of the mountains of evidence regarding the high payoff for early-childhood investments, one would think that the Michigan legislature would be eager to provide the resources for these investments. Yet unfortunately, funding for early-childhood programs has been cut. This trend is astonishingly shortsighted, and it should be reversed.

Just as there are advantages to early-childhood educational programs, there are also advantages to getting the most out of kindergarten. In terms of preparing children for subsequent grades in school, full-day kindergarten has advantages over half-day kindergarten. Currently, school districts in Michigan receive a set amount of funding for every kindergartner, even though the school districts have the option of offering kindergarten for only half of the day. In other words, when a school district offers full-day kindergarten, it does not receive any more funding than a district with half-day kindergarten, even though the full-day option is more costly. One possible reform would be for the state to require all kindergartners to participate in a full-day program. (If this is done, however, adequate funding must be provided.) Another possibility would be to provide greater funding for schools that offer full-day, as opposed to half-day, kindergarten programs.

The Critical Importance of Higher Education

In the last few years, a number of important studies have looked at higher-education issues. One of these is the report of the Lieutenant Governor's Commission on Higher Education and Economic Growth (known as the "Cherry Commission" after Lieutenant Governor John D. Cherry Jr.).[31]

Lou Glazer of Michigan Future Inc. (MFI) has probably done more than anyone to publicize the importance of highly educated, talented, and creative people. The MFI Web site (http://www.michiganfuture.org) is full of data, stories, and presentations, all emphasizing the importance of talent. According to MFI, one of the critical components for returning Michigan to high prosperity is to ensure "the long-term success of a vibrant and agile higher education system. This means increasing public investments in higher education. Our higher education institutions—particularly the major research institutions—are our most valuable assets."[32]

Both the Cherry Report and the MFI Web site (in addition to other resources) contain an enormous wealth of information and analysis, along with articulate commentary. It is far beyond the scope of this short book to summarize these sources adequately. However, I would like to emphasize a few points:

- First, as is clear from some of the data presented earlier in this chapter, an individual's *earnings in the labor market* are greater when she or he has more education. This occurs at all levels of education, but the most important jumps in earnings occur for people who go beyond high school. It should also be noted that the benefits of higher education do not solely accrue to those who are in school in their late teens and early twenties. In today's economic environment, learning is a lifelong enterprise, and increasing numbers of people are returning to college after many years away from school.

- Second, research universities perform a crucial function for society through the development of *basic science and technology*. So many aspects of the high-tech economy, from digital electronics to gene therapies to advanced cancer treatments to logistical management techniques, were built on a foundation of basic research carried out at universities.

- Third, research universities provide an ideal environment for developing *applied science and technology*. Basic research is an essential foundation for the new technologies that are transforming our lives. In addition, it is also essential to add to this basic research, so that new products and techniques can be developed and brought into the market. Michigan's research universities are devoting increased resources to programs for transferring new technologies from the laboratory to the marketplace.

Michigan is fortunate to have a multitiered group of publicly supported institutions of higher learning. The first tier includes the community colleges. These colleges provide a host of opportunities, including hands-on training for the skilled technical jobs that are increasingly important in today's economy. The community colleges also provide many students with a springboard to further education. The second tier of Michigan's higher-education system includes twelve regional universities, such as Eastern Michigan University, Grand Valley State University, and Northern Michigan University. The third tier of the system consists of three research universities: Michigan State University, the University of Michigan–Ann Arbor, and Wayne State University.

The research universities provide educational opportunities for large numbers of students. They also provide research capabilities that can have a profound economic impact. The research universities bring hundreds of millions of dollars of federal research funds into the state every year. Moreover, many laboratory discoveries made at research universities have commercial applications. These universities are also very actively engaged with the rest of Michigan in terms of economic, social, and cultural outreach programs. You can get a sense of the breadth and depth of these connections by going to the

Web site of University Outreach and Engagement at Michigan State University, at http://outreach.msu.edu.

Even though the research universities contribute greatly to the general well-being of the state, many of Michigan's people are not very familiar with these contributions. I have had many conversations with Michigan residents who reveal that they have only a very limited idea of the range of work done at the research universities. Although this brief book is not the place for a comprehensive catalog of all the beneficial activities of the research universities, I hope that I have made clear that the scope of these activities is vast.

Zones of Innovation

The Silicon Valley is a narrow strip of land along the southern and western shores of San Francisco Bay. It is home to Google, Hewlett-Packard, Intel, Oracle, and many other dynamic, innovative companies. The Silicon Valley is at the cutting edge of technology, not only for the United States but for the entire world.

Why is the Silicon Valley located where it is? Why is it not in Idaho, Nebraska, or Alabama? One important reason is the close proximity of Stanford University and the University of California at Berkeley. Across the country, when we find regions at the cutting edge in technology and innovation, universities are always nearby.

Could something similar to the Silicon Valley be formed in Michigan? To a certain extent, it is already happening. Michigan has already become a worldwide leader in automotive high technology, and the engineering programs at our universities have played a big role in this success. More important, Michigan has tremendous potential to become a much greater center of innovation. If this is to occur, Michigan's universities are certain to play a crucial role. For instance, during the winter of 2008–2009, when almost all the economic news was bad, there were two pieces of very good news in East Lansing. IBM announced that it would open a major software development facility in East Lansing. Also, Michigan State University won a federal contract for more than $500 million for the Facility for Rare Isotope Beams. Neither IBM nor the U.S. Department of Energy chose East Lansing at random. In each case, the choice was made because of the presence of a university with lots of scientists, engineers, and scientific infrastructure.

When we as Michigan citizens truly take time to analyze the benefits and potential of the University of Michigan, Michigan State University, and Wayne State University, we realize that we have three institutions of a caliber that is absent in most of the other forty-nine states. These institutions can provide a platform for future economic growth in Michigan. Unfortunately, policy makers in Michigan have slashed higher-education budgets in recent years. Yet the precious resource of our colleges and universities has not been squandered, at least not yet. The colleges and universities still provide tremendous benefits to the Michigan economy, and they have even greater potential.

The Brain Drain

If Michigan is to achieve its full economic potential, it is crucial for us to both *train* and *retain* educated workers. When highly educated workers migrate to other regions of the country, Michigan loses out. In fact, the migration of young people is a serious problem for Michigan. Michigan suffered a net loss in the 1990s of nearly sixty thousand residents aged 20 to 31.[33]

This outward migration is partly due to military service: young Michigan residents who enter the armed forces will almost always leave the state for military bases in the south and west. However, much of this outward migration has nothing to do with military service. In order to retain talented young people, Michigan has to create and maintain the kind of atmosphere that will make these people want to stay here. In the best-selling book *The Rise of the Creative Class*, Richard Florida emphasizes the increasingly important economic role played by creative people in science and engineering, design, education, arts, and entertainment. Mr. Florida stresses the "3 Ts" of economic development—technology, talent, and tolerance.[34]

Increasingly, young college graduates do something that I never would have had the courage to do when I graduated from college in 1976. These young folks often move to a new place *before* finding a job. This clearly indicates that, while jobs are important, the success of a region involves more than just jobs. When a young graduate of a college or university in Michigan moves to Chicago, it is safe to say that he or she did not pick Chicago by throwing darts at a map. Instead, the choice of Chicago (or Austin, Boston, New York, San Francisco, or any number of other cities) is based partly on cultural considerations. Talented people want to live in vibrant places. That's why if we want to keep our talented young people in Michigan (and attract others from outside the state), we need to make investments to make sure that our cities are vibrant and exciting places to be.

In spite of the increasing importance of higher education, the Michigan legislature has pursued a policy of systematic disinvestment in its universities. One possible explanation has to do with the outward migration of some of our college-educated young people. Maybe the legislators are saying, "Some of these young people leave Michigan, so let's stop educating them." In my opinion, this is an extremely unwise decision. I think we should double our efforts to educate our children and also double our efforts to keep them here.

The proportion of Michigan residents who have a college education *has* increased over the years. However, it is lower than it would be if more of our young people stay in Michigan. To capture a brighter future, we must attack the problem on three fronts: We need to educate our young people. We need to create a business environment that will bring jobs to the state. Finally, we need to improve the cultural vitality of our cities.

The Relative Decline in College Attainment for Men

Before closing this discussion of colleges and universities, I want to mention one more issue, which is illustrated in Figure 2.5. This figure shows that in the last few decades men in the United States have attained far fewer college degrees than women.[35]

Figure 2.5 is the result of both good news and bad news. The good news is that American women have increased their educational attainment dramatically. About 140,000 women got a bachelor's degree in 1961. This number increased steadily to about 420,000 in 1976 and about 875,000 in 2007. The bad news is that American men have not advanced nearly as much. The number of bachelor's degrees awarded to American men was almost exactly the same in 1999 as it had been in 1973. A similar trend has occurred in the awarding of associate degrees, about 62 percent of which now go to women. In 2007, for the first time ever, women received more than half of the doctorate degrees. In other words, American women have achieved exceptional increases in their educational attainment, while men have made much less progress.

Why have men become less likely to embrace higher education than women? One possible explanation is consistent with our analysis of many of

FIGURE 2.5. Bachelor's degrees awarded in the United States by sex, 1973–2007

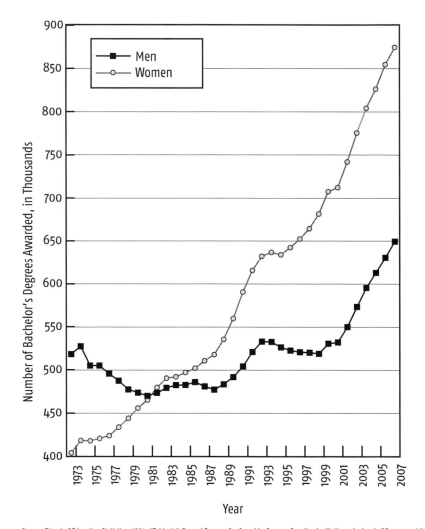

Source: Digest of Education Statistics: 2004, "Table 247. Earned Degrees Conferred by Degree-Granting Institutions, by Level of Degree and Sex of Student: Selected Years, 1869–1870 to 2013–2014," National Center for Education Statistics, http://nces.ed.gov/programs/digest/d04/tables/dt04_247.asp; and Digest of Education Statistics: 2008, "Table 248. Earned Degrees Conferred by Degree-Granting Institutions, by Level of Degree and Sex of Student: Selected Years, 1869–1870 to 2017–2018," http://nces.ed.gov/programs/digest/d08/tables/dt08_268.asp.

Michigan's problems. The manufacturing workforce of the 1950s and 1960s was dominated by men. Therefore, men became more attached to the old economy than women did. Men, more than women, seem to have nostalgia for the old days when it was possible to earn a good living with relatively little education. Old attitudes die hard. However, if Michigan is to achieve its economic potential, we need to change these attitudes. If we want to improve the economic strength of Michigan and the rest of the United States in the future, we need boys to strive for higher education just as much as we need girls to do so.

Financing Education in Michigan

I have stressed the importance of education at all levels, including early-childhood, elementary, secondary, and postsecondary education. Now we turn to the question of how to pay for it.

Greater Administrative Efficiencies in K–12 Education

If we can reduce our expenditures on administrative overhead, more money will be left over for the classroom. In recent years, there has been a great deal of discussion about sharing services across school district lines, as well as the consolidation of school districts. Both of these ideas have some potential to reduce costs without reducing the quality of instruction. However, we should not delude ourselves into thinking that either of these is a magical solution to all the problems of education finance.

When we think about school-district consolidation, we need to remember that most of the low-hanging fruit has already been picked. In the 1949–1950 school year, Michigan had more than 4,900 school districts. That number fell to about 2,100 in 1960–1961 and to 630 in 1970–1971.[36] After 1970, the pace of consolidation slowed down substantially. Michigan now has about 550 traditional school districts. This wave of consolidations helped to achieve economies of scale. By now, however, most of the economies of scale have already been achieved. The minimum efficient scale for a school district is probably about one thousand students, and the vast majority of schoolchildren in Michigan are already in districts that are well above the minimum efficient size. Thus further school-district consolidations are only likely to provide us with modest savings. I believe we should push for consolidations, where it can be shown that significant cost savings will occur, but we should understand that the cost savings, by themselves, will not be large enough to solve the problems of education finance in Michigan. (And if we can find those savings, we should put the money into increased classroom instruction.)

Sharing of accounting and administrative services can also lead to cost savings. Once again, however, many of the savings have already been achieved by previous efforts. Additional savings can be achieved in some cases, although it will take time. For instance, a group of school districts can become more efficient if they all use the same computer software. But the transition to a new software system takes both time and money.

As I see it, the cost-effectiveness of education in Michigan has already been enhanced tremendously by consolidations and sharing of services. Substantial savings have already been achieved. It is true that even more savings can still be achieved through selected consolidations and sharing of services. And, if cost-effectiveness can be enhanced, we should do it. But even if we achieve every possible administrative efficiency, many of the problems associated with educational funding will remain.

Educational Productivity

Another possible way to achieve better educational outcomes at a lower cost is to improve productivity in the delivery of instruction. However, there are serious limits to our ability to improve productivity in education.

In Chapter 1 of this book, we discussed huge productivity improvements in agriculture and manufacturing. The average farm worker in Michigan today can produce far more food than the average farm worker from a century ago. Likewise, the average factory worker of today can produce far more manufactured goods than the average factory worker from a century ago. But today's average classroom teacher does not (and should not) teach several times as many children as the average classroom teacher of long ago. If educational productivity had increased at the same rate as productivity in manufacturing and agriculture, elementary and secondary class sizes would be in the hundreds or even in the thousands.

It is *sometimes* possible to automate the educational process. Educators are experimenting with all sorts of new teaching methods, some of which involve instruction with computers and the Internet. I use online tutorials and problem sets in my own classes. Nevertheless, in many cases the learning process is best carried out through one-on-one contact between a teacher and a student.

This is especially true at the elementary level. Because of the importance of personalized instruction, the long-run trend in K–12 education in the United States has been toward *smaller* class sizes, and rightly so.

Thus there are limits on the extent to which we can improve education through cost-saving improvements in productivity.[37] This means that if we want to make major improvements in our educational system, it will probably cost money. In the rest of this section, we turn to the money issues.

No, the Lottery Won't Solve the Problem

All the profits of the Michigan Lottery are devoted to education. On the basis of this, some Michigan residents have reached the conclusion that the lottery is supposed to pay for education completely. This is a fallacy. (Here is a similar logical fallacy: all robins are birds; therefore, all birds are robins.) Just because 100 percent of the lottery profits go to education, that does *not* mean that 100 percent of education funding is provided by the lottery. In fact, the lottery only provides enough funds to keep our schools going for about a week of the regular school year.

It's easy to see why people would be attracted to the idea that the lottery will pay for all of education. Lots of people don't play the lottery, or if they play it at all, they don't play much. Many of those folks may think, "This is great; the lottery pays for schools, and I don't have to pay anything!" It's a nice fantasy, but it just isn't true. Thus as we grapple for solutions to the problems of educational funding, we need to look beyond the idea that the lottery is a cure-all solution. We will need to cut our educational expenditures, reform our tax system to get more revenues, or both.

Teacher Salaries and Class Sizes

Table 2.6 compares the average teacher salaries for public elementary and secondary school teachers in the fifty states and the District of Columbia in 2006–2007.[38] The table shows the wide variation in teacher salaries across the United States. The national average was a little more than $50,000 in 2006–2007. The average salary in the highest state (California) was nearly 80 percent higher than the average salary in the lowest state (South Dakota). The average teacher salary in Michigan was a little less than $55,000 in 2006–2007. This

TABLE 2.6. Average annual salaries (in dollars) of teachers in public elementary and secondary schools, 2006–2007

RANK	STATE	SALARIES	RANK	STATE	SALARIES
1	California	63,640	27	Colorado	45,833
2	Connecticut	60,822	28	Nevada	45,342
3	New Jersey	59,920	29	Florida	45,308
4	District of Columbia	59,000	30	Texas	44,897
5	Massachusetts	58,624	31	Virginia	44,727
6	New York	58,537	32	Arkansas	44,245
7	Illinois	58,246	33	South Carolina	44,133
8	Maryland	56,927	34	Tennessee	43,816
9	Rhode Island	55,956	35	Kentucky	43,646
10	Pennsylvania	54,970	36	Alabama	43,389
11	**Michigan**	**54,895**	37	Kansas	43,334
12	Delaware	54,680	38	Iowa	43,130
13	Alaska	54,658	39	Louisiana	42,816
14	Ohio	51,937	40	Idaho	42,798
15	Hawaii	51,922	41	New Mexico	42,780
16	Oregon	50,911	42	Oklahoma	42,379
17	Wyoming	50,692	43	Nebraska	42,044
18	Georgia	49,905	44	Missouri	41,839
19	Minnesota	49,634	45	Maine	41,596
20	Vermont	48,370	46	Montana	41,225
21	Wisconsin	47,901	47	Utah	40,566
22	Washington	47,882	48	West Virginia	40,531
23	Indiana	47,831	49	Mississippi	40,182
24	New Hampshire	46,527	50	North Dakota	38,822
25	North Carolina	46,410	51	South Dakota	35,378
26	Arizona	45,941		**U.S. average**	**50,816**

Source: Digest of Education Statistics: 2008, "Table 79. Estimated Average Annual Salary of Teachers in Public Elementary and Secondary Schools, by State or Jurisdiction: Selected Years, 1969–1970 through 2006–2007," National Center for Education Statistics, http://nces.ed.gov/programs/digest/d08/tables/dt08_079.asp.

makes Michigan the state with the eleventh-highest teacher salaries, about 8 percent above the national average.

In my 2006 book, I reported the same data for 2002–2003. In that school year, Michigan had the fourth-highest teacher salaries, about 18 percent above the national average. Thus Michigan's relative position has slipped substantially in only four years.

In response to the fact that teacher salaries are still relatively high, it would not be surprising for school districts in Michigan to try to control expenditures by having larger class sizes. Indeed, in the 2006–2007 school year, elementary and secondary class sizes in Michigan were about 13 percent larger than the national average.[39] As I see it, a strong case can be made for keeping class sizes small. This will require some combination of additional financial resources for the schools and increased moderation in teacher compensation.

Later in this chapter, we will discuss pension and health-care benefits for teachers. These expenditures are increasing at a rapid rate and wreaking havoc for school-district budgets around the state. Fringe benefits need to be brought under control. On the salary side of things, however, I very much hope that Michigan's people will not push too hard for cutbacks. Although I don't want to give teachers a blank check, I also don't want to see teacher salaries slashed. We won't get top-quality people into the classroom unless we pay decent salaries.

From my perspective, the average level of teacher salaries is not the biggest problem. The biggest problem is that in most districts, teacher salaries are set according to rigid, bureaucratic pay scales. In most of the state, teacher salaries depend chiefly on the number of years of service. This means that a high school chemistry teacher may be paid the same as a second-grade teacher with the same seniority, even though the equilibrium salary is higher for the chemistry teacher.

Some folks may object to the statement I just made. After all, the second-grade teacher probably works just as hard as the chemistry teacher. But that's not the point. Even though I may work just as hard as a surgeon, the surgeon makes more than I do. And even though a short-order cook may work just as hard as I do, I am paid more than the cook. The point is that the chemistry teacher probably has alternative employment possibilities (outside the classroom) that pay more than the alternatives available to the second-grade teacher. If we are to get top-quality people for different types of teaching positions, we need to have flexibility in our pay scales.

More generally, we should move toward pay scales that have the flexibility to reward the very best teachers. In other words, we need some sort of "merit pay." Of course, merit pay is not a panacea. But the concept makes a great deal of sense. My own pay is based on an annual merit evaluation, and the same is true for many others. It is not easy to evaluate teacher performance, but that does not mean that we should not even *try* to evaluate performance.

Proposal A and the Financing of K–12 Education

In 1994, Michigan voters approved Proposal A, which brought about dramatic changes in the financing of elementary and secondary education. Prior to Proposal A, local public schools in Michigan were financed mainly by local property taxes. Under this system, there were huge disparities between the funding levels in rich school districts and poor school districts. As a result of Proposal A, *local* property taxes were reduced dramatically while several *state* taxes were increased. Consequently, much of the power to make decisions about the public schools was shifted from the local level to the state level. After Proposal A, a large part of the decision-making process for school finance was moved from hundreds of local school boards to the Lansing offices of the legislature and the governor.[40]

Since the passage of Proposal A, the state government has provided a system of per-pupil "foundation allowances" for operating expenses in the public schools. The minimum foundation allowance, which goes to low-revenue school districts, has increased much more rapidly than the allowances for higher-revenue districts. After adjusting for inflation, the per-pupil funding levels in the poorest school districts have (until recently) increased substantially, while the funding levels in many affluent districts have increased at a much slower pace, and the funding for some of the richest districts has decreased. Thus the difference between the funding levels in the rich districts and the poor districts has fallen dramatically. In 1994, the per-pupil operating revenues in the ten highest-revenue districts were about 2.8 times as large as those in the ten lowest-revenue districts. By 2003, the foundation allowances for the top ten districts were still larger than the allowances for the bottom ten districts, but only by a factor of 1.7.[41]

Before Proposal A, it was difficult for Michigan's poorest school districts to provide even minimally acceptable levels of instruction. Of course, the increases in funding for the poorest districts do not *guarantee* that the children in these districts will be educated adequately, but at least the additional funding improves the chances that these children will get a good education. In fact, the evidence suggests that the increased funding for schools *did* improve educational outcomes. Leslie Papke of Michigan State University has studied the effects of spending on pass rates for the standardized fourth-grade math test. She uses data for individual schools in Michigan, for the years before and after the passage of Proposal A. Papke finds that an increase in real, inflation-adjusted spending leads to an increase in the percentage of students who pass. Importantly, these increases were larger for the schools that were performing poorly before Proposal A was instituted.[42]

I have emphasized the fact that the distribution of income has become much more unequal over the last thirty-five years. The trend toward greater inequality has actually been exacerbated by some of the policies undertaken in Michigan. However, the move toward more uniform levels of funding across school districts is an important and beneficial exception to this pattern.

Financing Capital Expenditures in Michigan's Public Schools

Proposal A reduced the school-funding disparities between rich districts and poor districts for *operating expenditures*. However, Proposal A did not apply to *capital expenditures*. As a result, the revenues for school construction, school renovation, and other capital expenditures are still drawn almost exclusively from local sources. Although the poorer school districts are now better able to pay for operating expenditures, they are still at a tremendous disadvantage when it comes to capital spending.

This issue is analyzed in an excellent report by the Citizens Research Council of Michigan (CRC) and the Educational Policy Center (EPC) at Michigan State University (herein referred to as the CRC/EPC report).[43] The report's authors emphasize that there are huge differences in the amount of taxable property in the various school districts in Michigan. In the twenty-nine wealthiest districts, the value of taxable property per student is more than $500,000. In the seventy-five poorest districts, there is less than $100,000 of taxable property per pupil. The six poorest districts (which include Detroit) have less than $50,000 per student. As a result, many of the poorest districts have aging and inadequate school facilities. This is not because the poor districts have low tax rates. In fact, the property-tax rates in many of the poorest districts are well above the state average. The problem is that these districts simply do not have a tax base that is large enough to pay for adequate school facilities, regardless of their property-tax rates.

Inadequate school facilities are not merely an economic issue. They are a moral issue. The taxpayers of East Lansing are wealthy enough that my son was able to attend school in facilities of high quality. However, many of Michigan's schoolchildren go to school in buildings that are out of date or even dilapidated. In a place as affluent as Michigan, I find it morally offensive that any child would have to attend school in a substandard building.

In school districts with high levels of taxable property, it has been possible to build newer and better facilities without raising property-tax rates to prohibitive levels. These new facilities can then be used to attract additional students from poorer nearby districts, under Michigan's program of "public schools of choice," under which parents can apply to send their children to public schools in a different school district from the one in which they reside. This puts the poorer districts in a vicious cycle: Unable to build new facilities, they lose students. When they lose students, they also lose the foundation-grant funds that go with those students. The loss of foundation-grant funds puts even more financial pressure on the poor districts, and the cycle continues.

The authors of the CRC/EPC report calculate the cost of providing every K–12 student in Michigan with an adequate physical infrastructure at school. (Note that these calculations are based on conservative assumptions about the quality of the new facilities that would be built. If the capital expenditures envisioned in the CRC/EPC report were undertaken, the new facilities would be better than the old ones they replace, but they would not be as elaborate as some of the facilities that have been built recently in some affluent districts.) The CRC/EPC report estimates that the value of unmet capital needs in Michigan public schools is about $8.9 billion. A substantial amount of the total need is in low-income school districts in central cities. However, this is not merely an inner-city issue. Inadequate school facilities are scattered all over the state, and many are in rural areas.

The figure of $8.9 billion of unmet capital needs may sound daunting. However, we should remember that capital expenditures can be financed over a long period of time. The CRC/EPC report's authors note that if we were to finance these new capital investments over a period of thirty years at 5 percent interest, it would add less than 5 percent to the annual amount that is now spent on public schools in Michigan.

Any successful reform of Michigan's school-finance system must shift some of the financial responsibility for school capital infrastructure from the local districts to the state government. As long as capital projects are exclusively a local responsibility, there is simply no way that the poorest districts can provide adequate facilities for their children. The authors of the CRC/EPC report discuss various proposals for addressing the unmet capital needs in Michigan's public schools. One option would be a system of "district power equalization." Under this plan, the state would subsidize the per-pupil yield of each mill of the local property tax in order to bring each district's revenue-raising capacity up to a guaranteed minimum level. Other proposals range from modest changes in the state's School Bond Loan Fund program, to a more drastic proposal under which the state would assume full responsibility for all financing of investments in public-school infrastructure.

Regardless of which plan is adopted, *something* needs to be done. The current policy says, in effect, that some Michigan children do not deserve to be educated in decent facilities. Michigan's children cannot reach their full educational potential when they are stuck in dilapidated and antiquated facilities. It is crucial to recall that even though Michigan's economy has not performed very well in recent decades, we are not a poor state. We *can* afford to send all of our children to school in decent facilities. And yet we choose not to. No one has forced us to leave some of our children in substandard facilities. We have *chosen* to leave them in substandard facilities because we have lacked the political will to do the right thing.

How Equal Should School Funding Be?

Until the mid-1990s, there were enormous disparities among Michigan school districts, both in per-pupil operating expenditures and per-pupil capital expenditures. As we have seen, Proposal A reduced the disparities for operating expenditures but not for capital expenditures. I have praised the move toward greater equality in operating expenditures, and I have proposed that we also move toward greater equality in capital expenditures.

However, I want to make the case *against* equalizing *completely*. It is absolutely appropriate to bring every student up to a substantial standard of funding, regardless of how wealthy or poor the child's school district might be. But once we provide a solid level of expenditure for every child in the state (for capital needs as well as for operating needs), I have no objection to allowing voters in individual school districts to spend some more on their own children, if they choose to do so. In fact, it might actually be counterproductive to insist on completely equal per-pupil expenditures throughout the state. If middle-class and upper-middle-class voters reach the conclusion that they are unable to provide the desired level of educational expenditures for their own children, there is a danger that they would withdraw their political support for public education in general. (This may already have occurred to a certain extent.)[44]

On the other hand, I do *not* support giving unlimited fundraising authority to individual school districts. If we do not impose any restrictions, we run the risk of seeing our system of school finance return to the vast inequities that existed before Proposal A.

For many years, Michigan tilted heavily toward local control of all types of school spending, with only a minor role for state government. Proposal A took Michigan to the other extreme for school operating expenditures, and left very little maneuvering room for the individual school districts. I have made a case here for a more balanced mixture of state control and local control of public-school financing, both for operating expenditures and for capital expenditures. There are vast differences among school districts in the ability to raise revenue. This suggests that there is an important role for state financing, so that even the children in the poorest areas can receive an adequate education. However, if every school district in Michigan is given the financial resources to educate its children to an acceptable level, there are good reasons to allow individual districts to spend more on their own students, if that is what their voters decide to do.

One other aspect of school funding needs to be addressed. Under the current system, the number of dollars that a school district receives is based on only two things: the funding formula established by the legislature and the number of students enrolled in the district. No adjustments are made for special circumstances. For example, some districts have much higher transportation costs. Other districts have far more special-needs students. The funding formula does not take these factors into account. If we want our public schools to be as effective as they can be, we need to adjust our system of school finance to do a better job of accounting for transportation, special needs, and other factors that influence costs.[45]

Financing Retirement Benefits for Michigan Teachers

Michigan has also made one other important change in the division of school-financing responsibility between the state government and the local school districts. Prior to Proposal A, the state government and the school districts shared in paying for the employer portion of contributions to the Michigan Public School Employees Retirement System (MPSERS). However, after Proposal A was approved, the full responsibility was placed on the shoulders of the local districts. Thus at the very time when local districts were losing their ability to raise their own revenues (because Proposal A reduced reliance on local property taxes), the local districts were given an additional financial responsibility. This has intensified the financial squeeze on school districts. The percentage of payroll going to contributions for retirement programs has been rising, and it is expected to continue to rise.[46]

The health-care benefits of retired teachers present a more serious problem than the pension benefits. The health-care benefits have always been handled on a pay-as-you-go basis. Whereas Michigan teacher pensions are paid from assets accumulated in advance, health-care benefits are paid out of current revenues. Health-care costs in the United States have been rising rapidly over a long period, and they are expected to continue to rise at a faster rate than the general rate of inflation. Since health-care costs have been escalating rapidly, and since they are only paid out of current revenues, local school districts have experienced an increasing financial squeeze.

Burgeoning pension and health-care costs are forcing many school districts to make painful reductions in their instructional programs. Since 2003, the foundation grants given by the state have had modest increases in some years and reductions in other years. The net effect is that the foundation grants have fallen well short of keeping up with inflation. Thus it has been extremely difficult for school districts to cover the rising pension and health-care costs. Under the current system, where public schools are not given additional resources to pay for these costs, it appears likely that the pressure on instructional programs will only become more severe over time.

In many of Michigan's school districts, inflation-adjusted funding levels went up substantially during the 1990s. This made it possible to improve instruction. However, much of the progress has since been wiped out by a combination of limited funding and rising pension and health-care costs. In recent years, I have had many discussions with public school business officials from around the state. It is widely predicted that if Michigan's public schools do not get some sort of relief in the next year or two, dozens of districts will be financially insolvent.

These financial troubles may actually be worse than they are sometimes said to be. Robert Lawrence (a member of the Board of Birmingham Public Schools) has written a thought-provoking piece for The Center for Michigan.[47] MPSERS reports that its unfunded liabilities are $35 billion. However, this figure is based on assumptions about future investment returns that may be unrealistic, and it is based on accounting procedures that may not be appropriate. Lawrence suggests that the true unfunded liability may be as large as $60 billion.

Ultimately, the people of Michigan will have to face up to some very difficult choices. It will be necessary to increase educational funding greatly, reduce teachers' benefits drastically, or choose some combination of spending increases and benefit reductions.[48] In my opinion, a combination of spending increases and benefit reductions is the best way to go.

If taxes are not returned to their earlier levels or at least stabilized, then the brunt of the problem will most likely be borne by teachers (in the form of reduced pay and benefits) or by schoolchildren (in the form of larger class sizes and lower-quality instruction). If teacher pay and benefits are protected completely, then the brunt of the problem will most likely be borne by taxpayers or schoolchildren. I firmly believe that school budgets should not be balanced on the backs of schoolchildren. If the children are spared, then the largest effects will probably be higher taxes or lower pay and benefits for teachers. I suggest that the burden should not fall exclusively on taxpayers, nor should it fall exclusively on teachers. Yes, there should be some tax increases. (In fact, as we saw in Chapter 1, tax effort in Michigan has fallen substantially in the last few decades. I will return to this issue in Chapter 6.) But teachers should not be immune. It is not asking too much for teachers to pay more for their health care, especially at a time when many private-sector workers are doing the same. My health-insurance premiums and copays have gone up, and I expect they will continue to rise. In view of the tremendous pressure that increasing health-care costs are putting on the budgets of employers all across the country, premiums and copays *should* increase.[49]

Financing Higher Education

I have repeatedly emphasized the crucial importance of higher education. In this light, it makes sense that Michigan should strive to achieve a substantial increase in the annual number of college graduates in the state. The Cherry Commission[50] recommends that the annual number of college graduates should be doubled. This raises the question of how we would pay for the increasing numbers of college students.

The first point to understand is that the most of state-supported universities in Michigan are already at or near capacity. If we were to double the number of students, it would be necessary to hire new faculty members and build new classrooms and laboratories. This will cost money. Second, federal funding for higher education is shrinking. This is a serious mistake on the part of the federal government, but it is doubtful that Michigan can change the direction of federal policy. Third, the universities are aggressively engaged in private fundraising, and the money raised through those channels is making a big difference. However, if enrollment at Michigan's universities were to increase substantially, it is very unlikely that private endowments could cover all the additional costs. Thus if the *people of Michigan* are serious about improving our higher-education outcomes, it will almost certainly be necessary for the *people of Michigan* to provide additional financial resources.

Remarkably, however, the Michigan legislature has undertaken a policy of systematic disinvestment in higher education. In the introduction to this book, I pointed out that the cuts to university budgets in the last eight years are equivalent to *completely eliminating* state support for ten of the fifteen universities.

Figure 2.6 shows that this trend of the last eight years is not exactly new. In fact, the trend of the last eight years is a continuation and acceleration of a very long-term trend. Figure 2.6 shows the percentage of the budget at Michigan State University that comes from state support and the percentage that comes from tuition. The fraction coming from the State of Michigan has declined fairly steadily for half a century but at an especially rapid rate in the last decade.

FIGURE 2.6. Sources of funds for Michigan State University, 1959 to 2009

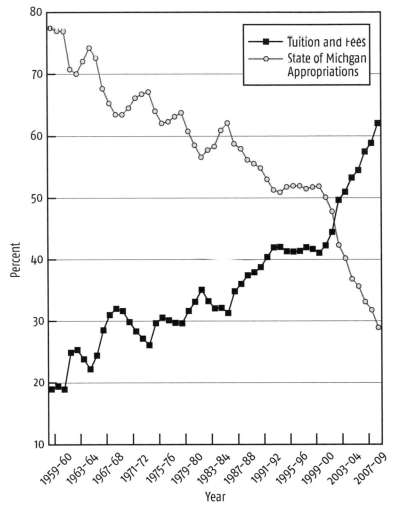

Source: Office of Planning and Budgets, Michigan State University.

I believe that the policy of disinvestment in higher education is a mistake. By saying this, I know that I run the risk of appearing biased, since I work for a university that is supported (at least somewhat) by the State of Michigan. My advocacy for better financial support for higher education might appear to be motivated out of sheer selfishness. If that's your view, I don't know if I can say anything that will change your mind. It is probably true that stronger state support for higher education would work out to my personal benefit. However, the ones who are harmed most by the budget cuts are the students. The students are the ones who suffer academically when programs are cut. The students are the ones who suffer academically when they have to work long hours during the school year to pay their bills. The students are the ones who are often forced to accumulate large amounts of student-loan debt.

If the state government were to increase its support for higher education, it would be easier for the colleges and universities to accommodate an increase in the number of students. In addition, the colleges and universities themselves can increase the affordability of a college education by adjusting their tuition and financial-aid policies. At many institutions of higher learning, large numbers of students pay less than the full amount of tuition because they receive a price discount in the form of financial aid. Under a program of need-based financial aid, students from the most affluent families would pay the full amount of tuition, and students from families of modest means would pay less, on net.

A large percentage of students from the most affluent families will go to college in any event. Students from low- and middle-income families are the ones who are making decisions about attending college on the basis of financial considerations.[51] Thus if we are to increase the number of college graduates, special attention must be focused on students from low- and middle-income families. The best combination of policies would involve strong financial support from the state so that tuition can remain at moderate levels, coupled with aggressive financial aid. Regardless of the tuition policies of the colleges and universities, it makes sense to increase the percentage of our financial-aid dollars that are allocated on the basis of need.

In this discussion of higher-education funding, I have focused mainly on public policies. However, private efforts can also be extremely important. In 2005 a group of anonymous donors initiated the "Kalamazoo Promise," which pays up to 100 percent of tuition at Michigan colleges and universities for graduates of Kalamazoo public schools. These farsighted donors deserve our thanks and praise. It is hoped that the spirit of the Kalamazoo Promise will one day extend to the entire state. If private donors and public officials can summon the wisdom and courage, it may someday be possible that no child in Michigan will be denied a college education for financial reasons.[52]

Getting Value for Our Education Dollars

Although funding is important, *student effort, student motivation,* and *parent involvement* are also extremely important. It is not easy to increase effort, motivation, and involvement in today's culture where skipping school is often seen as cool, and studious youngsters are lampooned as nerds. It may be a tall order, but it is one we cannot ignore. In this chapter, I have made the case for stable and adequate funding for education in Michigan. However, even if we increase spending tremendously, we will not get the desired outcomes unless parents turn off the television and help children with their homework. In other words, we need more than funding for education—we need a *culture* that values education.

Student effort has many dimensions, but certainly an important dimension is the amount of time spent in school. In Michigan, as in most states, students are supposed to have 180 days of instruction per year, with a three-month summer vacation. This schedule may have made sense in the nineteenth century, when most children were expected to spend the summer working in the fields, but it is badly out of step with today's needs. Huge amounts of time are wasted every autumn, reviewing the things that were learned the previous year but forgotten over the summer. In addition, the long summer of mental hibernation does more harm to some groups than to others. The economist Alan Krueger suggests that students from families of low socioeconomic status learn about as much during the school year as those from families of high socioeconomic status, but the students from low-status families fall behind during the summer months.[53]

Many of our international competitors have school years that are substantially longer. It's 190 days in England, 200 days in Australia and the Netherlands, and 220 days in South Korea.[54] If the people of Michigan are serious about preparing their children for the future, they should increase the length of the school year. As I see it, our school year should be increased to 190 or 200 days.[55] I don't follow the education debates in these other countries very closely. However, I am pretty sure that there aren't many folks in Australia who are saying, "We're educating our kids too much! We should have a shorter school year, like they have in Michigan! We should have a much longer vacation, so the children can forget a lot more of what they learned in the past year! That way, we'll get to spend the first few months of each new school year reviewing things that the students forgot over the break!"

The number of years of schooling is every bit as important as the number of school days per year. The evidence suggests that compulsory schooling laws are effective in getting some students to stay in school. Furthermore, the students who are compelled to stay in school earn higher wages as a result of their extra schooling.[56] In 2010, a bill was passed to raise the age of compulsory attendance in Michigan from 16 to 18. This is a step in the right direction, but if we manage to keep more children in high school, it will cost money to provide them with an education. If more students stay in school but we continue to cut funding, the new law will be a cruel joke.

An increase in the age of compulsory attendance is one method by which we can reduce the number of high school dropouts, but more still needs to be done. The public schools in Michigan should increase their efforts to identify at-risk students at an early age. Alternative high schools can provide an appropriate environment for students who struggle in regular high schools. (Of course, these programs will only succeed if they are adequately funded.) Curriculum reform is another method by which we can reduce the number of dropouts. In the next section, I will discuss specific curriculum issues in more detail.

While we are on the subject of student effort, I would like to mention the issue of repetition (or the lack thereof). Most of us get better and better as we do things over and over again. Yet based on my personal observations, it appears that repetition is out of fashion in the public schools. All of my students at Michigan State University have been exposed to math at the high school level, but it appears that many of them did not work on it long enough to learn the material in a solid way. Repetition is not very fun or exciting, but it is essential. Interestingly enough, no one ever questions the importance of repetition and drill in sports. *Of course* the football coach has the players practice the sweep play again and again. *Of course* the basketball coach has the players practice the in-bounds play again and again. We all understand that football and basketball teams will have a better chance of winning games if the players practice their drills over and over again. The same determination to improve through practice does not seem to be applied in the academic setting, but it should be.

Repetition and drill are often caricatured as "rote learning," which is viewed as less important than the learning of concepts, problem solving, and higher-order thinking. I have nothing against concepts, problem solving, and higher-order thinking. However, many students who have a diploma from a high school in Michigan don't know their multiplication tables, don't know how to use fractions, and can't do even the simplest arithmetic without a calculator. Unless a student knows the basics, it doesn't matter how much the student has worked with "concepts."

If the people of Michigan are serious about improving our position in the global economy, I believe we must do all the things suggested in the previous few pages. We need more early-childhood education. We need full-day kindergarten. We need a longer school year. And we need to decrease the number of dropouts. I very much doubt that we will be able to do these things without spending money, which means we will need to reverse the trend toward shrinking tax revenues. As of now, we are moving in exactly the opposite direction. Since its peak, the School Aid Fund, through which elementary and secondary schools in Michigan are financed, is down by about 15 percent and is expected to decline by another 4 percent this year.

Curriculum Issues in the Public Schools

I have suggested that children should spend more time in school, but I haven't said as much about which subjects the students should study. In my view, more time should be devoted to mathematics and science. (A friend once said that children ought to take every math course twice. In view of the poor math skills of some students, that does not seem like much of an exaggeration.)

However, I want to stress that students should *not* all be shoehorned into a one-size-fits-all curriculum. The high school graduation requirements in Michigan have recently been made more stringent.[57] Basically, every child is now required to take college-preparatory curriculum. In my view, it made a tremendous amount of sense to increase the graduation requirements. (The old requirements were pathetic.) However, it also makes sense to maintain some flexibility for those children for whom a college-preparatory curriculum may not be the best.

It may seem ironic that I am expressing skepticism about the new curriculum, since I have spent so much of this chapter emphasizing the benefits of a college education. However, just because Michigan would benefit from a large increase in the size of its college-educated population, it does not follow that every single child must go to college. A more vocationally oriented high school curriculum may be better for some children.[58] This viewpoint could be caricatured as saying that we should send the dumb kids to wood shop. That is *not* what I am saying. I *am* saying that a one-size-fits-all approach involves risks.

Earlier in this chapter, I have made the case for a longer school year. I believe that the new curriculum is more likely to succeed if we have a longer school year. Some students who might struggle to master a high school math class in a school year of 180 days would have a better chance of success with a longer year.

The new curriculum puts us *much* closer to where we need to be. Michigan's educational leaders are aware of the need for a curriculum that is rigorous but also maintains flexibility. I am optimistic that the effects of the new curriculum will be evaluated closely and that modifications will be made, if necessary, so we can serve the needs of *all* of Michigan's children.

The Race to the Top

The Obama Administration, under the leadership of Secretary of Education Arne Duncan, has encouraged states to reform their systems of elementary and secondary education. If Michigan wins a Race to the Top Grant (RTTT), the state will receive nearly $400 million in federal funds to implement school reforms. In order to be eligible for the RTTT funds, Michigan had to submit a very detailed proposal to the U.S. Department of Education. More details about this proposal are available at the Web site of the Michigan Department of Education (http://www.michigan.gov/mde).

Michigan's first RTTT application did not win, but I am very hopeful that the second application, submitted in May 2010, will win. It is an excellent proposal, and I applaud all who worked to put this proposal together, including the State Board of Education, State Superintendent of Public Instruction Mike Flanagan, the Department of Education staff, and the folks from MSU's College of Education. It's also worth noting that an overwhelming majority of school districts have given the proposal their support. Regardless of whether we win the additional RTTT federal funding, I hope that the common-sense reforms listed in the RTTT application are carried out for the betterment of our schools.

Conclusion

In this chapter, we analyzed Michigan's human resources. We began with a survey of the trends in population and the labor force. The population of

Michigan grew very rapidly for most of the twentieth century, but the rate of population growth dropped off sharply after 1970 and has fallen since 2005. In the last few decades, the greatest amounts of population growth have occurred in counties on the fringes of the metropolitan areas in the southern Lower Peninsula. The population of the Upper Peninsula has been stagnant for a century, and the populations of some central cities have declined since the 1950s. Detroit's population has fallen by about one million since 1950.

Michigan's population is aging, and the trend toward an older population is expected to accelerate in Michigan, as in the rest of the United States. About one out of every seven Michigan residents is African American, which is a slightly higher proportion than in the United States as a whole. The number of Hispanics in Michigan has grown rapidly in recent decades, but Hispanics still account for only about 4 percent of the Michigan population, which is far less than in the United States as a whole.

As in the rest of the country, the labor-force participation of Michigan women has increased rapidly. Today nearly half of the workers in Michigan are female. Also, the gender gap in pay has reduced as women have increased their education and their labor-market experience, and labor-market discrimination against women has lessened.

Michigan's labor force has long been more heavily unionized than the labor force of the rest of the United States. However, the percentage of workers who are in unions has decreased over time, both in Michigan and elsewhere. By 2009, 18.8 percent of Michigan workers were union members, compared with 12.3 percent of workers in the United States as a whole. In Michigan, as in the rest of the country, unionization is far more prevalent in the public sector than in the private sector.

After the initial sections on population and labor force, the bulk of this chapter has been devoted to educational issues. Although the percentage of adults with a high school education is higher in Michigan than in the rest of the United States, the percentage of Michigan residents with a college education has lagged persistently behind the national average. This has powerful implications for incomes, since the earnings gap between workers with a college education and those without a college education has been growing for the last thirty-five years.

There are huge disparities in labor-market earnings among groups with different levels of education. Therefore a strategy to increase the educational attainments of Michigan workers could produce benefits at *all* levels. Essentially, Michigan is underinvested at every level of education, from cradle to career. The State of Michigan will have a stronger economy if we do the following:

- Use early-childhood education programs to make sure that every child gets off to a good start in school.
- Increase the amount learned by students in our K–12 schools, regardless of whether they continue their education beyond high school.
- Reduce the number of high school dropouts.
- Increase the proportion of high school graduates who go on to college.
- Increase the proportion of college students who complete a degree.
- Increase the proportion of college graduates who continue their education beyond a bachelor's degree.

These improvements will only occur if the people of Michigan are willing to work for them and pay for them. In other words, they will only happen if we can achieve *changes in our culture* as well as *changes in our methods of financing education.* If our culture moves in the right direction, some of the financial issues may take care of themselves. Nevertheless, the financial issues are important in their own right. Thus we end this chapter with a brief summary of ideas regarding the financial side of the educational system:

- It is much more difficult to improve productivity in education than in agriculture or manufacturing. Therefore, we probably will not be able to make the necessary improvements to our educational system without devoting more resources to education.
- Since the passage of Proposal A in 1994, the lowest-spending school districts in Michigan have seen substantial increases in their per-student operating expenditures. A recent study has shown that this has succeeded in improving test scores. This is a major step forward. However, Proposal A has concentrated the power to make decisions about school operating expenses in the hands of the state government. Some districts would probably choose to increase their expenditures if they were allowed to do so. I have made the case for slightly loosening the restrictions on local school districts, while maintaining strong state funding for all districts.

- As a result of Proposal A, the gap in per-student spending between the highest-spending school districts and the lowest-spending districts has been reduced substantially for *operating expenditures*. However, Proposal A does not apply to *capital expenditures*. Thus many of the poorest school districts have aging and inadequate facilities. A recent study suggests that it would cost about $8.9 billion to provide every student in Michigan with adequate school facilities.[59] To address this problem, it will be necessary to shift some of the financial responsibility for school *capital* spending from the local school districts to the state government.
- The total unfunded liability for future health benefits for retired teachers is in the tens of billions of dollars. This is another area where it will be necessary to shift some financial responsibility from local school districts to the state government. It will also be necessary for teachers to shoulder more of the cost of their health care.
- The Cherry Commission has identified the need for a substantial increase in the number of Michigan residents who receive education beyond high school. It will not be possible to make progress in this direction without spending money. Unfortunately, the State of Michigan has drastically reduced its higher-education spending in recent years. Tax revenue will need to be increased to achieve a higher college attainment rate for Michigan residents.

In terms of the development of human resources, Michigan is at a crossroads. Our educational system and our attitudes toward education are better suited to the economic realities of fifty or even one-hundred years ago than to the realities of today. An extremely important challenge facing Michigan today is to provide adequate funding for education at all levels and to make sure those funds are well spent.

NOTES

1. For a much more detailed discussion of Michigan demographics, see Kenneth Darga, "Population Trends in Michigan," in *Michigan at the Millennium: A Benchmark and Analysis of Its Fiscal and Economic Structure,* ed. Charles L. Ballard, Paul N. Courant, Douglas C. Drake, Ronald C. Fisher, and Elisabeth R. Gerber (East Lansing, MI: Michigan State University Press, 2003).

2. U.S. Bureau of the Census, "Population Estimates," http://www.census.gov/popest/states/ states.html. Michigan has been the eighth most populous state for many years. However, if recent trends continue, Michigan is likely to be leapfrogged by Georgia very soon and by North Carolina in a few years.

3. The migration to the Sun Belt stems from a wide variety of sources, including the desire of businesses to locate in areas with cheap land and labor. Another influence is the widespread use of air conditioners. If air conditioning had not been invented, I am extremely doubtful that Arizona would now have a population of more than six million.

4. For data on the age distribution of the population, see the U.S. Bureau of the Census, "Selected Age Groups by States and Puerto Rico: 2008," http://www.census.gov/popest/ states/asrh/SC-EST2008-01.html.

5. Projections for the age distribution of the population for the fifty states can be found at the U.S. Bureau of the Census, "Population Pyramids and Demographic Summary Indicators for States," http://www.census.gov/population/www/projections/statepyramid.html.

6. Because so many properties in Detroit have been foreclosed upon or abandoned, it is difficult to get an accurate count of the city's population. One recent estimate put Detroit's population at about 912,000, while another study estimated the population at about 777,000. However, both of these estimates confirm that Detroit's population has plummeted in the last fifty years.

7. This figure is taken from figure 3.22 in Kenneth Darga's chapter "Population Trends in Michigan" in *Michigan at the Millennium*. Darga's figure, in turn, is based on data from the 2000 U.S. Census.

8. David Crary (Eastern Michigan University), George Erickcek (Upjohn Institute), and Allen Goodman (Wayne State University), "Economic Performance of Michigan Cities and Metropolitan Areas," in *Michigan at the Millennium*, 237.

9. Because the labor market is so important, many chapters in *Michigan at the Millennium* deal with labor-force issues, and three chapters are especially noteworthy for their in-depth discussions of labor-related issues. George Johnson of the University of Michigan surveys the overall labor-market situation in "The Evolution of the Michigan Labor Market from 1970 to 2001." Rebecca Blank, also of the University of Michigan, focuses on the low-wage, low-skill labor market in "The Less-Skilled Labor Market in Michigan." And Stephen Woodbury of Michigan State University considers unemployment insurance, workers' compensation, and reemployment programs in "Income Replacement and Reemployment Programs in Michigan."

10. These data are taken from selected issues of the U.S. Census Bureau's *Statistical Abstract*, http://www.census.gov/statab/www.

11. For an excellent discussion of the changing gender gap, see Francine Blau and Lawrence Kahn, "Gender Differences in Pay," *Journal of Economic Perspectives* 14 (2000): 75–99.

12. These data are from the U.S. Census Bureau, "Statistical Abstract: Table 19. Resident Population by Race, Hispanic Origin, and State: 2008," http://www.census.gov/compendia/statab/2010/tables/10s0019.pdf.

13. For more details, see Kenneth Darga, "Population Trends in Michigan," in *Michigan at the Millennium;* and George Johnson, "The Evolution of the Michigan Labor Market from 1970 to 2001" in *Michigan at the Millennium.*

14. This result comes from an unpublished research paper, "The State(s) of Inequality: Changes in Income Distribution in the Fifty States and the District of Columbia, 1976–2006," which is available upon request.

15. A wealth of data on rates of unionization can be found in a database constructed by Barry Hirsch and David Macpherson at http://www.unionstats.com. The unionized percentage of the labor force is highest in New York state, where 25.2 percent of workers were union members in 2009. New York is followed by Hawaii, Alaska, Washington, and then Michigan. At the other end of the scale, North Carolina has the smallest proportion of union members, at 3.1 percent.

16. George Johnson, "The Evolution of the Michigan Labor Market from 1970 to 2001" in *Michigan at the Millennium.*

17. For example, see Thomas Holmes, "The Effects of State Policies on the Location of Industry: Evidence from State Borders," *Journal of Political Economy* 106 (1998): 667–705. The loss of employment among union members can also have spillover effects on the nonunion labor force. If there are job losses among unionized workers, at least some of the displaced workers will then look for work in the nonunion sector of the economy. Since more workers will then be competing for the nonunion jobs, the wages in those jobs can be expected to decrease.

18. In the previous section, I mentioned research I have done with Paul Menchik. This result on the equalizing effect of unions is based on that same research. Our paper, "The State(s) of Inequality: Changes in Income Distribution in the Fifty States and the District of Columbia, 1976–2006," is available on request.

19. The data in Tables 2.2 and 2.3 are from the U.S. Census Bureau, "Table 13. Educational Attainment in the United States by Sex and State: 2005–07," National Center for Education Statistics, http://nces.ed.gov/programs/digest/d09/tables/dt09_013.asp. In this case, the Census Bureau takes an average of estimates over three years, in order to increase accuracy.

20. See the Center for Educational Performance and Information. "State of Michigan 2008 Cohort Four-Year and 2007 Cohort Five-Year Graduation and Dropout Rate Reports," State of Michigan, http://www.michigan.gov/documents/cepi/2008-2007_MI_Grad-Drop _Rate_283914_7.pdf. For an excellent discussion of related human-capital issues, see

Rebecca Blank and James Sallee (University of Michigan), "Labor Markets and Human Capital Investment in Michigan: Challenges and Strategies," http://closup.umich.edu/research/conferences/wdwgfh/blank.pdf.

21. Every year, I teach a course in introductory microeconomics to large numbers of students at Michigan State University. The overwhelming majority of my students went to high schools in Michigan. The best of these students are outstanding, but far too many have serious deficiencies, especially in mathematics. At MSU, as at many other colleges and universities, a tremendous amount of time, energy, and money is spent on remedial instruction. In other words, some college students have to be taught things they should have mastered in high school. Some data on the extent of this problem can be found in Charles Ballard and Marianne Johnson, "Basic Math Skills and Performance in an Introductory Economics Class," *Journal of Economic Education* 35 (2004): 3–23.

22. Of course, not every single person with a college education makes more money than every single person with less education. For example, National Basketball Association stars Kobe Bryant and Kevin Garnett make a lot more money than I do, even though each of them has only a high school education, and I have a PhD. But Bryant and Garnett have special skills that cannot easily be duplicated. For most people of ordinary size and strength, a college education is extremely valuable in today's economy.

23. These data were taken from the Bureau of Labor Statistics, "Labor Force Statistics from the Current Population Survey," http://data.bls.gov/cgi-bin/surveymost?ln.

24. See Timothy Bartik, "Increasing the Economic Development Benefits of Higher Education in Michigan" (working paper no. 04–106, Upjohn Institute, Kalamazoo, MI, September 27, 2004), Upjohn Institute, http://www.upjohninst.org/publications/wp/04–106.pdf.

25. See Claudia Goldin, "Egalitarianism and the Returns to Education during the Great Transformation of American Education," *Journal of Political Economy* 107 (1999): S65–S94.

26. See Robert T. Michael, *The Effect of Education on Efficiency in Consumption* (New York: Columbia University Press for the National Bureau of Economic Research, 1972).

27. See Haveman and Wolfe, "Schooling and Economic Well-Being: The Role of Nonmarket Effects," *Journal of Human Resources* 19 (1984): 377–407, and Wolfe and Haveman, "Accounting for the Social and Non-Market Benefits of Education," in *The Contribution of Human and Social Capital to Sustained Economic Growth and Well Being*, ed. J. F. Helliwell (Vancouver: University of British Columbia Press, 2001: 221–250).

28. For discussion and references regarding the Perry preschool project, see Greg Parks, "The High/Scope Perry Preschool Project," U.S. Department of Justice, Office of Juvenile Justice and Delinquency Prevention, October 2000, http://www.ncjrs.gov/pdffiles1/ojjdp/181725.pdf.

29. Timothy Bartik, "The Economic Development Effects of Early Childhood Programs," Upjohn Institute, http://www.upjohninst.org/early_childhood_full_report-2-28-08.pdf.

30. See James Heckman, "The Economic Case for Investing in Disadvantaged Young Children," http://dss.mo.gov/cbec/pdf/stl-fed.pdf .

31. "Final Report of the Lt. Governor's Commission on Higher Education & Economic Growth," prepared for Governor Jennifer M. Granholm, December 2004, http://www .cherrycommission.org/docs/finalReport/CherryReportFULL.pdf.

32. Lou Glazer, "Michigan's Transition to a Knowledge-Based Economy: Third Annual Progress Report," Michigan Future Inc., May 2010, http://www.michiganfuture.org/new/ wp-content/uploads/2010/06/MiFutureProgressReport10FINAL.pdf.

33. See Kenneth Darga's chapter "Population Trends in Michigan," in *Michigan at the Millennium*.

34. See Richard Florida, *The Rise of the Creative Class* (New York: Perseus Books, 2002). This book lists rankings of cities along various dimensions associated with creativity. The highest overall scores go to San Francisco, Austin, Boston, San Diego, and Seattle, all of which are fairly large. However, Mr. Florida also mentions a number of smaller cities that score well in some of these dimensions. These include Ann Arbor and East Lansing, as well as Bloomington, Indiana (home of Indiana University); Champaign-Urbana, Illinois (home of the University of Illinois); Iowa City, Iowa (home of the University of Iowa); Madison, Wisconsin (home of the University of Wisconsin); and State College, Pennsylvania (home of Pennsylvania State University). Clearly, university communities have some of the greatest potential for harnessing the forces of economic innovation.

35. The data for Figure 2.5 are derived from the Digest of Education Statistics: 2004, "Table 247. Earned Degrees Conferred by Degree-Granting Institutions, by Level of Degree and Sex of Student: Selected Years, 1869–70 to 2013–14," National Center for Education Statistics, http://nces.ed.gov/programs/digest/d04/tables/dt04_247.asp; and from the Digest of Education Statistics: 2008, "Table 268. Earned Degrees Conferred by Degree-Granting Institutions, by Level of Degree and Sex of Student: Selected Years, 1869–70 to 2017–18," National Center for Education Statistics, http://nces.ed.gov/programs/digest/d08/tables/dt08_268 .asp?referrer=list. More generally, the Web site of the National Center for Education Statistics, http://nces.ed.gov, has a huge wealth of information on a wide variety of topics.

36. For data and discussion, see Lawrence W. Kenny and Amy B. Schmidt, "The Decline in the Number of School Districts in the U.S.: 1950–1980," *Public Choice* 79 (1994): 1–18.

37. This problem of limited productivity gains is sometimes referred to as the "Baumol Disease," after the economist William J. Baumol. See Baumol, "Macroeconomics of Unbalanced Growth: The Anatomy of Urban Crisis," *American Economic Review* 57 (1967): 415–426. The arts provide good examples of the problem. For example, a performance of Beethoven's Symphony No. 9 will take a few hundred performers, and it will take about 65 minutes. If anyone were to attempt to "improve productivity" by using fewer performers and cutting the time of the performance, the results would be very unsatisfactory.

38. These data are from the Digest of Education Statistics: 2008, "Table 79. Estimated Average Annual Salary of Teachers in Public Elementary and Secondary Schools, by State or Jurisdiction: Selected Years, 1969–70 through 2006–07," National Center for Education Statistics, http://nces.ed.gov/programs/digest/d08/tables/dt08_079.asp.

39. See the Digest of Education Statistics: 2008, "Table 66. Teachers, Enrollment, and Pupil/Teacher Ratios in Public Elementary and Secondary Schools, by State or Jurisdiction: Selected Years, Fall 2000 through Fall 2006," National Center for Education Statistics, http://nces.ed.gov/programs/digest/d08/tables/dt08_066.asp.

40. The governor and the legislature have a moral duty to decide on school funding in a timely manner. When the state government delays its decisions, school districts are placed in an extremely difficult position. On more than one occasion in recent years, the state government has been unable to make its decisions until well into the school year. This is outrageous, and it has to stop. Our state elected officials need to do their jobs.

41. For the data behind these calculations, along with a tremendous amount of additional information, see Office of Revenue and Tax Analysis of the Michigan Department of Treasury (December 2002), "School Finance Reform in Michigan: Proposal A: A Retrospective," http://www.michigan.gov/documents/propa_3172 7.pdf.

42. See Leslie E. Papke, "The Effects of Spending on Test Pass Rates: Evidence from Michigan," *Journal of Public Economics* 89 (2005): 821–39.

43. See David Arsen, Tom Clay, Thomas Davis, Thomas Devaney, Rachel Fulcher-Dawson, and David N. Plank (May 2005), "Adequacy, Equity, and Capital Spending in Michigan Schools: The Unfinished Business of Proposal A," http://www.crcmich.org/PUBLICAT/2000s/2005/schoolcapital.pdf.

44. Here I have argued against complete equalization of per-pupil expenditures across the state. A similar story can be told for the distribution of income in general. The distribution of income has become substantially less equal in the last three decades, and I argue in this book for policies that will restore more equality. However, I certainly do not advocate complete leveling of incomes. If all incomes were equal, the incentive to work, save, and invest would be destroyed, and the overall level of economic activity would be drastically reduced.

45. The actual cost of providing education is higher for high school students than for elementary students, but this is not taken into account, either. Many of Michigan's charter schools only provide elementary education, and yet charter schools and traditional school districts receive the same number of dollars per student. This gives an unfair advantage to some charter schools.

46. The pension plan for Michigan teachers is a prefunded plan, which means that real assets are accumulated over time. However, it is also a "defined-benefit" plan. This means that if the investment portfolio's performance is subpar, additional contributions have to be

made in order to reach a prespecified level of retirement benefit payments. Thus the investment risk is borne by the taxpayers. This stands in contrast to a "defined-contribution" plan, under which investment risk is borne by the beneficiaries. Examples of defined-contribution plans include 401(k) plans and the system that serves most college teachers, including me. Defined-benefit plans can quickly become underfunded, whereas defined-contribution plans are always fully funded, by definition. This is one of the reasons for the growing popularity of defined-contribution plans. For example, after 1997, newly hired employees of the State of Michigan were no longer eligible for a defined-benefit plan. Instead, they were given access to a defined-contribution plan. For more discussion of these issues, see Leslie Papke (Michigan State University), "Public Pensions and Pension Policy in Michigan," in *Michigan at the Millennium*.

47. Robert Lawrence, "A Bill Coming Due for the Michigan Public," The Center for Michigan, http://www.thecenterformichigan.net/blog/a-bill-coming-due-for-the-michigan-public.

48. The pension benefits are protected by a provision of the Michigan Constitution, but the health benefits do not have any such protection. Thus if there are reductions in benefits, they may be concentrated in the area of health benefits. Of course, the Constitution could be amended, in which case benefit reductions could occur for pensions as well as for health care.

49. In 2010, President Obama signed a health-care bill into law. This law will eventually increase the number of Americans who have health insurance. It will also prohibit insurance companies from denying coverage on the basis of a preexisting condition, or from cancelling coverage when a policyholder gets sick. These are important improvements. However, much remains to be done. The 2010 healthcare law did not do very much to address the long-term issue of skyrocketing health-care costs.

50. "Final Report of the Lt. Governor's Commission on Higher Education & Economic Growth," prepared for Governor Jennifer M. Granholm, December 2004, http://www .cherrycommission.org/docs/finalReport/CherryReportFULL.pdf.

51. Many of the students in my classes finance their education partly by working long hours during the school year, but this is a very unsatisfactory solution. A student who is working thirty-five hours per week during the school year may be able to limp through to graduation, but he or she will not be able to derive the full benefits of a college education. If tuition continues to increase and financial aid does not keep up, many students from families of modest means will find that a college education is out of reach, regardless of how many hours they might work during the school year.

52. For more information and research regarding the Kalamazoo Promise, see the Web site of the Upjohn Institute, http://www.upjohn.org/promise.

53. See Alan B. Krueger, "Reassessing the View that American Schools are Broken," (working paper no. 395, Industrial Relations Section, Princeton University, Princeton, NJ, 1998).

54. These data are from the International Review of Curriculum and Assessment, "Table 15: Organization of School Year and School Day," http://www.inca.org.uk/Table15.pdf.

55. Another problem in some school districts is the proliferation of "half days," during which school is only in session for a few hours. If the school year is lengthened, it would be important to avoid an offsetting increase in the number of half days.

56. See Joshua D. Angrist and Alan B. Krueger, "Does Compulsory School Attendance Affect Schooling and Earnings?" *Quarterly Journal of Economics* 106 (1991): 979–1014.

57. The new graduation requirements impose new costs on the school districts. All else equal, this will intensify the financial squeeze on the districts. If the State of Michigan is going to require school districts to expand their programs, then the State of Michigan should increase the foundation grant appropriately.

58. For a very interesting discussion along these lines, see Timothy Bartik and Kevin Hollenbeck (Upjohn Institute for Employment Research), "Graduation Requirements, Skills, Postsecondary Education, and the Michigan Economy," http://www.upjohninst.org/Bartik -Hollenbeck_testimony.pdf.

59. See David Arsen, Tom Clay, Thomas Davis, Thomas Devaney, Rachel Fulcher-Dawson, and David N. Plank (May 2005), "Adequacy, Equity, and Capital Spending in Michigan Schools: The Unfinished Business of Proposal A," http://www.crcmich.org/PUBLICAT/2000s/2005/ schoolcapital.pdf.

Michigan's Physical Resources: Transportation, Land, and Environment

C hapter 2 was concerned with Michigan's *human* resources. In this chapter, we turn to Michigan's *physical* resources. We begin with a discussion of the transportation system, with special emphasis on highway construction and maintenance. Later in the chapter, we consider the closely related issues of land use and the environment.

Michigan's Transportation System

If you drive often in Michigan, you probably know that many of our roads are bone-jarring, teeth-rattling nightmares. By not maintaining our roads and bridges, we in Michigan are doing damage to our economy. A well-maintained road system is extremely important to the success of many industries. When trucks and delivery vehicles are damaged by bouncing on Michigan highways, it hurts the economy. When companies have to use extra packaging material to avoid damage to their merchandise in transit, it hurts the economy. And when trucks and delivery vehicles waste time in traffic bottlenecks, it also hurts the economy.

It is not just that the roads in Michigan are poor in an absolute sense; they also are not as good as the roads in neighboring states. Kenneth Boyer of Michigan State University discusses Michigan's transportation system in detail in *Michigan at the Millennium: A Benchmark and Analysis of Its Fiscal and Economic Structure.*[1] Although Boyer discusses various aspects of the system, including air, water, and rail transportation, his main focus is on the roads. This is because automobile and truck travel account for such a large part of the travel that occurs in Michigan.

Rough Roads and the Policies that Encourage Them

Boyer presents data from the Federal Highway Administration for the percentage of roads that met various standards for roughness in the year 2000. Michigan's rural interstate highways are far worse than the rural interstates in the United States as a whole or in the other states of the Great Lakes region. The same is true for every type of major road in urban areas, including interstate highways, noninterstate freeways, and other arterial highways. The worst roads of all are the nonfreeway arterial highways in urban areas. A recent poll of truck owner–operators by Overdrive magazine ranked Michigan as having the second-worst roads in the United States.[2]

On the other hand, minor arterial roads in rural areas are somewhat better in Michigan than in the rest of the United States or the rest of the Great Lakes region. In Michigan, roads that carry a few hundred vehicles per day are likely to be in pretty good shape, but the roads that carry tens of thousands of vehicles per day are likely to be poor.

These data suggest a few questions that need to be answered. First, why are Michigan highways of generally poor quality? Second, why are the most lightly traveled rural roads relatively better than other roads? It appears that much of the problem comes from the way Michigan allocates its road dollars. Highway funds in Michigan are allocated on the basis of formulas that were developed many years ago. These formulas are biased in favor of rural counties. Under the formulas, the most heavily populated county in the state (Wayne County) gets less than $40 per person for its roads every year, while sparsely populated Schoolcraft County gets more than $1,000 per person per year.

Michigan also allows heavier trucks than most other states. The gross weight limit on trucks in Michigan is more than twice as heavy as the limit imposed on federal-aid highways in some states. (Michigan was allowed to keep its higher weight limits, based on laws from the 1960s.) It is hard to ignore the apparent relationship between the fact that Michigan allows unusually heavy trucks to travel on its highways and that Michigan's highways are unusually poor. However, the Michigan Department of Transportation (MDOT) claims that heavier trucks do not cause disproportionate damage, as long as the weight is evenly distributed over an appropriate number of axles. MDOT also points out that if the weight limits were reduced and the same total amount of freight is carried, there would have to be an increase in the number of trucks on the road. This could have negative implications for traffic congestion and safety.

In my view, first and foremost we need to change the formula by which state funds are allocated to the counties. The current formula shows a major bias in favor of thinly populated rural counties. As a result, Michigan's road dollars are misallocated, with too much money going to areas that do not need as much and too little money going to the areas with greatest need. By reducing the discrimination against urban counties, it will be possible for Michigan to improve many roads that are both heavily traveled and of poor quality without spending any additional money.

Road Finance

In the previous section, we emphasized ways to improve the roads in Michigan without spending additional money. This could be accomplished by reallocating the money currently spent on road construction and repair. However, even if policies change along these lines, Michigan's road problems will still not be solved entirely. Michigan's roads are in such bad shape that it will require more money to get our road system into acceptable condition. Thus in this section, we turn our attention to the sources of funds for road construction and repair.

In Michigan, as in the rest of the United States, most of the money for road construction and road repair comes from sources that can be thought of as "user fees." These include fuel taxes, registration fees, and tolls. Much of the funding for roads in Michigan comes from taxes and fees collected in Michigan, but a substantial amount also comes from the federal government. (However, the amount that Michigan receives from the Federal Highway Trust Fund has historically been less than the amount of the state's payments into the fund.)

As I have said earlier, Michigan is not poor, even despite the difficult times our economy has suffered in recent years. However, when it comes to road funding, some members of the legislature appear to believe that Michigan is so rich that we can afford to turn down large amounts of federal road money. As of the spring of 2010, the legislature has been wrangling for months over the question of whether to come up with $84 million in order to qualify for $475 million of federal matching transportation funds. Let's do the math: if we divide $475 million by $84 million, we have a ratio of about 5.65. In other words, for every dollar that Michigan puts up, the federal government will put up $5.65.

It is astonishing that any legislator would even *think* of passing up that kind of money. Over the next four years, Michigan is in danger of losing about $2 billion of federal transportation funds. This is insane.[3] Why would anyone even consider passing up huge amounts of money? The answer appears to lie in an ideology that is pathologically opposed to raising *any* taxes, even taxes that can keep our roads from crumbling. To these tax cutters I say, "You've already won! Taxes in Michigan are at their lowest level in generations! So please, declare victory in your war on taxes and come up with the revenue to qualify for the federal funds." Of course, one way to find the $84 million without raising taxes is to slash other programs, and that is what some in the legislature want to do. In today's environment, when all sorts of public services have already been drastically reduced, that is irresponsible.

A recent study by the Anderson Economic Group considered the economic benefits and costs of investing in road infrastructure. The title of the study says a lot: "Michigan's Roads: The Cost of Doing Nothing and the Rewards of Bold Action." The study found that taking bold action to fund road repair and improvement—at a level that would make infrastructure an asset to Michigan's business climate—would bring large economic and employment benefits to Michigan. These benefits would far offset the cost of the higher taxes necessary to support the expenditure.[4]

Road repair projects provide employment for construction workers, many of whom have been hit very hard by the tough economic times of recent years. The Anderson Economic Group study suggests that a policy of infrastructure investment would lead to a net increase of about fifteen thousand jobs. The study also documents the costs imposed on Michigan's economy because of poor road infrastructure, which include time and fuel wasted due to highway congestion. The study estimates that crashes involving poor road infrastructure resulted in $542 million of vehicle repairs in Michigan in 2006. I hope this study, wisely commissioned by the Michigan Chamber of Commerce, will help to inject some common sense into discussions about transportation infrastructure in Michigan.

Taxes on motor fuels have traditionally been one of the sources of funding for transportation infrastructure. A strong case can be made for increasing these taxes, as one way of providing the funds to save our roads. Also, Michigan is unusual in its generosity toward users of diesel fuel. In most states, the diesel tax is at least as large as the tax on gasoline. The federal diesel tax is higher than the federal gasoline tax. In Michigan, however, the tax on gasoline is 19 cents per gallon, and the tax on diesel fuel is 15 cents per gallon.[5] There is no clear reason why diesel motorists should receive this privileged treatment. Michigan should raise the tax rate on diesel fuel at least to parity with the gasoline tax. Beyond that, increases in both the diesel tax and the gasoline tax would provide additional funds for highway construction and maintenance.

All around the globe, road construction and maintenance are increasingly being paid for by modern toll-collection systems, such as E-ZPass. Tolls can raise a substantial amount of revenue, and they can also help to relieve congestion. Larger tolls can be used in the most heavily congested areas. Also, tolls could be reduced or eliminated at off-peak times of the day and week and increased during the periods of heaviest traffic. If tolls are adjusted in this manner, they will encourage drivers to drive during off-peak times, thus spreading out the volume of traffic across the day and week. Effectively, this increases the capacity of the roads.

Despite these advantages of tolls, they have never been popular in Michigan. Other states use tolls far more than Michigan. But there is no reason for Michigan to shy away from the use of tolls. Tolls can raise revenue for maintaining the roads, and they can help us to use the existing roads in a more efficient manner.

Public Transportation

So far, this section has concentrated exclusively on the quality of Michigan's roads. Thus the implied emphasis has been on transportation using private passenger vehicles, since most road traffic involves private cars and trucks. However, potentially at least, the people of Michigan could use public transportation. I say "potentially" because Michigan residents do not actually use public transportation very much. In *Michigan at the Millennium*, Kenneth Boyer compares public-transportation usage in various metropolitan areas in the Midwest.[6] He finds that public transportation is far less prevalent in the Detroit area and the Grand Rapids area than would be expected for metropolitan areas of their size. Detroit is the second-largest metropolitan area in the region, but the people in the Detroit area use public transportation far less than those in the Chicago area (which is the largest in the Midwest) or in the Cleveland area (which is third-largest). The big difference between Detroit and Chicago or Cleveland is that Detroit lacks a significant rail-transit system.

We in Michigan do not use public transportation very much. Should we? As usual in economics, the answer to the question depends on our estimates of the benefits and costs. Public-transportation systems cost money. Boyer emphasizes that public systems usually cover only a fraction of their operating expenses, which means that these systems have to receive government subsidies.

On the other hand, the true social costs of automobile driving are probably far greater than the costs borne privately by individual drivers. In making the decision about whether to drive, an individual motorist will only take into account the private operating costs of driving. The individual motorist does not take into account the external costs that he or she imposes on the rest of society in the form of traffic congestion, air pollution, and noise.[7] Thus, with all things considered, public transportation is worthy of very serious consideration, because it may prove to be a smarter choice for Michigan commuters from an economic and social standpoint.

The benefits of public transportation are somewhat different for rail systems and bus systems. Rail systems can encourage denser patterns of residential and commercial development, which may have advantages. (Later in this chapter, we will return to the issue of the density of development.) Bus systems can provide access to transportation for low-income people and others who are unable to travel by passenger automobile. In the long run, one possible advantage of both bus and rail systems is that they would reduce the need to pave over large sections of our downtowns for parking lots.

Clearly, major investments in public transportation are not appropriate in all parts of the state. For the foreseeable future, most travel in most parts of Michigan will continue to occur in private passenger automobiles. However, a case can be made for a rail transit system in the Detroit metropolitan area. From the perspective of the state, the case for a rail system depends partly on who pays for it. In the past, the federal government has paid a substantial portion of the capital expenses for many public-transportation projects. If this were to occur for a rail-transit system in the Detroit area, it would reduce the costs for the people of Michigan.

As this book is being written, the price of oil is above $70 per barrel. The price of gasoline is almost $3 per gallon in much of Michigan, and prices in excess of $3 per gallon have become commonplace in some parts of the country. A few years ago, prices briefly soared above $4 per gallon. If the price of gasoline stays high and trends higher, people will respond in a variety of ways. Some folks who have never been part of a carpool may decide to give it a try. Some may shop for more fuel-efficient vehicles. (More fuel-efficient vehicles will become more and more prevalent as a result of the increased fuel-economy standards that were recently passed by the U.S. Congress.) And some may become more interested in public transit. At this point, there does not seem to be much of a public clamor for increased investment in public transportation. However, if the price of gasoline stays high enough for long enough, we may see increased interest in public transportation.

Land Use

In Chapter 1 of this book, we looked at Michigan's population trends. The population of Michigan grew very rapidly in the middle of the twentieth century, but the growth rate slowed down dramatically after 1970. If the population growth rate had been the same after 1970 as it was between 1940 and 1970, Michigan would have about seven million more people today than it actually has. Lots of people in Michigan view the sluggish growth of our economy and population as a cause for concern. However, it should be recognized that there is a positive aspect to the slower growth: more people in Michigan would have meant more pressure on Michigan's land. It probably would have meant that more farms and forests would have been covered over with houses, stores, offices, roads, and parking lots.

The situation in Michigan stands in dramatic contrast to the situation in California. In 1960, California had about 15.7 million people. By 1984,

California's population had risen to about 25.8 million, and it had risen to about 35.8 million by 2004.[8] Thus between 1960 and 1984 the *growth* of California's population was as large as the *entire* Michigan population today. Then, between 1984 and 2004, California gained *another* Michigan population. Consequently, the attitude toward growth is very different in the two states. In Michigan, there is a strong desire to attract more businesses, more economic activity, and more people. On the other hand, the focus in California is very much on how to manage and control the growth and not so much on stimulating additional growth.

Despite the differences between Michigan and California, there are important similarities. Even though the total size of Michigan's population has not grown very rapidly, it is still true that the *geographical distribution* of the population has changed a great deal. In particular, Michigan has shared in the nationwide trend toward suburbanization and lower-density development.

Gary Sands of Wayne State University discusses land-use issues in *Michigan at the Millennium*.[9] Another valuable resource for those interested in land-use issues is "Michigan's Land, Michigan's Future: Final Report of the Michigan Land Use Leadership Council."[10]

Land Use: Facts and Trends

About 79 percent of the land in Michigan is privately owned, with another 12 percent owned by the State of Michigan, and 9 percent owned by the federal government. In the nonfederal lands in 1997, about one-half was forested and one-third was used for crops or pasture. Only 10.7 percent of the land was developed in 1997. (This was up from 8.3 percent in 1982.)

One of the most important land-use trends, both nationally and in Michigan, is toward reduced density of development in metropolitan areas. All metropolitan areas in Michigan experienced substantial increases in the amount of urbanized land area in the 1980s and 1990s, even though the populations of these areas grew fairly slowly. As a result, population density decreased in the metropolitan areas. For example, from 1982 to 1997 in the Lansing area, population grew by 6.8 percent, but urbanized land area grew by more than 50 percent! As a result, the population density declined by about 29 percent. For the entire United States, urban population density decreased by 20.5 percent during this period. Density decreased more rapidly in some areas of Michigan and less rapidly in others, but the trend toward decreasing density was seen in every metropolitan area in Michigan.

The trend toward low-density development is not due to any one single cause, but one that deserves mentioning is the price of gasoline. From about 1985 to 2000, gasoline was relatively inexpensive. This encouraged low-density development, because many people were able to commute long distances without exorbitant fuel costs. It remains to be seen whether the relatively higher gasoline prices of recent years will be maintained, but if the price of gasoline does remain relatively high, long-distance commuting will become less attractive. This could encourage some movement back toward the center of metropolitan areas, although there could also be an increase in the number of people who engage in telecommuting.

A possible advantage of low-density development is that it allows people to fulfill the "American Dream" of a big house on a large lot. However, low-density development also causes problems. One of the problems is increased congestion in the suburbs. In *Michigan at the Millennium*, Gary Sands presents evidence of the growing level of suburban congestion.[11] Another problem is the loss of open space. A third problem comes in the form of increased costs of infrastructure, since it becomes necessary to provide water, sewer services, and electricity to distant regions. Sands reports the results of a 1997 study carried out for the Southeast Michigan Council of Governments. The study found that compact, higher-density growth leads to reduced needs for infrastructure. This, in turn, has a positive fiscal effect on local governments.

Selected Land-Use Policies

One problem identified by Sands is that land use in Michigan has traditionally been characterized by a lack of planning and coordination. It was against this background that "Michigan's Land, Michigan's Future" was written by the Michigan Land Use Leadership Council in 2003.[12] This report contains dozens of recommendations, and is far too detailed to summarize here. But the report and the process that produced it show an increased recognition of the need for a rational and organized set of land-use policies in Michigan.

Out of the hundreds of issues relevant to land-use policy, I have selected a few to discuss in detail.

Open space. In 1974, Michigan passed Public Law 116, which allows owners of agricultural lands to apply for a development-rights agreement. Under such an agreement, the owner agrees not to develop the property in return for a reduction in property taxes. I do not want to speak in opposition to the preservation of agricultural land as such. However policy discussions in this area sometimes make it sound as if preservation of agricultural land and preservation of open space are identical. They are not.

There is nothing wrong with privately owned agricultural land. However, from the perspective of the vast majority of Michigan residents who live in metropolitan areas, parks may be more valuable than farms. One of the most distinctive features of the urban landscape in the entire United States is Manhattan's Central Park. This huge green rectangle contributes immeasurably to the character and quality of life of America's largest city. In fact, however, parts of what is now Central Park were once farmland. If enough subsidies had been provided to the farmers, Central Park might still be a farm instead of a park. And yet I doubt that the people of New York City would be better off if Central Park were an alfalfa farm instead of a park. Again, I want to stress that this is not a diatribe against agriculture. Instead, I am trying to raise an issue that is likely to become more and more important over time in Michigan: future population growth in Michigan is likely to be concentrated in the metropolitan areas of the southern Lower Peninsula. The future residents of these areas will benefit from open space, and not merely from open space in the form of farms. Now is the time to devote planning and financial resources to making sure that future generations of Michigan residents have sufficient amounts of convenient parks and recreational facilities. Note that the financial resources for these facilities do not necessarily have to come from public sources. State and local governments should be ready and willing to work constructively with private donors who express an interest in providing funds for such facilities.

The tax system's incentives for sprawl. In 1978, the voters of Michigan passed the Headlee Amendment to the Michigan Constitution. The Headlee Amendment placed restrictions on the property taxes that could be levied by jurisdictions in the state. Under certain circumstances, the Headlee Amendment can trigger an automatic reduction in the property-tax millage rate. However, the law also allowed for ways to avoid the restrictions. In particular, new construction is excluded from the Headlee calculations. This means that rapidly growing communities (which are more likely to be in the distant suburbs) are more likely to be able to avoid a "Headlee rollback." Older cities, which tend to grow less rapidly, are more likely to bump into the restrictions.

Most of the voters who approved the Headlee Amendment probably did so because of their desire to limit property taxes. My guess is that few of the voters saw it as a mechanism for encouraging suburban sprawl. And yet it appears that suburban sprawl may have been an unintended byproduct of the Headlee Amendment. The Headlee Amendment helped to perpetuate the inequalities in tax and spending levels that have existed in Michigan since 1978.[13]

What, if anything, should be done? The Headlee Amendment is only one piece of a broader set of policies, so it would be inappropriate to focus too narrowly on the amendment. In general, however, it would be wise for Michigan to develop a comprehensive strategy to put older, developed areas on an equal footing with newly developing areas.

Reinvigorating Michigan's cities. In Chapter 1 of this book, I described how the population of Detroit has fallen by about *one million* in the last sixty years. There is plenty of space for redevelopment in Detroit. Any rational strategy for land use in southeast Michigan would recognize the benefits of using the land throughout the region, including the land in Detroit. Mayor Dave Bing and others in Detroit are to be commended for their efforts to rationalize land use in the city.

In Chapter 1 and elsewhere, I have also described the huge increase in inequality, which has been one of the most important features of the economic landscape in America in the last thirty-five years. Not everyone who lives in a city is poor and not everyone who lives in a suburb is affluent, but the suburbs do tend to be richer than the cities. As the gap between rich and poor has widened, so has the gap between suburb and city.

In Chapter 2 of this book, I described the difficulties facing school districts with low levels of taxable property per student. Although local school districts do not have to depend on local property taxes for their *operating* expenses, they do have to rely almost exclusively on local property taxes for their *capital* expenditures. This means that many of the older urban districts are unable to provide adequate school facilities, even if they impose high tax rates. This can only exacerbate the flight to the suburbs and further weaken the cities.

Earlier in this chapter, I described the astonishing inequity in the formula for allocating state transportation funds. Urban counties receive far fewer dollars per resident than rural counties.

I hope the pattern is clear: again and again, we see an economic playing field that is tilted against the cities. Almost by definition, cities tend to be developed more densely than suburbs and rural areas. Thus economic policies to strengthen the cities will tend to lead to more compact development. If Michigan's cities are strengthened, many of the problems associated with low-density land use will be reduced, regardless of what other land-use policies might be undertaken. I do not claim that it will be easy politically to strengthen the cities, but I do believe it will be good policy.

Environment

I have divided this chapter into three sections—transportation, land use, and the environment. This division is clearly somewhat arbitrary, since the lines between these three subjects are often blurry. For example, low-density development is not merely a land-use issue. It is also an environmental issue, because low-density development is associated with destruction of wildlife habitat, as well as other pressures on the ecosystem. In this section, we now move on to a fuller discussion of environmental issues.

Increased Environmental Awareness

In *Michigan at the Millennium*, environmental issues are discussed by Gloria Helfand of the University of Michigan and John Wolfe of Limno-Tech Inc. (formerly of Michigan State University).[14] They describe some of the changes in the last few decades both in environmental policy and in the quality of the environment. Prior to the 1960s, environmental concerns were low on America's list of priorities. Environmental awareness increased substantially in the late 1960s and early 1970s. In 1968, Michigan voters passed a bond measure for the purpose of cleaning the state's waters. In 1970, the federal government passed the Clean Air Act and authorized the Environmental Protection Agency, and Michigan passed the Michigan Environmental Protection Act. The U.S.–Canada Great Lakes Water Quality Agreement followed in 1972, setting the goal of reducing phosphorus levels in the lakes. In 1976, Michigan became the first major industrial state to approve a deposit-refund system for beer and pop containers. (Ten other states have now joined Michigan in having a bottle bill.) With a deposit of ten cents per container, the incentive to recycle these containers is stronger in Michigan than in most other states. Over the last few decades, many communities have also established curbside and drop-off recycling programs for newspapers, corrugated cardboard, glass containers, tin cans, and a variety of other materials. The federal Comprehensive Environmental Response, Compensation, and Liability Act (commonly known as the "Superfund law") passed in 1980 has led to better handling of hazardous substances and the cleanup of some hazardous-waste sites, although many sites remain. In 1998, Michigan voters passed the $675 million Clean Michigan Initiative. Thus we now have nearly forty years of heightened awareness of environmental concerns, matched by a wide variety of policies designed to create a cleaner environment.

Trends in Environmental Quality: Air, Water, and Wetlands

Not all the policies mentioned in the previous section have been equally successful. Nevertheless, considerable progress has been made. In many ways, the environment of Michigan and the environment of the rest of the United States have greatly improved since 1970. Because of laws that require unleaded gasoline, lead levels in the atmosphere have decreased dramatically. Emissions of carbon monoxide, particulate matter, and volatile organic compounds have dropped since the 1980s, although emissions of nitrous oxides have increased.

The amount of phosphorus entering Lake Erie decreased by more than 80 percent between 1972 and 1982. As a result, the growth of algae in Lake Erie has been reduced very substantially, and fish populations have returned. However, uncontrolled discharges of nitrogen and phosphorus still do occur. In 1998, nearly 5 percent of Michigan's lakes were classified as hypereutrophic (i.e., characterized by excessive amounts of algae and other plant life). Nearly three-hundred beach closings were reported in a survey in 2000.

In *Michigan at the Millennium*, Helfand and Wolfe report that during the first two-hundred years of U.S. history, the lower forty-eight states lost about 53 percent of their wetlands. Michigan is close to the national average with a loss of about half its wetlands. On the other hand, Illinois, Indiana, and Ohio lost more than 85 percent of their original wetlands because these states engaged in much more drainage for farmland. In the last twenty years, policy initiatives have sought to reduce the loss of wetlands. Helfand and Wolfe present evidence that these policies have been partly successful; the rate of wetland loss has slowed down considerably.

Solid Waste and Landfill

Recycling programs generally reduce the demand for landfill because the recycled materials are no longer being thrown away. In addition to instituting recycling programs, in 1993 Michigan banned yard waste from its landfills. These changes led to excess landfill capacity in Michigan. This, in turn, put downward pressure on landfill prices, which played a role in attracting imports of waste from other states and Canada.

Imported waste, especially imported waste from Canada, has generated a lot of policy discussion in Michigan. Before we blame too many of our problems on the Canadians, however, it is good to have some perspective on the amount of trash that comes into Michigan from Canada. In 2001, about 80 percent of the solid waste that went to landfill in Michigan was from Michigan. About 10 percent was from Canada, 4 percent from Illinois, 3 percent from Indiana, 2 percent from Ohio, and 1 percent from Wisconsin. Thus if solid waste from Canada were eliminated completely, the total amount of waste going to landfills in Michigan would not be dramatically reduced.

A 2006 deal called for Canadian municipal trash sent to Michigan to be phased out by 2010, but the agreement did not cover industrial and commercial garbage. A 2009 report by the Michigan Department of Environmental Quality said that the amount of Canadian trash coming into Michigan had dropped more than 11 percent since peaking in the 2006 fiscal year.[15] But it is important to keep things in perspective, and to remember that the vast majority of trash that goes into Michigan landfills is from Michigan sources. Pound for pound, Michigan trash is likely to have environmental effects that are very similar to the effects of Canadian trash. If the people of Michigan want to reduce the amount of solid waste that goes to landfill, the biggest strides can be made through reducing the amount of stuff that gets thrown away by the residents of Michigan.

Cleaning Up Contaminated Sites: How Good Is Good Enough?

Unfortunately, cleaning up contaminated soil and groundwater is technically very challenging. As reported by Helfand and Wolfe, studies in the early 1990s suggested that there were more than 300,000 groundwater contamination sites in the United States, and that the cost of cleaning them up might be as high as $1 trillion.[16]

As scientists have learned more about the daunting technical difficulties of cleaning up subsurface contamination, it has been recognized that complete elimination of environmental contamination may be impossible or at least prohibitively expensive. At many sites, the best that can be done is to contain the contamination while engaging in more research to try to find better ways of cleaning up.

Protecting the Great Lakes

Few people would disagree that the Great Lakes are one of the finest resources not only for Michigan but for the entire world.[17] The Great Lakes Compact was signed in 2007 and 2008 by the governors of Illinois, Indiana, Michigan, Minnesota, New York, Ohio, Pennsylvania, and Wisconsin. After approval by both Houses of Congress and President George W. Bush, the Great Lakes Compact became state and federal law in 2008. This law provides the framework for protecting the Great Lakes for generations to come. In particular, it limits the possibilities of diverting the Great Lakes' water to other regions.

The Great Lakes Compact is a model for regional and national cooperation. In 2010, however, the lakes are being threatened by the Asian carp. If this invasive species were to become entrenched in the lakes, the entire ecosystem could be greatly damaged. Michigan's political leaders as well as members of Congress from other states in the Great Lakes basin are pressing for action to keep the Asian carp from infesting the Great Lakes. Ultimately, I believe it will be necessary to have a physical barrier to prevent species from the Mississippi River basin from getting into the Great Lakes. I just hope action is taken before it is too late.

In April 2010, an explosion and fire occurred at an oil rig in the Gulf of Mexico. As of this writing, the resulting oil spill has continued unabated for months, and it has become the largest oil spill in American history. It is doing untold damage to the fishing industry, tourism industry, and environment of the Gulf Coast. I hope this incident will put a stop to any discussion of oil exploration in the Great Lakes.

The Need for Environmental Policy Coordination

One theme that has come up repeatedly in this book is that Michigan is closely interconnected with the rest of the United States. In Chapter 4, we will discuss

Michigan's connections with the rest of the world, with special emphasis on Canada. Interconnectedness with other places has significant effects on our environment. Air pollutants travel with wind currents across state lines and national borders. Invasive species can travel on ship hulls, in ballast, or under their own power. Contaminated ground water can flow far from its original source. All of these issues point to the need for greater coordination among various regions, states, and between the United States and other countries.

No issue is more international in scope than climate change due to greenhouse gas emissions. Carbon dioxide that goes into the upper atmosphere from Michigan will have about the same ultimate effect on the climate as carbon dioxide from Wisconsin, Texas, Germany, or China. There is controversy in the scientific literature about how much we can expect global temperatures to rise in the next century. There are even a few who dispute whether climate change is an issue at all, but these folks are an increasingly small fringe. In recent years, the scientific community has reached a general consensus that global warming is already under way and that it will continue. The only real controversy is over how hot it will get.

What can we in Michigan do about climate change? We can plant trees. We can drive fewer miles, and we can drive in more fuel-efficient vehicles. However, because of the global nature of the problem, the actions of Michigan residents will have to be a part of a much broader national and international campaign. It remains to be seen whether national and world leaders will have the wisdom and courage necessary to make a serious effort to reduce emissions of greenhouse gases.

If the people of Michigan are sufficiently bold, we could take a leadership role by increasing our taxes on greenhouse gases. In this chapter, I have already advocated an increase in taxes on gasoline and diesel fuel, but that was primarily in the context of finding the money to keep our roads from crumbling. We could go further by instituting taxes that are motivated by a desire to clean the environment, and not merely by a desire to pave our roads. One obvious objection to such a policy is that the increased taxes might have a disproportionate effect on the budgets of low- and middle-income Michigan residents. This is a legitimate concern. To deal with this issue, we could offer a set of rebates through the income tax to offset the taxes on fossil fuels.

Conclusion

In this chapter, we have discussed some aspects of the physical environment in Michigan. We began with a look at the transportation system, with special emphasis on the quality of our roads. We then considered land-use issues, followed by other environmental issues. Here are some of the highlights:

- With the exception of minor highways in rural areas, Michigan's roads are worse than roads in the rest of the United States and the Great Lakes region. Michigan's lightly traveled rural roads are the only ones that are likely to be of comparable quality to those in neighboring states. If a road in Michigan serves tens of thousands of motorists every day, it is likely to be of poorer quality than a similar road in other states.
- A number of policies have an influence on the poor quality of Michigan's roads. The most important of these is the misallocation of state highway funds. The spending formula devotes hugely disproportionate amounts of money to sparsely populated rural counties. As a result, the more densely populated urban counties have less money for roads. A new formula that devotes relatively more money to urban areas would be both more equitable and more efficient.
- Currently, Michigan's tax on diesel fuel is 15 cents per gallon, which is four cents per gallon lower than the gasoline tax. In most states, the diesel tax is equal to or greater than the gasoline tax. There is no good reason to favor diesel users in this way. The Michigan diesel tax should be increased so that it is at least equal to the gasoline tax. Moreover, even though some of the reforms mentioned above would improve Michigan's roads without an overall increase in spending, the poor condition of the roads will require an increase the total amount of funding for road construction and repair. Additional revenue could be obtained by increasing the tax rates on both gasoline and diesel fuel.
- It would be crazy for Michigan to turn down federal road money. We should come up with the funds that are necessary to qualify for federal matching transportation funds, and we should not do so by reducing other public services in Michigan.
- Tolls can raise revenue for road construction and maintenance. Also, if tolls are varied according to the time of day and the day of the week, they

can help to spread out the volume of traffic thus increasing the effective capacity of the existing roads. Michigan has never made substantial use of tolls, but greater use of tolls should be actively considered.

- Unlike the Chicago area or the Cleveland area, the Detroit area does not have a rail-transit system. As a result, Michigan's use of public transportation is much less than the average in the Great Lakes region or in the United States as a whole. A federally funded Detroit rail-transit system could help stimulate jobs and lessen the strain on our roads and the environment, in addition to other benefits.

- In Michigan, as in the rest of the United States, population density in metropolitan areas has been decreasing. Low-density development is associated with increased congestion in the suburbs, loss of open space, and increased infrastructure costs.

- The Headlee Amendment to the Michigan Constitution restricts the ability of local jurisdictions to levy property taxes. New construction is excluded from the Headlee calculations. Thus the Headlee Amendment indirectly encourages growth in outlying areas. In fact, the Headlee Amendment is only one of several policies in Michigan that favor sparsely populated or newly developing areas over densely populated or older areas.

- Michigan would benefit from the development of a comprehensive strategy to level the playing field between older developed areas and newly developing areas.

- In many ways, the environment in Michigan is in better condition now than it was in 1970. Several categories of air pollution are down, the destruction of wetlands has slowed down, and discharges of phosphorus into lakes and streams have been greatly reduced. Also, far more containers and other materials are recycled now than ever before. Nevertheless, a significant number of serious environmental challenges remain.

- Michigan's laws originally had the goal of eliminating environmental contamination. Unfortunately, experience has shown that there are profound technical difficulties in cleaning up contaminated ground water and sediments. It is now recognized that a complete cleanup may be impossible or at least prohibitively expensive. The challenge is to identify the sites with the greatest risks and to find the best methods of reducing these risks.

- The Great Lakes Compact of 2008 was a major step toward protecting the Great Lakes for the long term. The greatest current threat to the lakes is the Asian carp. It is hoped that strong steps will be taken to keep the Asian carp out of the Great Lakes and to permanently separate the Great Lakes from the Mississippi River basin.

NOTES

1. Kenneth Boyer, "Michigan's Transportation System and Transportation Policy," in *Michigan at the Millennium: A Benchmark and Analysis of Its Fiscal and Economic Structure*, ed. Charles L. Ballard, Paul N. Courant, Douglas C. Drake, Ronald C. Fisher, and Elisabeth R. Gerber (East Lansing, MI: Michigan State University Press, 2003).

2. Max Kvidera, "Road Poll: The Good, the Bad, the Better," *Overdrive*, February 1, 2010, http://www.overdriveonline.com/the-good-the-bad-the-better.

3. "Come to Michigan, Where Our Roads Are Turning to Gravel" doesn't sound to me like a very effective theme for an economic-development advertising campaign.

4. Alex Rosaen, Caroline Sallee, and Justin Eli, "Michigan's Roads: The Cost of Doing Nothing and the Rewards of Bold Action," Anderson Economic Group, May 13, 2010, http://www.andersoneconomicgroup.com/Portals/0/upload/AEG-%20Michigans%20Roads%20-%20Cost%20of%20Doing%20Nothing.pdf.

5. Because of the stop-and-go nature of driving in cities, urban drivers get fewer miles per gallon than rural drivers, but rural and urban drivers pay the gasoline tax at the same rate per gallon. Thus the tax rate per mile is higher for urban motorists than for their rural counterparts.

6. Kenneth Boyer, "Michigan's Transportation System and Transportation Policy," in *Michigan at the Millennium*.

7. For more on the external costs of driving, see Todd Litman, *Transportation Cost Analysis* (Victoria, BC: Victoria Transport Policy Institute, 2002).

8. These population data are taken from various issues of the U.S. Census Bureau's Statistical Abstract, http://www.census.gov/statab/www. By 2009, California is estimated to have nearly thirty-seven million people.

9. Gary J. Sands, "Land Use in Michigan," in *Michigan at the Millennium*.

10. Michigan Land Use Leadership Council, "Michigan's Land, Michigan's Future: Final Report of the Michigan Land Use Leadership Council," http://www.michiganlanduse.org/MLULC_FINAL_REPORT_0803.pdf.

11. Gary J. Sands, "Land Use in Michigan," in *Michigan at the Millennium*.

12. Michigan Land Use Leadership Council, "Michigan's Land, Michigan's Future: Final Report of the Michigan Land Use Leadership Council," http://www.michiganlanduse.org/MLULC_FINAL_REPORT_0803.pdf.

13. In *Michigan at the Millennium*, an entire chapter is devoted to the Headlee Amendment. See Susan Fino (Wayne State University), "Tax Limitation in the Michigan Constitution: The Headlee Amendment." Some of these issues are also discussed in the *Michigan at the Millennium* chapter by Naomi Feldman, Paul Courant, and Douglas Drake, "The Property Tax in Michigan." Chapter 6 of this book further explores some of these issues.

14. Gloria E. Helfand and John R. Wolfe, "Environment and Natural Resources in Michigan," in *Michigan at the Millennium*.

15. See Jonathan Oosting, "Canadian Trash Sent to Michigan Drops by 2 Percent," Mlive.com, http://www.mlive.com/news/index.ssf/2009/01/canadian_trash_sent_to_michiga.html.

16. Gloria E. Helfand and John R. Wolfe, "Environment and Natural Resources in Michigan," in *Michigan at the Millennium*.

17. A great deal of information regarding the Great Lakes is available from the Alliance for the Great Lakes, at http://www.greatlakes.org.

■ 4

Michigan and the World Economy

I n earlier chapters, we discussed the effects of Michigan's geographical isolation from the rest of the United States. This presents a challenge since it
is difficult for some parts of Michigan to maintain economic connections
with the rest of the country. Therefore, it is important for us to take advantage of the connections that we *do* have. Our relationships with the rest of
the world, beyond the borders of the United States, present similar challenges
and opportunities. Once again, geography plays an important role. Michigan
is the leading gateway to Ontario, the economic heartland of Canada. Trade
with Canada is one of the central pillars of Michigan's economy.

Earlier in this book, I mentioned that the U.S. Constitution abolished the
trade barriers that had once existed between the thirteen states. This turned
the United States into a free-trade zone, and it greatly fueled the economic
growth of the new nation. These trade provisions of the constitution also gave
the federal government power to determine international trade policies for
the United States. Thus Michigan's governor and legislature have relatively
little control over international trade policy. Nevertheless, it makes sense to
comment on some issues of international trade policy for two reasons: First,
the issues are of crucial importance to Michigan. Second, the public debate on
trade is often marked by confusion and misunderstanding.

Before I go on, I want to acknowledge that international trade can be a subject that causes emotions to run high. As we have seen in earlier chapters, the automobile industry in Michigan has had great difficulty in facing competition from companies headquartered in Germany, Japan, Korea, and other countries. Many Michigan residents, including some personal friends of mine, are deeply suspicious of international trade. However, most economists are fairly positive toward international trade, and my comments in this chapter reflect that view. *No one* advocates completely unregulated trade. No one believes we should have free trade in nuclear weapons, helicopter gunships, or any number of other things. For economic reasons and security reasons, there are important limitations on activity that crosses international boundaries. On the other hand, there is great danger in putting too many restrictions on international movements of goods, services, capital, and people.

When we look around the world at economic successes, we see countries that have engaged with and learned from the rest of the world. On the other hand, many of the greatest economic failures are found in countries that have isolated themselves. The best example of this is found on the Korean Peninsula. When the Korean War came to an end in the 1950s, both North Korea and South Korea were devastated. The two countries then went on very different paths. South Korea deliberately set out to integrate itself with the world economy through trade and investment, while North Korea cut itself off almost entirely from the rest of the world. (North Korea eventually became known as the "Hermit Kingdom.") Now, more than half a century later, the level of income in South Korea has improved dramatically. South Korea's per capita income is now far higher than that of most countries. On the other hand, portions of North Korea's population have been on the brink of starvation in recent decades. North Korea is so thoroughly estranged from the rest of the world that it is difficult to know exactly how poor its people are. However, the U.S. Central Intelligence Agency estimates that North Korea's gross domestic product (GDP) was $1,900 per person in 2009.[1] This puts North Korea in a tie with Cambodia for 187th place among the world's 227 countries. By comparison, South Korea's GDP was $28,000 per person, which puts South Korea in forty-ninth place. If these estimates are correct, the average person in South Korea has about fifteen times as much income as the average person in North Korea.

American economic history includes many cases of interference with international trade. The most notorious of these was the Smoot-Hawley Tariff

Act of 1930, which raised tariffs to their highest levels in history. These tariffs made it difficult for European firms to sell their goods in the United States. Thus, European workers were laid off, and they had less income to buy American goods. Also, European governments viewed the Smoot-Hawley tariffs as a hostile act, and they retaliated with higher tariffs of their own. Thus the Smoot-Hawley tariffs helped to accelerate the downward spiral of the Great Depression. Fortunately, world leaders recognized the damage done by the high tariffs of the 1930s. Since the Second World War, the United States has been one of the leaders of a long series of negotiations for mutual tariff reduction. (The most famous of these was the "Kennedy Round," sponsored by President John F. Kennedy.) As the obstacles to international trade have been reduced, increasing trade has helped to propel the worldwide economic prosperity of the last sixty years.

Of course, this does not mean that international trade has no problems. Some individual businesses and individual workers have been harmed by competition from abroad. The question is, What is the best way to help these workers and businesses? There is general agreement in the economics profession that large trade barriers are not the best way. Instead, it makes sense to embrace international trade (because it increases the overall standard of living) and to provide targeted assistance to those who have been harmed by trade.

The reasoning used here in relation to international trade is similar to the reasoning used earlier in this book in relation to the transitions out of agriculture and manufacturing. The improvements in agricultural productivity have contributed greatly to the overall standard of living, but they also forced a transition that was difficult for some farm workers. The improvements in manufacturing productivity have contributed greatly to the overall standard of living, but they have also forced a transition that has been difficult for some factory workers. Similarly, international trade contributes greatly to the overall level of prosperity, but it can lead to difficult adjustments for some workers. In each case, the consensus in the economics profession is that it is good to embrace the mechanisms that create general economic prosperity, while also providing assistance (such as unemployment insurance and retraining programs) to those who are adversely affected.

Later in this chapter, we will look in detail at the importance of international trade for Michigan. However, we begin by describing the extent of international trade for the United States as a whole.

The Growing Importance of American Trade with the Rest of the World

Figure 4.1 shows exports from the United States and imports into the United States as a percentage of U.S. GDP. Gross domestic product is the total value of all the goods and services produced in the economy. In other words, Figure 4.1 shows the number of dollars generated by exports as a percentage of the total number of dollars in the entire economy, and it shows the same percentage for imports.

Figure 4.1 reveals that, over time, international trade has become an increasingly large part of the U.S. economy. In most years in the 1950s, exports accounted for about 4 or 5 percent of GDP, and imports were about 4 percent of GDP. By the mid 1970s, exports and imports were both about 8 percent of GDP, and the growth has continued since then. Imports have accounted for more than 10 percent of GDP in every year since 1986, and exports have accounted for more than 10 percent of GDP in all but two of the years since 1992. By 2008, exports were about $1.83 trillion. That is more than 13 percent of GDP, which is an all-time high. Imports were about $2.54 trillion, nearly 18 percent of GDP, which is also an all-time high.

Thus if we look at the last fifty or sixty years, we see a period in which international trade was growing more rapidly than purely domestic economic activity. As a result, we can say that international trade has been a major "engine of economic growth" for the United States, pulling the rest of the economy along. (The same is true for many other countries as well. Overall, international trade has been an engine of growth for the entire world economy.)

Trade Deficits

Figure 4.1 shows that exports and imports have both grown tremendously since the Second World War. However, imports have grown much more rapidly than exports, especially since about 1980. In many of the years in the 1950s and 1960s, America exported more than it imported. In this situation, we say that the United States had a "trade surplus." In the last thirty years, however, imports have been greater than exports; this means that we have had a "trade deficit."

Trade deficits are the subject of much confusion. If you listen to some commentators and politicians, it would be easy to think that exports are "good" because they create American jobs, and imports are "bad" because they create jobs for people in other countries. Thus it is sometimes asserted that imports

FIGURE 4.1. U.S. exports and imports as a percentage
of gross domestic product, 1950–2008

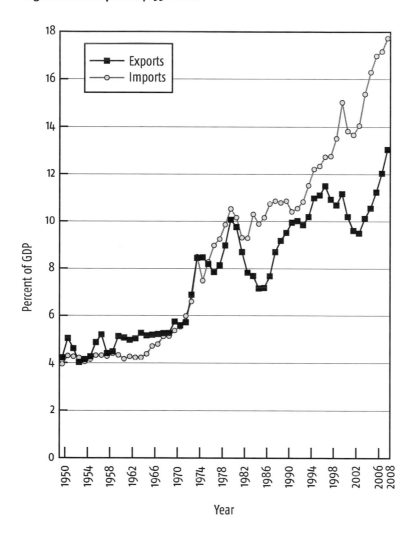

Source: U.S. Department of Commerce, Bureau of Economic Analysis, "Table 1.1.5: Gross Domestic Product," http://www.bea.gov/national/nipaweb/
SelectTable.asp?Selected=N.

are a major cause of unemployment. If exports are "good" and imports are
"bad," then it must be that trade surpluses are good and trade deficits are bad.

This sort of thinking can be very misleading. First of all, the United States
has had substantial trade deficits in many years when the unemployment
rate has been low. It is simplistic to think that trade deficits inevitably lead to

unemployment. The recent recession and the resulting high unemployment were caused by a speculative bubble in the housing market and a poorly regulated financial system. The financial crisis of 2008 was not caused by imports.

Second, although employment considerations are worth worrying about, they are not the only important thing when gauging the benefits of international trade. Consumer satisfaction is also important. Americans import goods from other countries because they believe those items provide a good level of satisfaction for the dollar. Part of the trade deficit is caused by imports of coffee from Brazil, wooden bowls from Thailand, radios from South Korea, and cheese from Denmark. It is very difficult to argue that American consumers would be better off if we were to cut off these imports. Part of the trade deficit is caused by imports of oil. In recent years, the United States has been importing more than ten million barrels of oil per day. (We get the oil from all over the world, but our four biggest suppliers are Canada, Mexico, Saudi Arabia, and Venezuela.) We could "solve" a part of the trade deficit by prohibiting imports of oil, but would that make us better off? Instead of making us better off, a prohibition on oil imports would just make us cold in the winter because it would become difficult to find enough energy to heat our homes. The long-term solution to our energy problems will involve greater energy efficiency and conservation, as well as the development of solar power and other alternative energy sources. Merely banning oil imports won't solve the problem.

A third important point is that there is no way for the world as a whole to run a trade surplus. By definition, one country's surplus is another country's deficit. This means that the world as a whole has a trade balance of exactly zero: for the world as a whole, total imports have to be exactly equal to total exports. Thus there is no way for all countries to reduce deficits (or increase surpluses) simultaneously. If lots of countries were to try to increase their surpluses (or reduce their deficits) at the same time, the results could be disastrous. In the 1930s, a number of countries increased their barriers against imports in the false belief that this would increase employment at home. This led to a downward spiral as economic activity decreased around the globe. Thus trade restrictions (in addition to many other factors) contributed to the Great Depression of the 1930s.

Figure 4.1 shows two time periods when trade deficits increased dramatically. The first of these was in the 1980s, and the second was shortly after 2000. Each of these episodes of increased trade deficits came at about the same time that the federal government had big tax cuts, which led to greatly increased government budget deficits. This is not a coincidence. In recent decades, American households have been on a consumption spending binge, and the private savings rate has fallen steadily. When the federal government piles a large budget deficit on top of the low private savings rate, the result is that the nation is consuming more than it produces.

When a household spends more than it makes, it has to borrow. The same is true for a nation. When the United States spends more than it makes, it has to borrow from other countries. The trade deficits and our growing indebtedness to the rest of the world are mainly driven by America's consumption binge, and not by anyone's trade policies. If we really want to address the trade deficit, the best way would be for American households to save more and for the federal government to get its deficit spending under control. The solution is to reduce our nation's consumption spending binge, rather than to erect artificial barriers to trade.

The Geographical Distribution of U.S. Imports and Exports

Figure 4.1 presents the time trend for the *overall* level of exports and imports for goods and services combined. Table 4.1 gives a *country-by-country* breakdown of exports and imports in 2008. In this table, the countries are listed in order of their amounts of U.S. exports.

The first thing to notice in Table 4.1 is that trade is very dispersed. Although some countries clearly have a lot more trade with the United States than other countries, it is not as if one or two countries are really dominant. The country with the greatest amount of exports and imports is our next-door neighbor, Canada. Our other next-door neighbor, Mexico, ranks second as a recipient of American exports and third as a provider of American imports. But there is also considerable trade with countries that are much farther away.

Table 4.1 also shows that many of our biggest trading partners are other affluent countries, such as Australia, Belgium, Canada, France, Germany, Italy, Japan, the Netherlands, and the United Kingdom. A lot of our trade is with other rich countries, because that's where a lot of the money is.

Although the United States has an overall trade deficit, it does not have a deficit with every country. As shown in Table 4.1, the United States had substantial surpluses in 2008 with Argentina, Australia, Belgium, Brazil, the Netherlands,

TABLE 4.1. U.S. exports and imports of goods and services
(in billions of dollars) for selected countries, 2008*

COUNTRY	EXPORTS	IMPORTS	TRADE SURPLUS (+) OR TRADE DEFECIT (−)
Canada	309.0	363.1	−54.1
Mexico	176.2	235.3	−59.1
United Kingdom	117.2	104.0	+13.1
China†	115.2	362.1	−246.9
Japan	108.6	166.9	−58.4
Germany	82.3	131.8	−49.5
Middle East‡	76.4	132.5	−56.2
Netherlands	54.9	30.9	+24.1
South Korea	49.4	57.5	−8.1
France	47.4	59.9	−12.5
Brazil	45.4	35.6	+9.8
Africa‡‡	39.9	120.0	−80.1
Singapore	37.1	21.0	+16.0
Australia	35.0	17.6	+17.4
Taiwan	33.3	44.4	−11.1
Belgium	33.3	21.3	+12.0
India	29.2	37.9	−8.7
Italy	25.3	45.0	−19.7
Venezuela	17.4	52.3	−34.8
Argentina	10.9	7.4	+3.6

* Surpluses or deficits may not agree exactly with export and import levels because of rounding.
† Includes Hong Kong.
‡ Includes Iran, Iraq, Israel, Saudi Arabia, United Arab Emirates, and ten other countries.
‡‡ Includes more than fifty countries.
Source: U.S. Department of Commerce, Bureau of Economic Analysis, "International Economic Accounts," http://www.bea.gov/
　　international/index.htm#trade.

Singapore, and the United Kingdom. Even when the United States has had an overall trade balance of zero, with total exports equal to total imports, we have always run deficits with some countries and surpluses with others. In fact, although the United States should strive to reduce its overall trade deficit, it does not make any sense to try to achieve bilateral trade balance with every country.

In particular, our largest trade deficit is with China, but that does not mean that we would be better off by clamping down on imports from China.[2] It's best to view our trade deficit with China as only one part of our overall trade imbalance. The overall trade imbalance is driven by America's consumption spending binge. These days, one sometimes hears angry talk that blames our problems on the Chinese. I think such talk will only distract Americans from the real solutions to our trade deficits. The real solutions have to do with the behaviors and policies of Americans, far more than with the behaviors and policies of people in China or other countries. It is almost always best to correct one's own mistakes instead of blaming them on someone else.

Now that we have seen some of the basic facts about America's international trade posture, we turn our attention to Michigan.

Some Facts about Michigan's Trade with the Rest of the World

In Chapter 2, we saw that Michigan has the *eighth-largest population* among the fifty states. However, because of the poor performance of our economy, Michigan had the *twelfth-largest economy* in 2008.[3] Still, in spite of its twelfth-place ranking in terms of the overall size of the economy, Michigan is the eighth-largest state in terms of the dollar value of international merchandise exports.[4]

Table 4.2 shows the value of international merchandise exports for the twenty states with the largest amounts of exports in 2008. (These twenty states had more than 81 percent of the total exports for the United States.) Michigan is in eighth place with about $45 billion in exports in 2008.

If we express exports as a percentage of the state's economy, we get a somewhat different picture. Table 4.3 shows the twenty states in which international exports make up the largest fraction of the economy of the state. In other words, Table 4.2 shows the states that are biggest in the *absolute size* of their exports, whereas Table 4.3 shows the states for which exports are *relatively* most important to the state's economy. One of the most notable things about Table 4.3 is that many of the biggest states don't make it to the list. For example, California, Florida, New York, and Pennsylvania are all missing from Table 4.3. All four of these states are among the top six states in terms of the overall size of their economies, and Table 4.2 showed that all four of them also rank fairly high in terms of the dollar value of their international exports. However, these four states (and several other states with large economies)

TABLE 4.2. Value of merchandise exports (in billions of dollars) for the twenty states with the largest exports, 2008

RANK	STATE	EXPORTS
1	Texas	192.2
2	California	144.8
3	New York	81.4
4	Washington	54.5
5	Florida	54.2
6	Illinois	53.7
7	Ohio	45.6
8	**Michigan**	**45.1**
9	Louisiana	41.9
10	New Jersey	35.6
11	Pennsylvania	34.6
12	Massachusetts	28.4
13	Georgia	27.5
14	Indiana	26.5
15	North Carolina	25.1
16	Tennessee	23.2
17	Wisconsin	20.6
18	South Carolina	19.9
19	Arizona	19.8
20	Oregon	19.4

Source: U.S. Department of Commerce, International Trade Administration, "TradeStats Express," http://tse.export.gov.

do *not* rank very high when it comes to the *percentage* of their economies that come from international exports.

In Table 4.3, as in Table 4.2, Michigan is in eighth place. In 2008, nearly 12 percent of the Michigan economy was associated with exports. Tables 4.2 and 4.3 have shown that Michigan is a major exporting state, regardless of whether we look at the absolute dollar value of exports or at the relative importance of exports to our state's economy. Thus, more than most states, Michigan has a lot to lose from excessive interference with international trade and a lot to gain from trade improvements.

TABLE 4.3. Value of merchandise exports as a percentage of gross state product (GSP) for the twenty states with the highest percentage, 2008

RANK	STATE	EXPORTS
1	Louisiana	18.86
2	Washington	16.88
3	Texas	15.71
4	Vermont	14.53
5	South Carolina	12.69
6	Kentucky	12.22
7	Oregon	11.98
8	**Michigan**	**11.80**
9	Indiana	10.40
10	Kansas	10.20
11	Ohio	9.68
12	Idaho	9.49
13	Utah	9.39
14	Alabama	9.34
15	Tennessee	9.22
16	West Virginia	9.15
17	Iowa	8.93
18	North Dakota	8.88
19	Wisconsin	8.56
20	Illinois	8.47

Source: U.S. Department of Commerce, International Trade Administration, "TradeStats Express," http://tse.export.gov.

The Geographical and Industrial Composition of Michigan's Exports

It is probably not surprising that Canada stands head and shoulders above Michigan's other international trading partners. In 2008, Michigan exported more than $24 billion of goods to Canada. That works out to more than 53 percent of Michigan's total exports in that year. Mexico was in second place, with about $6.4 billion of exports or about 14 percent of Michigan's total exports. The others among the top five customers for Michigan's international exports are Germany, Japan, and China. When taken together, these five countries account for about 77 percent of Michigan's exports. The top twenty destinations for Michigan's international export goods are shown in Table 4.4.

Even though a relatively small number of countries receive the lion's share of Michigan's exports, it is still true that a very large amount of value is exported to an astonishing variety of countries. Michigan exported at least $100 million of goods to each of thirty-one countries in 2008. No fewer than seventy-one countries received at least $10 million of Michigan exports in

TABLE 4.4. The twenty countries that receive the most merchandise exports from Michigan, 2008

RANK	COUNTRY	MICHIGAN EXPORTS (IN MILLIONS OF DOLLARS)	PERCENTAGE OF MICHIGAN EXPORTS
1	Canada	24,073.0	53.3
2	Mexico	6,414.6	14.2
3	Germany	1,562.1	3.5
4	Japan	1,437.7	3.2
5	China	1,287.6	2.9
6	Saudi Arabia	840.5	1.9
7	United Kingdom	693.9	1.5
8	France	627.1	1.4
9	South Korea	621.7	1.4
10	Venezuela	563.4	1.2
11	Belgium	531.8	1.2
12	Netherlands	489.5	1.1
13	Brazil	438.7	1.0
14	United Arab Emirates	388.6	0.9
15	Russian Federation	364.9	0.8
16	Australia	357.5	0.8
17	Kuwait	240.1	0.5
18	Austria	235.3	0.5
19	Argentina	228.7	0.5
20	Taiwan	208.2	0.5
Total for these countries		**41,604.9**	**92.2**
Total for all countries		**45,135.5**	**100.0**

Source: U.S. Department of Commerce, International Trade Administration, "TradeStats Express," http://tse.export.gov.

2008, and two-hundred countries paid for at least some exports from Michigan. Michigan exports cover the entire world, going to an alphabet soup of countries including Albania, Bolivia, Cyprus, Denmark, Egypt, and Fiji.

Table 4.4 shows the top twenty countries that pay for Michigan's exports. In turn, Table 4.5 shows the top twenty industries for Michigan exports.

TABLE 4.5. The twenty industries that account for the most merchandise exports from Michigan, 2008

RANK	INDUSTRY	MICHIGAN EXPORTS (IN MILLIONS OF DOLLARS)	PERCENTAGE OF MICHIGAN EXPORTS
1	Transportation equipment	21,065.7	46.7
2	Machinery manufactures	4,244.7	9.4
3	Chemical manufactures	4,017.5	8.9
4	Oil and gas extraction	3,148.9	7.0
5	Primary metal manufactures	2,398.5	5.3
6	Computers and electronic products	1,747.0	3.9
7	Fabricated metal products	1,447.4	3.2
8	Electrical equipment, appliances, and parts	977.8	2.2
9	Processed foods	823.0	1.8
10	Plastic and rubber products	756.2	1.7
11	Nonmetallic mineral manufactures	677.8	1.5
12	Mining	619.9	1.4
13	Furniture and related products	502.9	1.1
14	Miscellaneous manufactures	447.5	1.0
15	Crop production	379.7	0.8
16	Waste and scrap	368.5	0.8
17	Paper products	343.4	0.8
18	Petroleum and coal products	197.6	0.4
19	Leather and related products	188.7	0.4
20	Wood products	159.8	0.4
Total for these industries		**44,512.4**	**98.6**
Total		**45,135.5**	**100.0**

Source: U.S. Department of Commerce, International Trade Administration, "TradeStats Express," http://tse.export.gov.

In 2008, about 47 percent of Michigan's international exports were in the transportation-equipment industry. Another 18 percent were in machinery manufacturing and chemical manufacturing. Thus Michigan's international exports are dominated by a fairly small number of industries, just as they are dominated by a fairly small number of countries. However, just as Michigan had at least some exports to each of a large number of countries, Michigan had at least some exports in each of dozens of industries. In addition to the industries shown in Table 4.5, Michigan also exported leather products, printing products, beverages, textiles, apparel, and other goods.

Immigration

The United States is a nation of immigrants. Native Americans make up about 1 percent of the U.S. population, but the vast majority of the people in the United States came from somewhere else, or are descended from people who came from somewhere else in the last five-hundred years. Until well into the 1800s, most immigrants to the United States came from Great Britain (voluntarily) or from Africa (in chains). In the middle of the nineteenth century came waves of immigrants from Germany, Holland, and Ireland. Still more immigrants came in the late nineteenth and early twentieth centuries from Finland, Greece, Italy, Poland, Russia, and many other countries.

America's immigration laws were tightened in the 1920s. As a result, immigrants came at a slower rate from the 1920s to the 1960s. However, the immigration laws were loosened again in 1965. Since then, the rate of immigration has been somewhat higher, although not as high as in the early 1900s. Also, the mix of immigrants has changed. Until 1965, most immigrants came from Europe, but the largest numbers of immigrants in recent years have come from Latin America and East Asia.

Michigan has people with roots all over the world. For those interested in learning more about the rich diversity of Michigan's ethnic heritage, an excellent source is a series of books published by the Michigan State University Press. These include *African Americans in Michigan*, *Arab Americans in Michigan*, *Dutch in Michigan*, *Finns in Michigan*, *Greeks in Michigan*, *Irish in Michigan*, *Mexicans and Mexican Americans in Michigan*, *Poles in Michigan*, and several others.[5]

Most Michigan residents are descended from Europeans, although relatively few came directly from Europe. It was more common for the first waves of immigrants to land in New England and New York and then make their way westward. In the nineteenth century, Michigan's population included large numbers of transplanted New Englanders and New Yorkers. This made Michigan one of the staunchest centers of antislavery sentiment, and it meant that the Republican Party (founded in Jackson, Michigan with an antislavery platform) dominated Michigan politics for many decades.

Another noteworthy migration came from the South in the middle of the twentieth century. This brought large numbers of African Americans to Michigan for the first time, and it also brought large numbers of white southerners.

According to the Census Bureau, about 583,000 people residing in Michigan in 2008 were born in other countries. That works out to about 5.8 percent of the population. That is less than half of the average for the country. In 2008, it is estimated that about thirty-eight million foreign-born persons lived in the United States, which works out to about 12.5 percent of the national population. In terms of the foreign-born percentage of the population, Michigan ranks twenty-seventh among the fifty states, or twenty-eighth if we include the District of Columbia.[6]

Table 4.6 shows the percentage of the population that is foreign-born for the fifty states and the District of Columbia. The table reveals tremendous variation across the different regions of the country. California is estimated to have nearly ten million foreign-born residents. This is by far the most in absolute numbers, and it is also the highest percentage—the estimates indicate that nearly 27 percent of California's people were born in other countries. At the other end of the scale, the smallest absolute number of foreign-born residents is in Wyoming, where only about twelve-thousand people were born in other countries. The smallest foreign-born percentage is in West Virginia, where only about 1.3 percent of the people were not born in the United States.

Table 4.6 indicates that, for better or worse, Michigan is not one of America's major centers for immigrants. Thus fewer of the benefits of immigration and the problems caused by it are experienced in Michigan. In the next section, I briefly discuss some of the economic benefits and costs of immigration.

TABLE 4.6. Percentage of the population who are foreign born in the fifty states and the District of Columbia, 2008

RANK	STATE	PERCENTAGE	RANK	STATE	PERCENTAGE
1	California	26.8	26	Idaho	5.9
2	New York	21.7	27	Kansas	5.9
3	New Jersey	19.8	**28**	**Michigan**	**5.8**
4	Nevada	18.9	29	Nebraska	5.5
5	Florida	18.5	30	Pennsylvania	5.3
6	Hawaii	17.8	31	Oklahoma	5.0
7	Texas	16.0	32	New Hampshire	5.0
8	Massachusetts	14.4	33	Wisconsin	4.4
9	Arizona	14.3	34	South Carolina	4.4
10	Illinois	13.8	35	Indiana	4.0
11	District of Columbia	13.2	36	Tennessee	4.0
12	Connecticut	13.0	37	Vermont	3.9
	United States	**12.5**	38	Arkansas	3.8
13	Maryland	12.4	39	Iowa	3.7
14	Washington	12.3	40	Ohio	3.7
15	Rhode Island	12.2	41	Missouri	3.6
16	Virginia	10.2	42	Louisiana	3.1
17	Colorado	10.1	43	Maine	3.0
18	Oregon	9.7	44	Alabama	2.8
19	New Mexico	9.6	45	Kentucky	2.8
20	Georgia	9.4	46	North Dakota	2.3
21	Utah	8.3	47	Wyoming	2.3
22	Delaware	7.7	48	Montana	2.2
23	North Carolina	7.0	49	Mississippi	2.1
24	Minnesota	6.5	50	South Dakota	1.9
25	Alaska	6.5	51	West Virginia	1.3

Source: Migration Policy Institute, "2008 American Community Survey and Census Data on the Foreign Born by State," http://www.migrationinformation.org/datahub/acscensus.cfm#.

The Economic Effects of Immigration

Throughout American history, there has been tension between newcomer immigrants and established citizens. The tensions have often had to do with culture, language, or religion. These tensions have also had to do with economic issues. The most important of these issues is the fear that immigrants will reduce the wages of established citizens. Economic theory does indeed suggest that an increase in the supply of labor will lead to lower wage rates, all else equal. (This is true for *any* increase in the supply of labor, regardless of whether it is brought about by immigration, by the natural increase of the native-born population, or by anything else.)

However, it is important to remember that not all workers are the same. Immigration is likely to have more of an effect in some labor markets than in others, and some native workers will be affected by immigration more than others will. In fact in the last few decades, a large fraction of the immigrants have been less educated than most of the native population. Consequently, we would expect that recent immigrants would have more of an effect on less-skilled Americans than on those of greater skill. This appears to be the case. Overall, immigration of low-skilled workers has probably led to reductions in the wage rates of native-born Americans who do not have a high school education. However, we should note that the last few decades would have been bad times for poorly educated native-born Americans, even if there had not been any immigration.

In spite of the fact that immigration may exert some downward pressure on the earnings of some native-born workers, it is incorrect to see the less-skilled immigrants as a heavy weight, dragging down the economy. They provide valuable services (often doing work that native-born Americans are not enthusiastic to do), and they pay taxes. Many of the immigrants own their own homes and businesses. Also, while many of the immigrants are unskilled, some are very highly skilled. At American universities, a large fraction of the new PhDs in the sciences and engineering are foreign-born, and many of these people stay on to contribute strongly to the U.S. economy.

Certainly, if we look at Table 4.6, it would be difficult to assert that immigrants have wrecked the American economy. Many of the states with the most vibrant economies have relatively large immigrant populations.

Illegal Immigration

In recent years, much of the debate about immigration has focused on illegal or undocumented immigrants. The Center for Immigration Studies (CIS), a think tank based in Washington, DC, estimates that 10.8 million immigrants were in the United States illegally in early 2009.[7] This is actually a decrease from a peak of 12.5 million in 2007.[8] The CIS estimates that more than 60 percent of the illegal immigrants are in a very particular demographic group: Hispanics, ages 18 to 40, with no education beyond high school.

Since so many of the undocumented immigrants are Hispanic, it is not surprising that states in the south and west are estimated to have far more illegal immigrants than Michigan. According to a recent report issued by the Pew Hispanic Center, the top three states (California, Texas, and Florida) have a total of 5.2 million illegal immigrants.[9] At the other end of the spectrum, fewer than ten-thousand undocumented immigrants are estimated to be in each of Alaska, Maine, Montana, North Dakota, South Dakota, Vermont, West Virginia, and Wyoming. Michigan is estimated to have 110,000 illegal immigrants, which puts us in a tie for twentieth place with Connecticut, Minnesota, and Utah.

In 2010, Arizona passed a law to crack down on illegal immigrants. The Arizona law has caused a great deal of often-heated debate, so it is appropriate to comment on it briefly. The first thing to say is that regardless of the details of the Arizona law, it is easy to understand the frustration felt by many people in Arizona. Their state's long border with Mexico includes some extremely rugged country that is very difficult to patrol. As a result, the border country is rife with drug trafficking and human trafficking, and there are occasional incidents of horrific violence.

Many supporters of the Arizona law acknowledge that border security and immigration control are really matters that ought to be handled by the federal government. However, the federal government has thus far not devoted sufficient resources to secure the border. (It is not clear whether any amount of border patrols could secure the border entirely, but additional patrols would undoubtedly make some difference.) Congress is stalemated, caught between those whose main concern is to secure the border and those whose main concern is to provide a pathway to citizenship for at least some of the undocumented immigrants.

In my view, the Arizona experience is just not very relevant for Michigan. Lots of people try to get into Arizona from Mexico, whereas there is not much evidence that large numbers of illegal immigrants are trying to get into Michigan. The Arizona–Mexico border has hundreds of miles of open country, where it is relatively easy to sneak across. Michigan, on the other hand, is mostly surrounded by water. Our border crossings with Canada at Sault Ste. Marie, Port Huron, and Detroit are all at places where the Great Lakes narrow down to a river. These "choke points" are much easier to control.

I see no need for Michigan even to consider an Arizona-style law. In fact, Michigan is losing population. If we could get a few hundred thousand immigrants to come here and help rebuild our state, it would be a good thing (especially if these immigrants are skilled).

Border Security

Security concerns are very important, and they are one of the reasons that international trade has to be regulated. The challenge is to achieve the greatest possible economic benefit from international trade while preserving security. In the aftermath of the events of September 11, 2001, heightened security led to considerable congestion at border crossings. Some of the congestion was relieved by the opening of new U.S. Customs booths on the Detroit side of the Ambassador Bridge in 2004. Nevertheless, the Michigan–Ontario economy will be greatly enhanced by construction of a new bridge in the Detroit area. When producers in Ontario want to ship goods to the eastern third of the United States, they have a choice of sending the goods through border crossings in Detroit or Port Huron, or through crossings in the region of Buffalo–Niagara Falls, New York. For the sake of the future economic health of Michigan, it makes sense to ensure that the Michigan border crossings are modern, fast, and efficient.

Our friends on the Canadian side of the Detroit River are ready to build the new bridge, and they will put up a great deal of money to fund the project. The bridge will provide thousands of jobs during the construction phase, and it will strengthen our economy for decades to come. We need to sign on.

Conclusion

America's number-one trading partner is Canada, and the number-one gateway to Canada is Michigan. That's the main reason I am very uneasy when I hear talk about reducing international trade. More than most states, Michigan has a great deal to gain from international trade and much to lose from excessive interference with trade.

But even if we weren't right next door to Canada, many of the arguments in favor of relatively free trade would still apply. As shown in this chapter, international trade has been an engine for the growth of the world economy for more than half a century. A major retreat from international trade could have devastating effects on the entire world economy.

Some folks believe that restricting international trade will "save Michigan jobs," but the evidence for that assertion is sketchy at best. In this chapter, I have tried to make the case that the economy will actually work better if we allow people to trade. It is natural to feel uncomfortable about people who look different, speak different languages, and have different customs. But we can learn from people of different backgrounds, and by learning, we can make the entire world economy work better.

I know that suspicion of international trade is very deeply ingrained in the minds of some of Michigan's people. If you were in favor of greatly reduced trade when you began reading this chapter and I haven't already changed your mind (at least a little bit), I'm not sure that I will be able to do so. However, let me make one final attempt. The argument that some folks make is that restricting trade with other countries will "save American jobs." But if that argument is true, then it simply *must* be true that restricting trade with Ohio will "save Michigan jobs." And if that is true, then by the same logic, it simply *must* be true that restricting trade with Livingston County will "save Ingham County jobs." And if that's true, it must be true that restricting trade with Lansing will "save East Lansing jobs." In fact, none of the above is true.

Of course, there should be some regulations on international trade and immigration. In this chapter, I have presented many of the arguments that economists make in favor of *relatively* free movements of goods and people across international boundaries, but that does not mean that these movements should be completely unrestricted. The point is that, subject to reasonable regulations, people should be allowed to choose what products to buy.

However, there is absolutely nothing wrong with encouraging Michigan's people to buy Michigan products, as long as no coercion is involved. The farms, factories, laboratories, and offices in Michigan produce a staggering array of excellent goods and services. I have had several conversations with Michigan merchants who once used ingredients and materials made in other places, but have now found high-quality Michigan products. I encourage all of Michigan's people to keep their eyes out for the wonderful goods and services produced in Michigan.

NOTES

1. For the CIA's rankings of countries for a wide variety of indicators, see the Central Intelligence Agency, "The World Fact Book," https://www.cia.gov/library/publications/the-world-factbook/index.html.

2. The United States has signed multilateral trade agreements. If we abide by those agreements, we cannot single out any one country for special punishment. As a citizen of Michigan, one of my fears is that concern about trade disputes with China will lead to a political atmosphere that is hostile to trade in general. I do not want to see increased restrictions on trade with Canada as a result of trade disputes with China.

3. This ranking is based on the data for "gross state product," which is a measure of the total value of the goods and services produced in each state. Gross state product for Michigan is analogous to gross domestic product for the United States as a whole. See the Bureau of Economic Analysis, "Regional Economic Accounts," http://www.bea.gov/regional/index.htm#gsp.

4. *Michigan at the Millennium* includes an excellent discussion of international issues by Alan Deardorff of the University of Michigan. See Alan Deardorff, "Michigan's Stake in International Trade and Investment," in *Michigan at the Millennium: A Benchmark and Analysis of Its Fiscal and Economic Structure*, ed. Charles L. Ballard, Paul N. Courant, Douglas C. Drake, Ronald C. Fisher, and Elisabeth R. Gerber (East Lansing, MI: Michigan State University Press, 2003). In this chapter, Deardorff reports on export data for 2000. At that time, Michigan was the eighth-largest economy in the United States, but it was the fourth-largest exporter. Thus exports continue to be a larger portion of the economy in Michigan than in the nation as a whole. However, Michigan's ranking among the states has fallen for exports, just as it has fallen for the overall economy.

5. See the MSU Press Web site, http://msupress.msu.edu. The titles in the area of Michigan history can be found at http://msupress.msu.edu/subjectIndex.php?subjectID=35.

6. These data are from the Migration Policy Institute, "2008 American Community Survey and Census Data on the Foreign Born by State," http://www.migrationinformation.org/datahub/acscensus.cfm#.

7. See Steven A. Camarota and Karen Jensenius, "A Shifting Tide: Recent Trends in the Illegal Immigrant Population," Center for Immigration Studies, http://www.cis.org/IllegalImmigration-ShiftingTide.

8. These estimates, like any estimates of illegal activity, are bound to be imprecise. The difficulties in estimating the number of illegal immigrants are similar to the difficulties in estimating the size of the underground economy or the extent of income-tax evasion. One of the most prominent scholars on income-tax evasion, enforcement, and compliance is Joel Slemrod of the University of Michigan. See Slemrod, ed., *Why People Pay Taxes* (Ann Arbor: University of Michigan Press, 1992).

9. See Jeffrey S. Passel and D'Vera Cohn (April 2009), "A Portrait of Unauthorized Immigrants in the United States," Pew Hispanic Center, http://pewhispanic.org/files/reports/107.pdf.

■ 5

Other Budget-Related Issues
and Policies in Michigan

D irectly or indirectly, almost every issue of economic policy in Michigan is affected by the budgets of the state government and local governments.[1] In Chapters 2 and 3 of this book, we have already touched on several issues of importance to Michigan's government budgets. Chapter 2 covered education, which is an especially important category of government expenditure in Michigan. The various policy issues discussed in Chapter 3 also have implications for the budget. In this chapter, we turn to some other aspects of budget policy. We begin with an overview of the state budget, followed by a discussion of the state's chronic structural budgetary imbalances. We then look at corrections and health care, before turning to programs aimed at low-wage workers and low-income families. Finally, we discuss the shrinkage of the state government workforce.

The State Budget in Michigan

In Table 5.1, we show the total amounts of spending by the various departments and agencies of the state government for the 2010 fiscal year.[2] These

TABLE 5.1. Budget for departments and agencies of the State of Michigan, fiscal year 2010 (dollar amounts in millions)

DEPARTMENT	AMOUNT	PERCENTAGE OF TOTAL
Community Health	13,073	28.89
School Aid	12,826	28.34
Human Services	5,917	13.08
Transportation	3,260	7.20
Corrections	1,956	4.32
Universities and Financial Aid	1,612	3.56
Treasury	1,535	3.39
Energy, Labor, and Economic Growth	1,463	3.23
Technology, Management, and Budget	728	1.61
Natural Resources and Environment	712	1.57
State Police	536	1.18
Community Colleges	299	0.66
Judiciary	259	0.57
Secretary of State	209	0.46
Military and Veterans Affairs	146	0.32
Education	113	0.25
Legislature	106	0.23
Agriculture	80	0.18
Debt Service	80	0.18
Attorney General	74	0.16
Legislative Auditor General	15	0.03
Civil Rights	14	0.03
Executive Office	5	0.01
Total	**45,254**	**100.00**

Source: Michigan Department of Technology, Management, and Budget, "Executive Budget, Fiscal Year 2011," State of Michigan, http://www.michigan.gov/documents/budget/2_310743_7.pdf.

spending categories are ranked by size. The largest is the Department of Community Health, which includes the Medicaid program, with more than $13 billion of expenditures. The School Aid Fund (state aid to K–12 education) is the second-largest category, with about $12.8 billion. These two categories accounted for about 57 percent of gross expenditures by the state in fiscal year 2010. Note, however, that not all of these expenditures are actually paid for by Michigan taxpayers. In particular, the Medicaid program is a joint federal–state program, and the federal government picks up a large portion of Medicaid costs. In fact, the General Fund/General Purpose budget for the State of Michigan was only about $8 billion in 2010. Thus, when discussing budgets in Michigan, it is important to specify which budget is being considered. The State of Michigan has control over the School Aid Fund and the General Fund, which together add up to about $20 billion. However, the rest of the budget is mostly aid from the federal government, which usually comes with specific strings attached.

When I wrote my earlier book about the Michigan economy in 2005 and 2006, School Aid was larger than Community Health. However, in the intervening four years, Community Health grew by 27 percent, while School Aid grew by only about one-half of a percent. In other words, health-care spending grew substantially, even after adjusting for inflation, but the minuscule growth of state aid to K–12 schools was not nearly enough to keep up with inflation. This is a stark indication of the extent to which health-care spending is crowding out other things. This is happening at the federal level as well as in all fifty states.

Figure 5.1 shows some of the same information that was shown in Table 5.1 but in a different form. The point of Figure 5.1 is to illustrate that the state budget is dominated by a relatively small number of expenditure categories.

Spending on the legislature and the executive office account for a total of only about $111 million, which is less than one-fourth of a percent of the state budget. We often hear complaints about the amount spent on elected officials. However, relative to the rest of the budget, the amounts spent directly on elected officials are a tiny drop in the bucket. If the salaries of legislators, legislative staff, the governor, and the governor's staff were eliminated completely, the direct effect on the state budget would be negligible. In fact, even though I know that many of these officials are unpopular, I would like to argue against substantial cuts in their pay. I believe we are likely to get what we pay for. Right

FIGURE 5.1. Categories of expenditure in the budget
of the State of Michigan, fiscal year 2010

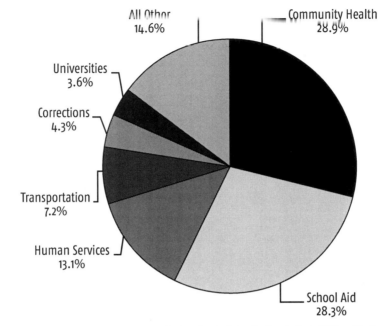

Source: Michigan Department of Technology, Management, and Budget, "Executive Budget, Fiscal Year 2011," State of Michigan, http://www
.michigan.gov/documents/budget/2_310743_7.pdf.

now, public service is unattractive to many good and talented people because
they would have to take a pay cut if they were to enter the legislature. If we
cut the pay of elected officials, we are more likely to have a government dominated by those who are independently wealthy or those who don't have very
good earnings prospects in the private sector.

Structural Budget Deficits

Since the Second World War, the U.S. economy has experienced twelve recessions.
During a typical recession, there is a reduction in employment and economic
activity. As a result, if tax rates do not change, there is a reduction in tax revenues.
Recessions also typically bring an increase in the number of people seeking social
services. The budgetary problems caused by a recession are known as "cyclical"
budgetary pressures because they are caused by the business cycle.

The recent recession created tremendous cyclical problems for government budgets in Michigan and in other states. Without very substantial help from the federal government, the effects on budgets in Michigan would have been devastating. However, the budget difficulties faced by today's governments in Michigan are *not* fundamentally cyclical in nature—Michigan's budgetary problems will continue long after the recession is over. Michigan faces a "structural deficit," which means that the cost of maintaining programs is increasing relative to revenues, even when the economy is expanding.

Every budget has a revenue side and an expenditure side. In Michigan, both sides of the budget contribute to the structural deficit. On the revenue side, the percentage of personal income that goes to state and local governments has been shrinking. The shrinkage has been caused largely by structural weaknesses in Michigan's major taxes. Consequently, tax revenues in Michigan grow more slowly than the overall economy, even when tax rates remain the same. We will discuss the tax system in Michigan in much greater detail in Chapter 6 of this book. In the current chapter, most of our attention is focused on the expenditure side of the budget.

The Michigan Constitution requires a balanced budget.[3] However, falling tax revenues do not necessarily translate into immediate cuts in programs. Instead, it may be possible to use up financial reserves (such as the "Rainy Day Fund") or to make accounting or timing changes. Over the five-year period from 2001 to 2005, Michigan used $6.6 billion of these one-time actions.[4]

This extraordinary series of temporary measures made it possible for the state government to support spending at a higher level than could have been supported by recurring tax revenues. However, the day of reckoning could not be postponed forever. As mentioned in Chapter 2, education budgets have been cut in recent years, and the pressure on the education budget is expected to rise dramatically in the next fifteen years. Many other spending categories have been cut as well.

In the next two sections, we discuss corrections and health care, each of which has an important effect on the budget.

Corrections

In the last thirty years, the corrections system has been one of the fastest-growing categories of government spending in Michigan. Corrections grew especially rapidly in the 1980s and 1990s. Even after adjusting for inflation, state-government expenditures for corrections were more than four times as large in 2009–2010 as in 1982–1983.[5] The tilt toward corrections has been just as dramatic for the state government's work force. Between 1980 and 2002, corrections employment more than tripled, while employment in all other categories of state government fell by more than one-third.

These increases in the corrections budget and workforce have been caused primarily by the tremendous increase in the number of inmates. In 1982, some 13,372 prisoners were under the jurisdiction of the State of Michigan. By 2002, this figure had risen to 48,920. In other words, the number of inmates in Michigan was more than 3.6 times as large in 2002 as it had been twenty years earlier. In the last decade, however, the number of prisoners has leveled off.

Prison populations grew very rapidly in the 1980s and 1990s throughout the United States. However, the rate of growth was even faster in Michigan than in most other states. Thus the prison population per 100,000 residents is higher in Michigan than in the rest of the United States, and substantially higher than in the other states in the Great Lakes region. In large part, this is due to the use of longer prison sentences in Michigan. One result of these sentencing policies is that Michigan's prison population is getting older. In turn, the aging of the prison population means that we can expect further increases in the portion of the corrections budget to be devoted to health care. Expenditures on health care for prisoners in Michigan are already in excess of $200 million per year.

If the incarceration rate were the same in Michigan as in the other states in the Great Lakes region, prison expenditures in Michigan would be reduced by several hundred million dollars per year.[6] Of course, this does not necessarily mean that Michigan should adopt the less-stringent sentencing policies used in other states. It is possible that the people of Michigan are better off as a result of these incarceration policies. In other words, it is possible that the added expense is worth it in terms of reduced crime. However, in view of the relatively large amount of spending on corrections in Michigan, it makes sense to think extremely carefully about the benefits and costs of Michigan's corrections policies.

The cost of keeping an inmate in prison in Michigan is well above $30,000 per year. In other words, the annual cost of incarcerating a prisoner is roughly equivalent to the annual cost of educating a student at a good college or university. Because of these high costs, the criminal-justice system in Michigan has already increased its use of alternatives to incarceration. These include probation, halfway houses, electronic monitors, and other methods of dealing with offenders. In the years to come, Michigan would do well to continue to consider ways to ensure public safety at lower cost.[7]

Health and Health Care

Governments, companies, and private citizens in the United States spend about $2 *trillion* per year on health care. Of course, health is affected by many things and not just by health-care spending. In recent years, Michigan has raised the cigarette tax substantially. This is one of the most important public-health initiatives in Michigan's history, even though it does not show up in the budget as an explicit health-care expenditure.[8] (We will return to the cigarette tax in Chapter 6.) In 2010, Michigan instituted a smoking ban, so that patrons of restaurants and bars will no longer be inflicted with second-hand smoke.

Similarly, the population's health will be improved if we can find ways to get Michigan residents to get more exercise and eat a healthier diet, even though this will not necessarily have a direct effect on the health-care budget.[9]

As mentioned earlier in this chapter, Community Health spent more than $13 billion in fiscal year 2010, making health care the largest category of spending for the State of Michigan. In fact, if we look at the data in a slightly different way, health-care spending is even larger. As discussed in Chapter 2, much of the money sent to school districts through the School Aid Fund is actually spent on health care for school employees and retirees. And, as we saw in the preceding section, a substantial amount of the corrections budget is devoted to inmate health care. If we were to put everything associated with health care under one heading, it would greatly outrun all other expenditure categories.

Health and health care in Michigan are discussed in *Michigan at the Millennium* by John Goddeeris of Michigan State University.[10] He shows that the trend toward increased health-care spending has been going on for a very long time in Michigan and in the rest of the United States. From 1960 to 1993, after adjusting for inflation, real health-care expenditures per person in the United States grew by an astonishing 454 percent. Health-care spending moderated in the mid- and late 1990s, but then came a new surge of expenditures.

There are many reasons for the trend toward increased health-care expenditure. Part of the increase is a natural result of rising incomes: as American society has become more affluent, the demand for health care has grown rapidly. Changes in medical technology have also played a very large role in the expenditure increases. Some new medical technologies actually lead to cost reductions. (For example, a well-timed dose of antibiotics can be a low-cost way of stopping a sinus infection before it worsens into bronchitis or pneumonia.) But many of the new diagnostic and therapeutic technologies developed in the last generation are very expensive. These new techniques, medicines, and devices have made it possible for the medical profession to provide better care—in many cases, patients have been saved who once would have died. As John Goddeeris points out, age-adjusted death rates fell substantially in the 1980s and 1990s. Death rates fell at about the same rate in Michigan as in the rest of the country. But the advances did not come cheaply, and future medical advances are also expected to come at high cost.

Health-care expenditures per person are much higher for elderly people than for younger ones. The elderly will account for an increasingly large percentage of the population in the future, and this will put further upward pressure on health-care spending. In the United States, health expenditures are currently in the vicinity of 17 percent of gross domestic product (GDP). Projections suggest that health expenditures may rise to more than 25 percent of GDP in the next twenty-five years or so. According to some projections, it is possible that health-care spending in the United States may eventually rise to 40 percent of GDP or more. The budgetary pressures are already enormous, and they will be far worse if health-care spending rises at that rate.

Public and Private Health-Insurance Coverage

These medical expenditures must be paid for. In 2008, about 67 percent of the American population had private health-insurance coverage. The vast majority of these people received their coverage through an employer, former employer, or through the employer of a family member. About 29 percent of Americans received health-insurance coverage through government programs (primarily Medicare, which serves elderly and disabled Americans, and Medicaid, which serves low-income children and adults as well as several other categories of beneficiaries). If we add together the 67 percent with private coverage and the 29 percent with government coverage, it might appear that 96 percent of Americans have some sort of coverage. However, some people receive coverage from multiple sources. After we account for those who have both private coverage and public coverage, only about 85 percent of the U.S. population has health insurance.[11]

In Michigan, the proportion with insurance is higher than the national average. On average in the years from 2006 to 2008, nearly 89 percent of Michigan residents had health insurance. This is good news. In this book, we have seen an uncomfortably large number of statistics for which Michigan does not compare well with the rest of the country. It's good to know that Michigan is ahead of the national average in this very important aspect.

However, if we look at the same data another way, we see that more than one million Michigan residents lack health insurance, along with about forty-five million Americans in other states.[12] Among the advanced industrial countries, the United States is unique in having such a large proportion of the population without health insurance.

From the perspective of the Michigan budget, the Medicaid program is by far the most important form of health insurance. Most Medicaid *beneficiaries* are low-income children and adults. However, most Medicaid *expenditures* are for other, more costly groups. These include low-income disabled individuals, low-income elderly people who receive coverage supplementary to Medicare, and elderly people who have exhausted their own ability to pay for long-term care. Both federal and state payments for Medicaid grew very rapidly until the mid-1990s. The rapid growth paused briefly for a few years in the late 1990s and then took off again in the early years of the twenty-first century. Michigan's payments for Medicaid were about 8 percent of General Fund revenues in 1980. This figure rose to about 17 percent in 1992 and about 25 percent in 2002.

Michigan's Medicaid caseloads have increased substantially over the years. In 1980, the Medicaid caseload was about 927,000. Over the next twenty years, the caseload grew slowly, reaching about 1,068,000 in 2000. However, by 2011, the Michigan Medicaid caseload is projected to reach about 1,754,000.

There is every indication that health-care spending will put even more pressure on the budgets of Michigan and the other states, as well as on the federal budget in the coming years. For example, the federal government spent about $516 billion on Medicare and Medicaid in 2005. This rose to about $730 billion by 2009. According to estimates by the federal Office of

Management and Budget, this is projected to increase to about $1.05 trillion by 2015.[13] This is a remarkable growth rate of about 8 percent per year.

Michigan will have to respond to the pressures created by Medicaid. There are only a few choices for how to do this, and the choices are not easy ones. As John Goddeeris puts it in Michigan at the Millennium, "There are no magic bullets or politically easy answers. Responses must be some combination of the following: (1) Increasing state revenues, which probably implies raising taxes as a share of income in the state; (2) Reallocating revenues from other state priorities to Medicaid; (3) Reducing the number of Medicaid beneficiaries; or (4) Reducing the growth of Medicaid expenditures per beneficiary."[14]

As we survey these choices, a note of caution is in order. Medicaid is a joint state–federal program, but the federal government picks up most of the tab. Thus if the State of Michigan tries to solve its budget problems by making big cuts in its Medicaid expenditure, it stands to lose the federal matching funds. Michigan is not a poor place, but we aren't so rich that we can easily turn down federal money.

In 2010, President Obama signed a health-care bill into law. During the bitter partisan wrangling that led up to passage of the law, the bill was often called a "massive government takeover of health care."[15] In fact, the new law is not even remotely similar to a massive government takeover. If the United States were to institute a single-payer type of health-care system like the ones in Canada and the United Kingdom, that would indeed be a government takeover. But a single-payer plan was never seriously considered. A "public-option" health-insurance plan was considered for a while but eventually scrapped. The public option would not have been a "massive takeover," but it would have been a modest extension of government involvement (into a sector of the economy in which government is already very much involved).

While some caricatured the health-care law as "massive," I find it rather modest and incremental. If the law is carried out as planned, it will eventually increase the proportion of the American public with health insurance from the current 85 percent to about 95 percent. It will also make it much more difficult for insurance companies to deny coverage to people with preexisting conditions or to terminate coverage when someone gets sick. These are important improvements. However, the law does not fundamentally change the fact that health insurance in the United States is delivered through a bewildering array of public and private plans. As a result, it will still be true that the

United States will spend far more on administration of the health-insurance system than is spent in most other countries.

The biggest shortcoming of the new health-care law is that it did so little to control costs. Thus even after the new law is implemented, it will almost certainly still be true that the United States will *waste* more health-care dollars than any other country *spends*. (Some sensible proposals were set aside after opponents inaccurately called them "death panels.")[16] Many economists believe that one of the biggest causes of wasteful health-care spending is the fee-for-service system, under which many doctors are paid on the basis of the procedures they perform, regardless of patient outcomes. However, the new law does only a little to move toward rewarding doctors on the basis of health outcomes.

Ultimately, Americans will have to face some difficult choices. As our population ages, and as more and more expensive medical technologies become available, spending pressures are expected to rise dramatically. It will be necessary for the private sector, state governments, and the federal government to come up with additional resources; or we will have to ration access to health care by other means.

Michigan Policies Relating to Income Support

I emphasized the importance of education in Chapter 2 because education is the surest path to a high-wage future. However, the payoff from education comes over a period of decades. We now turn our attention to some labor-market policies that affect low-wage workers in the shorter term. The first of these policies is the minimum wage, which has relatively small effects on government budgets. The minimum wage fits within a broader context of programs for low-wage workers, many of which do have budgetary implications, that we will discuss in this section.

The Minimum Wage

Since 2009, the federal minimum wage has been $7.25 per hour. Since 2008, the minimum wage in Michigan has been $7.40 per hour. Rebecca Blank of the University of Michigan discusses the minimum wage in *Michigan at the*

Millennium[17]. Minimum-wage laws have different effects on different groups of workers. For the vast majority of workers in Michigan (and in the rest of the United States), wage rates are well above the minimum wage. The minimum-wage law has no direct effect on these workers. The only workers who are affected directly by the minimum wage are those who face low wage rates. Fortunately, this is a relatively small group of workers.

Some low-wage workers will be helped by an increase in the minimum wage because they will continue to work while receiving a higher wage rate. For a person working a forty-hour week for fifty weeks per year, the increase in the minimum wage from $5.15 (the rate that obtained a few years ago) to $7.40 would increase annual earnings from $10,300 to $14,800. That is an increase of $4,500 per year. If the affected worker is the head of a low-income household, this would make a tremendous difference.

However, this positive result will not occur if the worker is unable to find or keep a job. The minimum-wage law will harm some low-wage workers because they will lose their jobs, or they will be unable to find work in the first place. Consider a worker who is able to produce $6 per hour of value for his or her employer. If the minimum wage were at its previous level of $5.15, or at any other level that is less than or equal to $6, this person would be employed and would earn $6 per hour. But when the minimum wage rises to $7.40, if employers obey the law, it may be very difficult for this worker to find and keep a job. As a result, instead of earning $6 per hour, this worker may earn zero.

This is one of the reasons why unemployment rates for teenagers are so much higher than unemployment rates for adults: teenagers are more likely to have the low levels of productivity that would merit a wage rate below the minimum wage. In the United States in April 2010, the unemployment rate was 25.4 percent for workers aged 16–19 versus 9.9 percent for the entire labor force.[18] Of course, the minimum wage is not necessarily the only reason for the difference between the unemployment rates of teenagers and adults, but minimum-wage laws probably explain an important part of the difference.

There is an active debate in the economics profession about the size of the employment losses that will be brought on by an increase in the minimum wage. When the minimum wage goes up, how many workers will keep their jobs and earn more, and how many will be out of work? Charles Brown of the University of Michigan has written a thorough survey of the literature on the subject.[19] According to many of the studies surveyed by Brown, a 10 percent increase in the minimum wage would lead to a loss of youth employment of 1 percent or less.

Of course, the existing literature consists primarily of studies based on data sets in which the wage rates are substantially lower than $7.40 per hour. Therefore we cannot be absolutely certain of the size of the employment losses that has occurred and will occur as a result of Michigan's minimum wage increase from $5.15 to $7.40. Nevertheless, it is useful to get a sense of what the effects might be if the existing literature turns out to be a reliable guide. The increase from $5.15 to $7.40 means that the minimum wage in Michigan rose by more than 40 percent. Based on Brown's analysis of the literature, we might expect to see a loss of youth employment of something like 2 to 4 percent.

Thus the good news is that the employment losses are likely to be relatively small. The bad news is that *any* increase in unemployment, especially among young people, would be an unfortunate side effect of the increase in the minimum wage. High youth unemployment can lead to a variety of long-term problems for society.

Proponents of the minimum wage increase often speak of it as an anti-poverty measure. However, it should be noted that the minimum-wage law does not specifically target poor families. Many of the people who receive the minimum wage and are able to keep their jobs are teenagers in affluent families. Minimum-wage laws are an inefficient method of fighting poverty since young people in high-income households may be among those who reap benefits from an increase in the minimum wage, while some people in low-income households may be unable to find work.

The Earned Income Tax Credit

I am hopeful that the increased minimum wage in Michigan will be beneficial to some low-wage workers, and that the employment losses will be relatively small. However, I am one of many economists who believe that the Earned Income Tax Credit (EITC) is a much more effective policy than the minimum wage. The federal EITC was instituted in 1975 during the presidency of Gerald Ford. The EITC was expanded in 1986 (under Ronald Reagan), in 1990 (under George H. W. Bush), and in 1993 (under Bill Clinton). Unlike the minimum wage, the EITC specifically targets low-income families. The EITC is an earnings subsidy for the workers with the lowest earnings in the labor market. Thus while the minimum wage is likely to *reduce* employment, the EITC actually *increases* employment for certain groups of low-wage workers.[20]

In 2006, Governor Granholm signed into law a new Earned Income Tax Credit for Michigan. It first became effective in 2008. The Michigan EITC is now equal to 20 percent of the federal EITC. On several occasions in this book, I have lamented the fact that those on the lowest rungs of the economic ladder have fared very poorly in the labor market for several decades. The EITC, both at the federal level and in Michigan, is one of the few bright spots for the working poor. I am proud that we in Michigan took this step.

Income-Support Programs

Rebecca Blank discusses both the minimum wage and the EITC in *Michigan at the Millennium*.[21] Blank also discusses a wide variety of other policies aimed at the low-wage labor market, including child-care and health-care programs. The effects of these policies for low-wage, low-skill workers are closely connected to the effects of public-assistance programs that provide cash support for low-income families and sometimes for low-income individuals. These programs sometimes involve people who are not working. However, as we shall see, income-support programs increasingly requiring benefit recipients to work.

Until 1996, the main cash-support program for non-elderly poor families in the United States was the Aid to Families with Dependent Children program (AFDC). The federal government provided much of the funding for the program, but the individual states had considerable freedom to set their own benefit rules. In the 1970s, AFDC caseloads doubled in Michigan, reflecting a nationwide trend. Many of the changes that have since been instituted in the program can be seen as an extended reaction to the rapid growth of the program in the 1960s and 1970s. In their chapter in *Michigan at the Millennium*, Kristin Seefeldt, Sheldon Danziger, and Sandra Danziger discuss the history of income-support programs, which have changed repeatedly in the last thirty years or so.[22] In 1981, a federal law tightened the eligibility requirements for recipients. A 1988 federal law put greater emphasis on education and training but did not alter the basic structure of eligibility.

In the early 1990s, much of the impetus for changes to public-assistance programs came from state governments. A major change occurred in Michigan in 1991 when the General Assistance program was eliminated. General

Assistance had provided benefits to low-income persons who were ineligible for AFDC or for federal disability programs. Some eighty thousand individuals lost their benefits when the program was terminated. Michigan was also one of several states that obtained "waivers," whereby the federal government allowed the states to experiment with changes in the AFDC rules. Michigan's waivers involved changes in the benefit formula in an attempt to encourage program participants to work. The waivers also increased penalties for not participating in education or training activities. Also, monthly benefits in many states (including Michigan) were staying the same or falling. After adjusting for inflation, real benefit levels decreased.

The largest change of all came in August 1996 when President Clinton signed a new law fulfilling his pledge to "end welfare as we know it." This law, the Personal Responsibility and Work Opportunity Reconciliation Act, replaced the federal entitlement to benefits with a set of block grants to the states. Thus laws on public-assistance programs continued to move in the direction of requiring participants to work in order to be eligible to receive benefits.

Seefeldt, Danziger, and Danziger suggest some ways in which we could improve the economic situation of the low-income population:

- *Education* is extremely important. Lack of a high school diploma is one of the most important difficulties faced by people at the bottom of the economic ladder. Over the long haul, the best policy is to reduce the number of high school dropouts. For those who have already dropped out, training and diploma-equivalent programs may help.
- *Transportation* is one of the largest barriers to employment for many people. Improved public transportation could make a big difference for some.
- *Streamlined procedures for assessment and referral* would help to identify welfare recipients who have mental-health or substance-abuse problems. Those who suffer from these problems are unlikely to improve their long-term economic situations unless they get treatment.
- *Community service jobs* have fallen out of favor, but public-service employment can be a first step toward better long-term employment prospects for some workers.
- *Supported-work situations* can help to provide supervision for individuals who are having difficulty in making the transition to work.

Some of the suggestions mentioned above are in line with programs that are already in place. However, few would say that the existing programs are doing everything they could possibly do. If the existing programs were expanded, or if new programs were established, it would cost money. In these tight budgetary times, it seems unlikely that large amounts of additional funding will be forthcoming. Nevertheless, if programs are carefully targeted it may be possible to generate a substantial benefit for modest cost.

Poverty in Michigan and in the Rest of the United States

So far in this section, we have discussed a number of laws and programs aimed (at least in part) at Michigan residents who are at or below the poverty line. In 2008, the official poverty line in the United States was about $10,000 for a one-person household, $21,000 for a four-person household, and $36,000 for a household with eight people. The Census Bureau calculates that about 1.3 million Michigan residents fell below the poverty line in 2008, for a poverty rate of 13 percent. The rate for the United States as a whole was 13.2 percent in 2008. The worst of the recession did not come until 2009. When the poverty data for 2009 become available, they will almost certainly show an increase in poverty, in Michigan and across the entire United States.

Figure 5.2 shows some trends in the poverty rate. The figure shows Michigan and the United States, and it also shows Mississippi (which usually has one of the highest poverty rates in the country) and Connecticut (which usually has one of the lowest rates).[23] The poverty rate in Michigan has historically been fairly close to the U.S. average.

The poverty rate in the United States fell sharply in the 1960s and early 1970s. Since then, the poverty rate has had its ups and downs, but the overall rate is actually higher today than in 1973. Clearly, our antipoverty programs have not been enough to overcome this disappointing trend. On the other hand, it is asking a lot to expect antipoverty programs to turn the tide when so many forces are pushing in the opposite direction. As mentioned earlier in this book, the gap between high-income and low-income Americans has been widening for more than thirty years. And the biggest antipoverty program of all—the educational system—has turned in a mediocre performance. Until we make major additional progress toward improving the skills of our population, the poverty rate is unlikely to drop substantially.

FIGURE 5.2. Poverty rates for selected states and the United States, 1981–2007

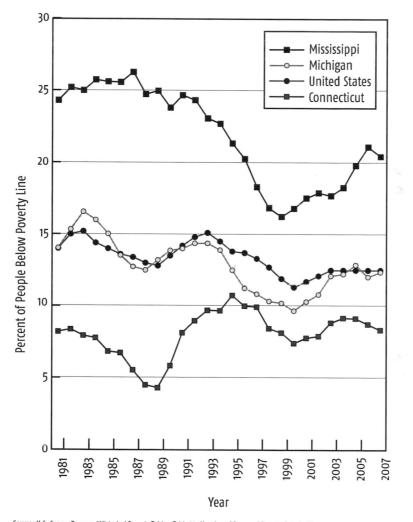

Source: U.S. Census Bureau, "Historical Poverty Tables. Table 21: Number of Poor and Poverty Rate by State, 1980 to 2008," http://www.census.gov/
hhes/www/poverty/histpov/perindex.html.

The Retrenchment of the State Employee Workforce

Figure 5.3 shows the changes over time in the size of the workforce employed
by the State of Michigan. The figure divides the state workforce into two

FIGURE 5.3. Size of the State of Michigan employee workforce, 1970–2008

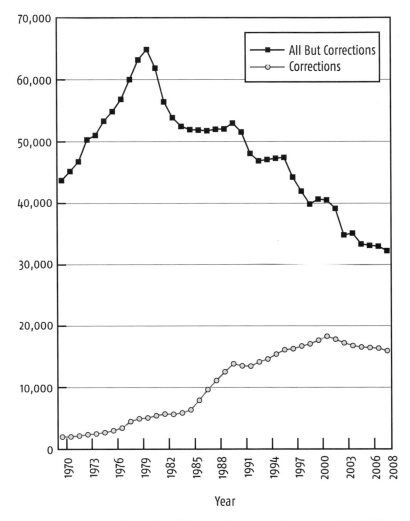

Source: Michigan Department of Civil Service, "Annual Workforce Report," selected years. These reports are available at http://www.michigan.gov/
mdcs/0,1607,7-147-6879_9329_48076---,00.html.

groups—those working for the Department of Corrections and everyone else. In 1970, the Department of Corrections had about 2,000 employees, and the other departments had a total of about 44,000. Thus the total state workforce was about 46,000. During the 1970s, both groups grew substantially. The total state workforce reached its all-time peak of nearly 70,000 in 1980. During the next twenty years, the overall size of the workforce fell, but the Department of Corrections' workforce grew tremendously. Thus the number of workers in departments other than corrections fell very substantially. Since 2000, the noncorrections workforce has continued to decline, and the number of corrections employees has also fallen. By now, the total state workforce is down by more than one-fourth since its peak thirty years ago, and the noncorrections workforce is only about half as large as it was at its peak.[24]

These reductions in the size of the state workforce are part of the general reduction in the size and scope of the public sector in Michigan. It is extremely difficult to identify the "optimal" number of public-sector employees. However, no one can deny that the decreases in the last thirty years have been very substantial. Overall, the number of state workers is about the same as it was in the early 1970s, when Michigan's population and economy were significantly smaller. Thus I am concerned that it is becoming more and more difficult to provide essential public services to the people of Michigan. It is possible that the state government workforce was "too big" thirty years ago. However, even if one believes it was "too big" in 1980, that does not necessarily mean that it is too big now. With each reduction in the size of the workforce, it becomes more likely that it is "too small."

In addition to the reductions in the workforce, state employees have accepted concessions in their wages and benefits, and they have accepted "furlough days" and other reductions in their compensation. Once again, it is difficult to identify the "optimal" level of compensation. However, I am concerned that these reductions in compensation will make it more and more difficult for the state to attract and retain the right employees. On average, the salaries of state employees are slightly higher than salaries in the private-sector workforce. However, if we only compare the averages, we are not making an appropriate comparison. That's because the educational attainment of the state employees is much higher than the educational attainment of the rest of Michigan's population. (When you think about the work that many state employees do, this probably makes sense. After all, if we were to hire an assistant attorney general who did not have a law degree, we would be looking for really big trouble. Many of the people who work for the State of Michigan are scientists, engineers, doctors, lawyers, and others with technical skills.) If we factor in the employees' levels of education, the state workers in the highest categories of educational attainment are actually paid less than their private-sector counterparts.

I believe that the people of Michigan are running some serious risks as a result of the ongoing retrenchment of the state workforce. Even though we have made dramatic cuts in the state workforce, the work that needs to be done has not decreased. In fact, when the economy is not doing well, the demands on state government workers tend to increase. In the words of one Child Protective Services officer who works for the State of Michigan, "unfortunately, child abuse does not take a furlough day." One popular method of reducing the size of the state-government workforce is to offer "retirement buyouts."[25] In my opinion, these policies are very short-sighted. The idea appears to be that we should get our most experienced people to retire, so that we can replace them with inexperienced workers who are paid less, or eliminate their position entirely. Any organization is likely to suffer when it loses large numbers of its most experienced workers. This creates an atmosphere of musical chairs, as people switch jobs within the organization in an attempt to deal with the loss of the retiree.

One other thing needs to be said regarding the state employees. If you follow some blogs and Internet postings, you are likely to find some really vitriolic and abusive stuff aimed at government employees. They are characterized as lazy and overpaid, often with very ugly language. This is completely unnecessary and very unfortunate. I know many state employees personally, and they are decent and honest people who are trying to do their best under difficult circumstances.

The Role of Government

The ugly stuff in the blogosphere is part of a trend that has been building for thirty years or more in the United States. In some parts of the political spectrum, "government" is almost a curse word. The antipathy toward "government" is sometimes comical, as in the case of a speaker at a health-care reform town hall meeting in Simpsonville, South Carolina, in July 2009, who said, "Keep your government hands off my Medicare.[26]

This person's desire to keep the government out of a government-run health-care program is remarkable. However, this sort of attitude is not really surprising in light of the profound disconnect that has grown up in America in recent years between antigovernment rhetoric and reality. In fact, this antipathy toward a vaguely menacing "government" does not extend to a host of actual government programs. For example, the two largest programs of the federal government, Social Security and Medicare, are very popular. Only a few antigovernment zealots want to dismantle Social Security and Medicare.[27]

The federal government came to the assistance of General Motors and Chrysler in 2009. This was criticized by some as "big government," and indeed it was an unprecedented action by the federal government. However, if we can put ideology and rhetoric aside for a moment and focus on the facts of the case, I believe that federal intervention played a very positive role in the case of GM and Chrysler. The troubles encountered by those companies created a profound danger for the Michigan economy and the economy of the entire United States. There was a real danger of a "hard landing," resulting in a fire sale of assets under chapter 7 of the bankruptcy laws. Instead, with federal help it was possible to get about as soft a landing as possible. In many ways, 2009 was the worst year for the economy in the lifetime of most of Michigan's people. Without federal action in the case of GM and Chrysler, it could have been much worse.

Although there is much hostility to "government" in general, most of the public services that are delivered by governments have broad public support. In 2009, a survey of Michigan voters was released by the Lansing-based public-opinion research firm, EPIC-MRA. When asked about solutions to Michigan's budget problems, 68 percent were opposed to eliminating the Michigan Promise scholarships. Seventy-seven percent opposed substantial cuts in state aid to K–12 schools, and 75 percent opposed a substantial reduction in Medicaid reimbursements to doctors and hospitals. Seventy-five percent opposed cutting funding for state police, and 66 percent opposed eliminating the Earned Income Tax Credit.[28] And the list goes on.

In today's overheated political environment, "government" has become a code word that plays into deep-seated resentments harbored by many Americans. It will be good for Michigan's economic future if we can strip away the slogans and focus on the things that governments actually do. In Michigan, governments are involved in educating our children, providing public safety, making sure our water supplies are safe, paving our roads, and many other important activities. We would do well to focus on those realities, rather than some abstract notion of "government."

Conclusion

In earlier chapters, we have taken a look at some programs that have important implications for government budgets in Michigan. In this chapter, we began by considering the overall budget of the State of Michigan. We then moved on to consider some other specific programs that have important effects on the budget, including corrections, health care, programs for low-wage and low-income residents, and the size of the state workforce.

The most important idea in this chapter is that the budget of the State of Michigan faces chronic *structural* deficits. The cost of maintaining programs is increasing relative to tax revenues, even in good economic times. By itself, robust economic growth will *not* be enough to change this situation. Of course, a higher rate of economic growth is better for the budget than a lower rate of economic growth. But the people of Michigan will be deluding themselves if they think that economic growth alone will solve these long-run budgetary problems. Instead, it will be necessary to make choices. The choices will not be easy, but they cannot be avoided.

In part, the structural deficits arise because of problems with the tax system. Every major source of tax revenue in Michigan has structural problems. The tax system will be discussed in much more detail in Chapter 6.

The rest of this chapter was devoted to looking at categories of government expenditure in Michigan. Here are some of the highlights:

- Gross expenditures by the State of Michigan are dominated by a small number of categories. In particular, well over half of these expenditures are for School Aid and Community Health. However, not all the gross expenditures are actually financed by Michigan taxpayers; a substantial portion comes from the federal government, especially in the Medicaid program.
- From 1982 to 2002, the number of prisoners under the jurisdiction of the State of Michigan increased from about 13,000 to about 49,000. The incarceration rate is substantially higher in Michigan than in neighboring states. This is partly due to the use of longer prison sentences in Michigan. If the incarceration rate were the same in Michigan as in the other states in the Great Lakes region, prison expenditures in Michigan would be reduced by several hundred million dollars per year.

- Community Health is the largest item in the Michigan budget, having recently surpassed state aid to K–12 education. If we were to construct a single category including all health-related expenditures (such as health care for prisoners and health care for current and retired government employees), it would dominate the budget to an even greater extent.
- Health-care spending has grown tremendously in the last several decades, and it is expected to continue to grow much more rapidly than the rest of the economy. This is partly because of the aging of the population, and partly because it is expected that expensive new medical techniques will continue to be developed. There is every indication that health-care spending (and Medicaid spending in particular) will continue to exert great pressure on the Michigan budget. It will either be necessary to increase revenues, or reduce spending on health-care and other programs. Neither of these options will be easy.
- Michigan raised its minimum wage to $7.40 per hour in 2008. Some low-wage workers will be able to earn more as a result. However, others may lose their jobs or have difficulty finding employment. Fortunately, the economic literature suggests that the job losses will be relatively small. However, *any* losses of employment would be an adverse side effect of the law. Another problem with the minimum wage is that it is not targeted toward low-income families. Some of the affected workers are teenagers in affluent families.
- Michigan recently adopted an Earned Income Tax Credit (EITC). The EITC has two distinct advantages over a minimum wage: First, the EITC is an earnings subsidy, and it tends to increase employment. In addition, the EITC is targeted toward low-income families. The EITC is the most important effort in recent years to help the working poor in Michigan.
- The number of people receiving public-assistance payments grew dramatically in the 1970s. Since then, a series of changes in state law and federal law have reduced the generosity of these programs. In Michigan, the General Assistance program was eliminated in 1991. A federal law in 1996 continued a trend toward requiring participants in public-assistance programs to work in order to be eligible for benefits.
- Improved education and training have the greatest potential to help the population of low-skill workers who have traditionally been served by public-assistance programs. Transportation, assessment and referral for

mental-health and substance-abuse programs, and supported-work situations could also improve the lives of people in low-income households.

- The state employee workforce reached its highest level in 1980. In the 1980s and 1990s, the number of employees in the Department of Corrections grew very rapidly, while staffing levels in other departments shrank. Since about 2000, the number of state employees has decreased in nearly every department. The overall workforce is now down by more than one-fourth, and the noncorrections workforce is down by about half. State workers have also made concessions in terms of pay and benefits. If further reductions are made, Michigan will increasingly risk having a state workforce that is unable to deliver important public services.

NOTES

1. See Charles L. Ballard, Paul N. Courant, Douglas C. Drake, Ronald C. Fisher, and Elisabeth R. Gerber, eds., *Michigan at the Millennium: A Benchmark and Analysis of Its Fiscal and Economic Structure* (East Lansing, MI: Michigan State University Press, 2003). Most chapters in *Michigan at the Millennium* deal with certain aspects of government budgets, and two chapters are devoted exclusively to budgetary issues. Gary Olson of the Senate Fiscal Agency reviews state government spending in his chapter "Overview of State Government Expenditures in Michigan." Local government expenditures are discussed by Earl Ryan and Eric Lupher of the Citizens Research Council in their chapter "An Overview of Local Government Expenditures in Michigan: Patterns and Trends." In addition, *Michigan at the Millennium* includes a chapter on intergovernmental fiscal relations, "Fiscal Relations among the Federal Government, State Government, and Local Governments in Michigan," by Ronald Fisher (Michigan State University) and Jeffrey Guilfoyle (formerly the Office of Revenue and Tax Analysis, currently the Citizens Research Council).

2. Department of Technology, Management, and Budget, "Executive Budget: Fiscal Year 2011," State of Michigan, http://www.michigan.gov/documents/budget/2_310743_7.pdf.

3. Gary Olson provides a detailed discussion of the constitutional and statutory rules governing the budget of the State of Michigan in his chapter "Overview of State Government Expenditures in Michigan," in *Michigan at the Millennium*.

4. For an excellent discussion of the structural deficit and related issues, see Citizens Research Council of Michigan, "Michigan's Budget Crisis and the Prospects for the Future," March 2006, http://www.crcmich.org/PUBLICAT/2000s/2006/sbn200601.pdf.

5. The nominal expenditure data are taken from Gary Olson's chapter "Overview of State Government Expenditures in Michigan," in *Michigan at the Millennium* and from the State of Michigan's Executive Budget for Fiscal Year 2011 (see Department of Technology, Management, and Budget, "Executive Budget: Fiscal Year 2011," State of Michigan, http://www .michigan.gov/documents/budget/2_310743_7.pdf). The inflation adjustment is based on data from the U.S. Commerce Department's Bureau of Economic Analysis, Table 1.1.4, "Price Indexes for Gross Domestic Product," http://www.bea.gov/national/nipaweb/ SelectTable.asp?Selected=N.

6. Citizens Research Council, "Michigan's Budget Crisis and the Prospects for the Future."

7. For a detailed discussion of these issues, see Sheila Maxwell, David Martin, and Christopher Maxwell, "Issues in Crime and Criminal Justice in Michigan," in *Michigan at the Millennium*.

8. The increase in the cigarette tax is certain to improve some aspects of the health of Michigan's people. The long-term effects on the budget are less clear. In the near term, higher taxes on cigarettes mean more revenue for the state government. However, cigarette-tax revenue may decline over a period of several years if there is a sufficiently large decrease in the number of smokers. Also, if people stop smoking, they will live longer. There may be a reduction in lung cancer, heart disease, and other tobacco-related illnesses, but those who live longer may eventually suffer from other diseases. These other diseases may increase health-care spending in the long run. For me, however, this is not a very important consideration. I would much rather have people live and deal with their old-age health problems when the time comes, rather than allow them to go to an early death from smoking.

9. According to a recent report issued by the Trust for America's Health and the Robert Wood Johnson Foundation, Michigan has an adult obesity rate of 28.8 percent. This makes Michigan the ninth fattest state in the country. By comparison, Mississippi is the fattest state, with an obesity rate of 32.5 percent. Colorado is the leanest state, with an obesity rate of 18.9 percent. There has been a shocking increase in obesity throughout the United States in the last few decades. In 1991, not a single state had an obesity rate above 20 percent. By 2009, Colorado was the only state where the obesity rate did *not* exceed 20 percent. For more information, see Trust for America's Health, "F as in Fat 2009: How Obesity Policies are Failing in America," http://healthyamericans.org/reports/obesity2009.

10. John Goddeeris, "Health Care in Michigan," in *Michigan at the Millennium*.

11. For details, see Carmen DeNavas-Walt, Bernadette D. Proctor, and Jessica C. Smith, "U.S. Census Bureau Current Population Reports, P60-236: Income, Poverty, and Health Insurance Coverage in the United States: 2008," U.S. Census Bureau, http://www.census.gov/ prod/2009pubs/p60-236.pdf.

12. Carmen DeNavas-Walt, Bernadette D. Proctor, and Jessica C. Smith, "U.S. Census Bureau Current Population Reports, P60-236: Income, Poverty, and Health Insurance Coverage in the United States: 2008," U.S. Census Bureau, http://www.census.gov/prod/2009pubs/p60-236.pdf.

13. Federal Office of Management and Budget, "Budget of the United States Government: Historical Tables Fiscal Year 2011," http://www.gpoaccess.gov/usbudget/fy11/hist.html.

14. John Goddeeris, "Health Care in Michigan," in *Michigan at the Millennium*, 179–80.

15. For example, see Michael D. Shear and Dan Balz, "Obama offers new health-care plan; GOP slams it as 'government takeover,'" *The Washington Post*, February 22, 2010, http://www.washingtonpost.com/wp-dyn/content/article/2010/02/22/AR2010022201731.html.

16. For discussion of the "death panel" rumors, see Jim Rutenberg and Jackie Calmes, "False 'Death Panel' Rumor Has Some Familiar Roots," *New York Times*, August 13, 2009, http://www.nytimes.com/2009/08/14/health/policy/14panel.html.

17. Rebecca Blank, "The Less-Skilled Labor Market in Michigan," in *Michigan at the Millennium*.

18. Bureau of Labor Statistics, "Labor Force Statistics from the Current Population Survey," http://data.bls.gov/cgi-bin/surveymost?ln.

19. See Charles Brown, "Minimum Wages, Employment, and the Distribution of Income," in *Handbook of Labor Economics*, vol. 3B, ed. Orley Ashenfelter and David Card (Amsterdam: Elsevier, 1999).

20. The EITC is another policy discussed in the *Michigan at the Millennium* chapter by the University of Michigan's Rebecca Blank, "The Less-Skilled Labor Market in Michigan." For further discussion of the EITC, see Joseph Hotz and Karl Scholz, "Not Perfect But Still Pretty Good: The EITC and Other Policies to Support the U.S. Low-Wage Labor Market," *OECD Economic Studies* 31 (2000): 26–42. Also, see Scott Darragh, "The Impact of the Earned Income Tax Credit on Poverty, Labor Supply, and Human-Capital Accumulation," (PhD diss., Michigan State University, 2002).

21. Rebecca Blank, "The Less-Skilled Labor Market in Michigan," in *Michigan at the Millennium*.

22. Kristin Seefeldt, Sheldon Danziger, and Sandra Danziger, "Michigan's Welfare System," in *Michigan at the Millennium*.

23. The data for Figure 5.2 are taken from the Census Bureau Web site. See the U.S. Census Bureau, "Historical Poverty Tables: Table 21. Number of Poor and Poverty Rate, by State: 1980 to 2008," http://www.census.gov/hhes/www/poverty/histpov/perindex.html. The data for individual states can fluctuate by a fairly large amount because of small sample sizes. Therefore, for the three states shown, we use a three-year average.

24. I document and discuss these and other changes in "The Economic and Fiscal Background of Metropolitan Policies in Michigan," in *Sustaining Michigan: Metropolitan Policies and Strategies*, ed. Richard W. Jelier and Gary Sands (East Lansing, MI: Michigan State University Press, 2009), 17–44. Also, I teamed with Nicole Funari to write "The Retrenchment of the State Government Workforce in Michigan," which is available on request.

25. Retirement buyouts are also being tried in the K–12 schools in Michigan. I was recently dismayed to see a press report that Cheryl Kreger, the dynamic Superintendent of Okemos Schools, had decided to accept a retirement deal after forty years of service to public education. See Dawn Parker, "Okemos School Board Loses Its Top Administrator," *Lansing State Journal*, May 30, 2010, http://www.lansingstatejournal.com/apps/pbcs .dll/article?AID=20105300377. According to the report, Kreger said, "I am sad to leave Okemos. I had planned to stay much longer." I am also sad that she and many other educators will be leaving early. Their experience will be sorely missed.

26. The precise identity of the speaker is apparently unknown. The incident, at a meeting with U.S. Representative Bob Inglis, was noted in the *Washington Post*, July 28, 2009. "Keep your government hands off my Medicare" was chosen as the top quote of 2009 by the Yale Book of Quotations, http://yalepress.yale.edu/yupbooks/book.asp?isbn=9780300107982. For further discussion, see Paul Krugman, "Health Care Realities," *The New York Times*, July 30, 2009, http://www.nytimes.com/2009/07/31/opinion/31krugman.html.

27. In this book, I mention on more than one occasion that the federal government needs to bring its budget into balance. That is very likely to include *reforms* of Social Security and Medicare. However, it is certainly not necessary to dissolve these programs.

28. Results from the EPIC-MRA survey, conducted from September 16 to 21, 2009, are described at http://www.epicmra.com/press/Stwd_Survey_Sep2009_Media_Freq.pdf.

The Tax System in Michigan

I n the words of Supreme Court Justice Oliver Wendell Holmes Jr., "Taxes are what we pay for civilized society." On the other hand, nobody enjoys paying taxes, and taxes can damage the workings of the economy. The tension between the benefits of public services and the costs imposed by taxes is one of the most important concerns of economics.

One of the central objectives of tax policy is to choose the *best possible overall level* of taxes. Another objective is to choose the *best possible mix* of income taxes, sales taxes, property taxes, and other revenue sources. These two issues are closely related, and I will discuss both of them in this chapter. I will argue for changes in the overall level of taxes, and I will also argue for changes in the mix of taxes in Michigan.

First, however, we begin with a brief tour of the tax system in Michigan.[1] When I discuss the tax system, I will usually focus on the *combined* tax systems of the state government and the various local governments. In Michigan (as in most states), local governments and school districts receive a great deal of their funding from the state government. Therefore it usually makes sense to think of the state tax system and the local tax systems as parts of a whole rather than as separate entities. This is especially important if we want to make comparisons among the states. There is great variation in the degree to which the tax system is centralized at the state level. If we compare states by focusing only on state taxes, or only on local taxes, we can get misleading results. In fact, with the passage of Proposal A, Michigan went from having one of the more decentralized revenue systems to having one of the more centralized systems.

A Brief Overview of the Michigan Tax System

In many ways, the Michigan tax system is quite similar to the state and local tax systems in most states. Michigan has an individual income tax, as do forty-two other states and the District of Columbia.[2] Michigan also has a general retail sales tax, as do forty-five other states and the District of Columbia.[3] Every one of the fifty states and the District of Columbia uses property taxes (which are especially important for local governments), as well as taxes on alcoholic beverages, tobacco products, and motor fuels.

Table 6.1 compares the state and local tax system in Michigan with the average of the state and local tax systems in the United States in 2006–2007. These data are from the U.S. Census Bureau's Census of Governments, which provides the highest-quality information on the finances of state and local governments.[4] The downside of having data of such quality is that the Census Bureau takes a long time to release the information.[5] Thus the information in Table 6.1 is three years old. Although we don't have information that is quite as complete for more recent years, we do know a fair amount about what has been going on since 2007, especially at the level of the state government. Thus, in the remainder of this chapter, I will also discuss many of the changes since 2007.

Table 6.1 shows that in 2007 property taxes accounted for a substantially higher percentage of tax revenues in Michigan than in the rest of the country. Property taxes were more than 39 percent of state and local tax revenues in Michigan but only about 30 percent for the United States as a whole. However, the percentage of the economy that goes to state and local taxes in Michigan is smaller than the national average. Thus when we take property taxes as a percentage of *income* (rather than as a percentage of *all taxes*), Michigan's property taxes are not quite as unusual, although they are still above the national average.

Michigan reduced its reliance on property taxes very substantially in 1994 with the passage of Proposal A. (We will discuss Proposal A in more detail below.) Thus if Proposal A had not passed and Michigan's government had

TABLE 6.1. Revenues for selected taxes as percentage of total tax revenues for Michigan and the United States, 2006–2007

TAX	MICHIGAN	UNITED STATES
Property	39.19	30.04
General retail sales	21.52	23.46
Individual income	18.63	22.68
Business income	4.82	4.74
Tobacco	3.07	1.24
Motor fuel	2.79	2.97
Motor vehicle license	2.45	1.63
Alcoholic beverage	0.38	0.44

Note: Column totals do not add to 100 percent because some small categories of taxes have not been included.

Source: Calculations based on U.S. Census Bureau, "State and Local Government Finances: 2006–2007," http://www.census.gov/govs/ estimate.

not made any other changes, Michigan would be even more out of line with the rest of the country. Also, without Proposal A, the recent decline in property values would have created an even more devastating financing crisis than the one we are currently experiencing.

Since property taxes are relatively *more* important in Michigan than elsewhere, it must be that some other taxes are relatively *less* important in Michigan than elsewhere. In 2006–2007, the general retail sales tax provided about 21.5 percent of the tax revenues in Michigan and about 23.5 percent of the state and local taxes in the United States overall. Individual income taxes accounted for about 18.6 percent of the tax revenues in Michigan and about 22.7 percent for the nation as a whole. These three main pillars of the state and local tax system in Michigan (property, general sales, and individual income taxes) add up to about 79 percent of the total state and local tax revenues, which is only slightly higher than the national average of 76 percent. Table 6.1 also has a line for business income taxes. In most states, this refers to a corporate income tax. In Michigan, the data are for the Single Business Tax, which was replaced by the Michigan Business Tax in 2007.[6] We will discuss the Single Business Tax and the Michigan Business Tax in detail later in this chapter.

Table 6.1 also shows that tobacco taxes account for a much larger percentage of tax revenues in Michigan than in the United States as a whole.[7] The tax system in Michigan also relies relatively heavily on motor-vehicle license taxes. In the next few paragraphs, we will discuss some other unusual aspects of the Michigan tax system.

The Centralization of the Tax System in Michigan

Michigan's state and local tax system is more dominated by *state* taxes than many other states. In 2006–2007, about 64.3 percent of the state and local taxes in Michigan were collected by the state government. This compares with about 59.3 percent for the nation as a whole. Michigan did not always have such a centralized tax system. However, as a result of the passage of Proposal A in 1994, local property taxes were reduced substantially. Proposal A replaced a portion of the lost revenue with increases in the sales tax and the cigarette tax, both of which are levied by the state government. Proposal A also introduced a new property tax at the state level, known as the "State Education Tax."[8] Consequently, control over revenues is more concentrated at the state level in Michigan than it used to be. As a result, local governments and public schools in Michigan have less direct control over their finances than local governments and public schools in much of the rest of the country.

Michigan's Flat-Rate Income Tax

Michigan is one of only seven states in which the individual income tax has only a single rate.[9] (Currently, the tax rate on all taxable income in Michigan is 4.35 percent.) By contrast, the individual income taxes in most other states have "graduated marginal tax rates." When an income tax has graduated rates, the tax rate on an additional dollar of income is higher for those with larger incomes. For example, in Wisconsin the tax rate on the first dollar of taxable income is 4.6 percent, but Wisconsin's income tax has five marginal tax rates. The highest of these is 7.75 percent, which takes effect when a married couple has a taxable income of more than $300,000. Michigan's flat income tax collects relatively more from low-income residents and relatively less from those with higher incomes, when compared to a graduated income tax system that would raise the same amount of revenue.[10]

The Level of Taxes

Figure 6.1 shows some of the trends in the percentage of personal income that goes to state and local taxes. The figure covers the years from 1972 to 2007.[11] Figure 6.1 shows the trends for Michigan and the United States as a whole, as well as for New York (because its taxes are persistently among the highest in the country) and Texas (because its taxes are persistently among the lowest).

Perhaps the most important trend shown in Figure 6.1 is the significant decrease in the percentage of income that goes to state and local taxes. For the United States as a whole, state and local taxes dropped from about 12.8 percent of income in 1972 to about 11 percent in 2007. Michigan's state and local taxes have been fairly close to the U.S. average for this entire period, especially when compared with the taxes in states like New York and Texas. However, the decrease in state and local taxes has been even sharper in Michigan than in the rest of the country. In Michigan, state and local taxes fell from about 13.2 percent of income in 1972 to about 10.7 percent of income in 2007. As a result of this substantial decline, taxes in Michigan fell from slightly *above* the national average in the 1970s and 1980s to slightly *below* the national average by 2007, at a time when the national average was falling.

Figure 6.1 shows a slight increase in state and local taxes as a percentage of income from 2002 to 2005. This was largely due to increases in property-tax revenues, which resulted from increases in property values. These increases in property values came to a halt in the last two years shown in the figure. When complete data for more recent years become available, they will almost certainly show substantial further decreases in property-tax revenues as a result of the real-estate crisis.

Figure 6.1 shows information for state and local governments combined. If we consider the state government by itself, tax revenues have been especially weak in recent years. Data from the House Fiscal Agency show that after adjusting for inflation, revenues for Michigan's School Aid Fund were down by about 15 percent from 2003 to 2009.[12] The decreases in revenue for the General Fund are far more drastic. Figure 6.2 shows that Michigan's General Fund revenues have fallen by more than 40 percent in less than a decade.[13] The latest Executive Budget reports that after adjusting for inflation, General Fund revenues are at their lowest level since 1965 when Michigan's economy was only about half as large as it is today.[14] By 2010 the combined total of Michigan's

FIGURE 6.1. State and local taxes as a percentage of personal income, 1972–2007

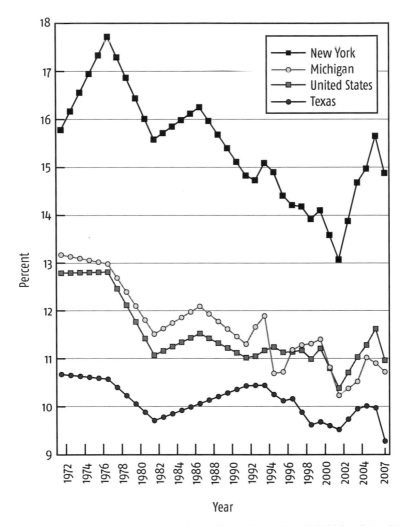

Source: For the years from 1992 onward, annual data are available at the Census Bureau Web site. See the U.S. Census Bureau, "State and Local Government Finances," http://www.census.gov/govs/estimate. For 1972, 1977, 1982, and 1987, the data are taken from the Census of Governments, vol. 4, no. 5, "Compendium of Government Finances," Washington, D.C.: United States Government Printing Office. In constructing Figure 6.1, the years between 1972 and 1977, 1977 and 1982, 1982 and 1987, and 1987 and 1992 were interpolated.

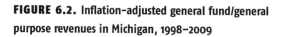

FIGURE 6.2. Inflation-adjusted general fund/general
purpose revenues in Michigan, 1998–2009

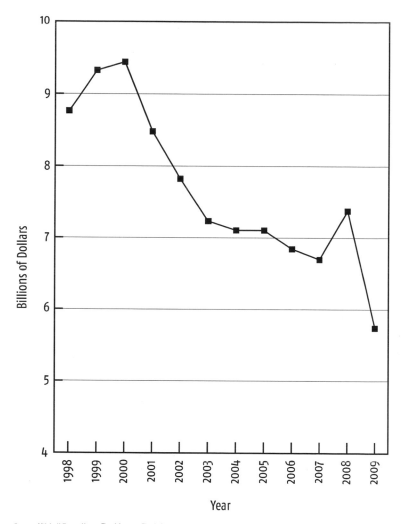

Source: Mitchell Bean, House Fiscal Agency. The inflation adjustment is made with the deflator for state and local government expenditures, from
U.S. Department of Commerce, Bureau of Economic Analysis, "Table 1.1.4 : Price Indexes for Gross Domestic Product," http ://www.bea.gov/
national/nipaweb/SelectTable.asp?Selected=N.

School Aid Fund and General Fund was smaller than the bonuses paid by the Wall Street firm of Goldman Sachs.

The Politics and Economics of Declining Tax Revenues

Thus a dwindling fraction of income is being devoted to the functions of state and local government in Michigan, affecting schools, roads, health care, police protection, and fire protection. If Michigan were to return to the relative levels of taxation that prevailed for most of the last generation, the budgets of the state and local governments and public schools would increase by something in the vicinity of $10 billion per year.

It has often been suggested that this decrease in tax revenues is due to the poor performance of the economy. In fact, however, the sluggish economy is only a *small* part of the explanation for the dramatic decline in tax revenues. It is true that Michigan's economy is smaller than it used to be. After adjusting for inflation, personal income in Michigan is down by a bit more than 4 percent. However, as we have just seen, the School Aid Fund is down by four times as much and the General Fund is down by ten times as much. Clearly, tax revenues are not just shrinking in line with the economy. Instead, tax revenues are falling much more rapidly than the rest of the economy, so that the percentage of the Michigan economy that goes to public services has plummeted. Later in this chapter, we will discuss the structural deficiencies in Michigan's taxes that have caused this situation.

Even as recently as a few years ago, I was cautiously optimistic about the budgetary situation in Michigan. My chapter in *Michigan at the Millennium* (written in 2003) does not ring with the same sense of alarm that I would like to convey here.[15] But the fiscal crises of recent years have been a sobering experience. As the resources available for public goods and services have continued to fall, the situation has become increasingly dire. Michigan's tax system is drastically out of step with the revenue needs of today and tomorrow.

Unless this trend is reversed, it will be more and more difficult for Michigan to provide a proper educational system and other public services that its citizens deserve. Of course, it is *always* good policy to examine and reexamine the expenditures of government in search of savings. However, the fiscal crises of recent years have already caused a tremendous amount of belt tightening in the budgets for state government, local government, and public schools in Michigan. Although further economizing must be a *part* of the solution, it cannot be the *entire* solution. If it was possible for the State of Michigan to provide the public services that are essential for Michigan's future without reversing the trend of plummeting taxes, I would be the first to say so. However, this just is not possible.

I understand that a call for more public revenues is controversial. However, I am not suggesting a radical increase in taxes in Michigan. The percentage of income that is paid in taxes in Michigan is lower now than it has been in decades. We could have a substantial *increase* in tax revenues and still be *well below* the tax levels of thirty or even ten years ago. Thus I am not calling for tax increases that would take us into uncharted waters. Instead I am calling for a return to the levels of taxation under which Michigan has prospered in the past.

I am not alone in saying that increased tax revenues have to be a part of the solution to Michigan's fiscal problems. In another of Michigan's recurring fiscal crises, Governor Granholm appointed an Emergency Financial Advisory Panel. The membership of the panel included many giants of Michigan's leadership over the last forty years. The lineup included former Governors Bill Milliken and Jim Blanchard, former Senate Majority Leader Dan DeGrow, former House Speaker Paul Hillegonds, former Attorney General Frank Kelley, former State Treasurer Doug Roberts, former State Senator and U.S. Congressman Joe Schwarz, Michigan State University President Lou Anna Simon, and others with a wealth of leadership experience in Michigan. The panel issued its report in February 2007. The report is worth reading in its entirety, but one especially important passage states, "Solving the state's budget crisis requires a combination of revenue increases, spending cuts, and reform of how public services are delivered. No single silver bullet incorporating only tax increases, only spending cuts, or only government reform will work in either the short term or the long term to solve the state's fiscal challenge."[16]

Those words were true when they were written in 2007, and they are even more truthful now. Unfortunately, many of the candidates for governor in 2010 are pledging to rely exclusively on spending cuts.

In my view, the main obstacles to improving the tax system in Michigan are political rather than economic. Earlier in this book, I mentioned a conversation with a student who suggested it would be "political suicide" to raise taxes. As I have said before, if it is political suicide to do what needs to be done for the future of Michigan's economy, then we're dead already.

In the next few pages, I will discuss some specific aspects of the Michigan tax system that have contributed to the decline in tax revenues. Throughout this chapter, the discussion will be framed in terms of the need to collect an adequate amount of revenue. However, it makes no sense to flail about wildly in search of tax revenues. The search must be focused. Thus some of the tax reforms discussed in this chapter do not involve additional revenues at all. I recommend reducing or eliminating the Michigan Business Tax (but only if we make up the resulting revenue losses with some additional revenues from other sources). And when I suggest a reform that does raise additional revenues, I do so because that reform would also advance other goals such as improving the efficiency or fairness of Michigan's tax system.

The Structural Deficiencies of Michigan's Taxes: Termites in the Tax Base

Policy changes in Michigan have led to revenue reductions on several occasions in the last few decades. In 1994, Proposal A involved some tax-rate increases as well as some rate cuts, but the net effect was a decrease in tax revenues. Then beginning in 1999, the marginal tax rate in the individual income tax was reduced repeatedly.[17] The income tax was then raised in 2007, but this barely slowed the downward trend in revenues.

Another possible explanation for the general decrease in tax revenues is that the Michigan economy has been weak. However, the poor performance of the overall economy does not even come close to explaining the precipitous decline in tax revenues. If the weak economy cannot explain the enormous decreases in tax revenues, than what is the explanation? The answer is that the tax system in Michigan has serious structural weaknesses. These weaknesses cause tax revenues to decline year after year—even when the economy is not sinking and even when there are no tax-rate cuts. There are structural weaknesses in the sales tax; the income tax; and the taxes on beer, wine, tobacco, and motor fuels. I will discuss the structural flaws of these taxes in the next few sections. The property tax also suffers from structural weaknesses, which I will discuss later on in this chapter.

Erosion of the Sales-Tax Base: Most Services and Entertainments Are Not Taxed

In Michigan and in most other states, most services and entertainments are exempt from the sales tax. Michigan's sales tax does not apply to accounting services, admissions to sports events, beauty parlors, car washes, carpentry services, dance lessons, dating services, health clubs, laundry and dry-cleaning services, lawn-care services, legal services, live-theater and movie-theater admissions, pet-grooming services, plumbing services, real-estate-agent services, tanning parlors, tax-return preparation services, veterinary services, and a host of other services and entertainments.

The Federation of Tax Administrators has published information on the taxation of services as of July 2007.[18] This report lists 168 service categories. Delaware, Hawaii, New Mexico, and South Dakota come close to comprehensive taxation of all 168 service categories. The median state taxes fifty-five categories. Michigan taxes only twenty-six of the 168 categories. (Some thirty-six states and the District of Columbia tax more service categories than Michigan.)

At one time, the nontaxation of services did not make a huge difference because services were a relatively small part of the economy. But services have grown more rapidly than the rest of the economy for the last couple of generations. As we saw in Chapter 1, services are now the biggest single part of the economy.

Thus the revenue losses from not taxing services are very large, and they grow larger every year. The Michigan Department of Treasury has estimated the size of the revenue losses in the "Executive Budget Appendix on Tax Credits, Deductions, and Exemptions, Fiscal Year 2010."[19] The Executive Budget Appendix lists dozens of holes in the Michigan tax system, totaling about $36 billion of annual revenue losses. By far the largest of these is the nontaxation of services in the sales tax, which is estimated to have accounted for more than $10 billion of lost tax revenues in 2010. (In other words, this annual revenue loss from not taxing services is much larger than the amount that is actually collected by the sales tax!)

Much of these revenue losses are the result of not taxing business-to-business services. In an ideal sales tax, business-to-business services should *not* be taxed.[20] Even if we exclude business-to-business services, however, the revenue losses are well in excess of $3 billion per year. This indicates that we should reform the tax system to include certain services. Instead of taxing some things at 6 percent and not taxing services and entertainments, we could bring more services and entertainments into the tax base and raise the same amount of revenue with a tax rate substantially lower than 6 percent. This has the potential to raise the same number of dollars that we raise now, in a much more efficient manner. In light of the ongoing budgetary crisis, an even more attractive policy would be the following: if the sales tax were extended to a broader range of services, it would be possible to raise *additional* revenue while still *reducing* the sales-tax rate on the things that are taxed.

In response to proposals to expand the sales tax to cover more services and entertainments, one sometimes hears the following objection: if we tax a sector of the economy that has previously been untaxed, there will be employment losses in that sector. That may be true (although those who raise the objection often have an incentive to overstate the problem in an attempt to maintain political support for their privileged treatment). However, it is important to keep this in perspective. For example, untaxed tanning parlors may very well have grown more rapidly than they would otherwise have grown, if they had been taxed. (It is not surprising that activities tend to grow faster when they receive preferential treatment.) Thus if the privileged tax treatment of tanning salons were removed, the tanning-salon sector would probably grow less rapidly, which might result in some employment losses.

However, this type of situation would be reversed in the sectors of the economy that have been taxed all along. Just as the untaxed services have benefited from the unlevel playing field, the taxed activities have been penalized by it. If the playing field were leveled, there might be job losses in the sectors that have previously been privileged, but there would also be job gains in the sectors that have previously been punished. There is no reason to believe that the *overall* level of employment would be harmed. In fact, overall employment might increase because the reformed tax system would create a more efficient allocation of resources in the economy.

In 2007, the state legislature passed a bill to extend the sales tax to some services, but the new law created a political uproar and was repealed before it ever went into effect. In 2010, Governor Granholm has proposed extending the sales tax to some services, while lowering the sales-tax rate from 6 percent to 5.5 percent. If enacted, this would be a big step in the right direction. However, as of this writing, this idea does not have good prospects in the legislature.

The *politics* of sales-tax reform are very difficult. Lobbyists fight hard to maintain the privileged status of the services that currently get preferential treatment. And yet the *economics* of sales-tax reform are absolutely and completely solid. Extending the sales tax to services is a slam dunk, both in terms of fairness and in terms of economic efficiency. If we create a level playing field by taxing goods and services in the same way, our tax system will be both fairer and more efficient. If we continue with the current system, which taxes some activities at 6 percent while other activities get special treatment, the long-term effect will be the continued erosion of the tax base. This will perpetuate economic inefficiency and an unfair tax system, and it will damage our ability to pay for public services in Michigan.

The Sales Tax Treatment of Food

Restaurant meals are subject to the Michigan sales tax, but food purchased for home consumption is not. This creates a loss of tax revenue of more than $1 billion per year. Thus although the revenue loss from not taxing food is substantial, it is much smaller than the loss incurred from not taxing services.

The policy of not taxing food is usually justified in terms of its effect on the distribution of income, since the percentage of income spent on food is highest for low-income people. That is a valid concern. However, the exemption of food from the sales tax is an inefficient instrument for helping those with low incomes. After all, middle- and upper-income people also eat food. As we move up the income scale, the decrease in the percentage of income devoted to food is surprisingly slow. Higher-income people do not necessarily eat *more* food, but they do eat *more expensive* foods. Of course, it might be possible to tax food items that are consumed mainly by high-income folks, but that would open up the sales tax to endless wrangling.

An alternative policy would be to tax food and offset the effect on low-income people by using a refundable credit in the income tax. This would make the sales tax more efficient, while still dealing with the concern about the way a tax on food would affect the poor. This kind of policy is worth thinking about. However, at this time, many other tax-policy issues are more pressing. The tax treatment of food is not near the top of my list of possible tax reforms.

Evasion of Taxes on Internet and Mail-Order Sales

When a purchase is made from an out-of-state mail-order service or over the Internet, the buyer is supposed to pay tax. However, these taxes are widely evaded because the U.S. Supreme Court has ruled that the states cannot enforce the taxes on these interstate purchases. In a report issued in 2009, the Michigan's Department of Treasury estimated that the tax revenue losses from mail-order and Internet sales were about $308 million in the 2008 fiscal year and that they are estimated to grow to about $355 million by 2011.[21]

Thus the nontaxation of Internet and mail-order sales is yet another structural deficiency of the tax system. The revenue losses grow, year after year. Like so many other structural problems, this is economically inefficient. It is also unfair. If a Michigan resident buys a sweater from a local retailer, the purchase is taxed. If the identical item is bought by mail order from L.L. Bean, the State of Michigan can't collect sales tax because L.L. Bean is headquartered in Maine. Local retailers are outraged by this and justifiably so.

Unfortunately, there is little that the State of Michigan can do about this unfair and inefficient aspect of the tax law, because it is the result of decisions by the U.S. Supreme Court. If the problem is to be fixed, it will require action by the U.S. Congress. This reform should be one of the top priorities of Michigan's congressional delegation.

Erosion of the Income Tax

In the Michigan individual income tax, the calculation of taxable income begins with adjusted gross income, which is taken directly from the federal tax return. This procedure simplifies the calculation of Michigan income-tax liability and therefore reduces the taxpayer's cost of complying with the tax laws. However, it also means that many types of income are excluded from the tax base of the Michigan income tax because they have already been excluded from the federal tax base. (The largest excluded items are the employer contributions for health insurance and pensions.)

The Michigan income tax also includes a personal exemption, which was $3,600 per person in 2009.[22] Additional exemptions are given for senior citizens, individuals with certain disabilities, and children under eighteen. Senior citizens are also allowed to deduct Social Security benefits, dividends, interest, capital gains, and most pension benefits. After these and a few other adjustments, the taxpayer calculates his or her taxable income. Taxable income is then multiplied by the flat tax rate, which is currently 4.35 percent. After that, taxpayers may further reduce their tax liabilities if they are able to claim certain tax credits. By far the largest of the tax credits is the Homestead Property

Tax Credit, which effectively reduces property-tax liabilities. The Homestead Credit is larger for senior citizens than for the rest of the population.

Because of the various exclusions, deductions, exemptions, and credits, the revenue-raising capacity of the individual income tax is much smaller than it would otherwise be. If the tax base were less eroded, it would be possible to raise more revenue with the same tax rate or raise the same amount of revenue with a lower tax rate.

The Generous Tax Treatment of Retirement Income

As mentioned in the previous section, senior citizens in Michigan receive a large number of special tax treatments. Seniors receive additional exemptions, and they are able to deduct large amounts of retirement income. Moreover, senior citizens receive extra Homestead credits. Senior citizens receive more generous treatment from the Michigan income tax than from the income taxes in virtually any other state. About nine out of every ten Michigan senior citizens pay no state income tax at all. In fact, the total net amount of income tax paid by Michigan seniors is *negative*. (In other words, their Homestead Property Tax Credits are larger than their tax liabilities, so they actually get a rebate.) This creates annual revenue losses estimated to be $700 million.

As discussed in Chapter 2, Michigan's population is growing older. The proportion of the Michigan population who are senior citizens will continue to increase. Therefore, unless the extraordinary generosity of the tax system toward senior citizens is reduced, the revenue-raising capacity of the income tax will continue to shrink.

It is important to address one potential objection to reducing the generosity of the Michigan income tax toward senior citizens. Many elderly people have modest incomes, and it is very reasonable to ask whether these folks should have to pay more taxes. However, the income tax already addresses this issue through the personal exemption. The purpose of the personal exemption is to shield low-income residents (young and old) from having to pay much income tax. Thus the low-income elderly have never paid much income tax, and they still would not pay much income tax if some of the special tax treatments discussed here were reduced. A large portion of the special tax breaks for the elderly are received by those with high incomes. Thus if these generous tax breaks were scaled back, most of the additional taxes would be paid by the affluent elderly.

Without question, reducing the tax breaks for elderly Michigan residents will be difficult politically. Nevertheless, if we fail to bring the taxation of seniors more into line with the taxation of the rest of the population, the long-term effect will be continued erosion of the tax base. In turn, this will compromise our ability to deal with Michigan's fiscal challenges.

I expect to retire in ten years or so. If Michigan's income-tax laws are not changed, the date of my retirement will mark the onset of a sudden change for me. Up to the time of my retirement, I will be paying several thousand dollars of Michigan income taxes every year. These taxes help pay for schools, roads, police protection, and other public services. Then when I retire, I will suddenly pay nothing or next to nothing. This is an unfair system, and it makes no sense. I hope that the Michigan legislature will have the wisdom and courage to scale back our extraordinary generosity toward senior citizens. Of course, if they do so, I will end up paying more taxes when I retire. Thus I do not advocate this reform out of narrow self-interest. I define my self-interest more broadly, as a citizen of Michigan.

Michigan's Flat-Rate Income Tax and the Shrinkage of Tax Revenues

In earlier chapters, I have emphasized that the distribution of income in the United States has become dramatically unequal in the last thirty-five years. The vast majority of the income growth has been experienced by those at the top of the income scale. Michigan's income tax is levied at a flat rate, which means that an additional dollar of taxable income for a millionaire is taxed at the same rate as an additional dollar of taxable income for the average worker. If Michigan had a graduated income tax, as most states do, an additional dollar of taxable income for the millionaire would be taxed at a higher rate than an additional dollar for the average worker.

If Michigan had a graduated income tax, the recent trend toward greater income inequality would have led to more tax revenue to support public services. The flat-rate income tax, like the nontaxation of services and the generous tax treatment of retirement income, has contributed to the decline of tax revenues in Michigan.

The Peculiar Taxes on Beer, Wine, and Tobacco

All fifty states have taxes on beer, wine, tobacco products, and motor fuels. It is important to understand a fundamental difference between these taxes and most other taxes. Income taxes are levied as a *percentage* of taxable income. Property taxes are levied as a *percentage* of the taxable value of the property. Sales taxes are levied as a *percentage* of the price of the item. But most of the taxes on beer, wine, tobacco products, and motor fuels are different. Instead of being levied as a percentage of some dollar value, these taxes are "unit taxes." For example, the tax rates are expressed as a number of dollars per pack of cigarettes or a number of dollars per barrel of beer.

For the taxes that are expressed as a percentage of value, an increase in the price of the item leads automatically to an increase in the amount of tax per unit. However, for the unit taxes, the amount of tax per unit is the same, regardless of the price. This creates two distinct problems. First, when inflation pushes prices higher, the unit tax becomes a smaller percentage of the total price. Thus the real revenue-raising capacity of these taxes is eroded over time, unless the legislature increases the tax rate explicitly. In the case of cigarette taxes, this effect has been offset by legislated increases in the tax rate.[23] However, the unit tax on wine has been unchanged since 1981, and the unit tax on beer has stayed the same since 1966 (when it was decreased). In the four-plus decades since 1966, the overall price level has increased by more than 430 percent.[24] As a result, inflation has reduced the effective tax rates substantially, and this has seriously eroded the real revenue-raising capacity of these taxes. Also, the taxes on beer and wine are probably motivated by a desire to discourage the antisocial behaviors associated with excessive drinking. As the effective tax rate is reduced over time, the disincentive for binge drinking is also reduced.[25]

The second problem with unit taxes is that they create a strange kind of inequity. The cigarette tax in Michigan is $2 per pack. If a smoker buys a pack of a discount brand of cigarettes for $4, the Michigan tax is one-half of the total price. On the other hand, if another smoker buys a pack of a premium brand of cigarettes for $6, the Michigan tax is only one-third of the price. Thus the buyer of premium cigarettes pays a lower effective tax rate than the buyer of discount cigarettes. The same thing happens when people buy wine, beer, or gasoline: the folks who buy high-priced wines face a lower effective tax rate than those who buy the cheaper varieties, and the folks who buy premium gasoline face a lower effective tax rate than those who buy regular gasoline.

There is a clear-cut solution to these problems. We should replace most of the unit taxes with taxes levied as a percentage of the sales price. That way, inflation would no longer erode the revenues from these taxes over time. In the case of the cigarette tax, I am in favor of using the percentage tax rate that would raise the same amount of tax revenue as the current unit tax. For the taxes on beer and wine, a strong case can be made for using a percentage tax rate that would raise *more* revenue than is currently raised, to offset some of the erosion of the last few decades.

Taxes on Motor Fuels

The excise taxes on motor fuels are also levied on a per-unit basis, although most states also add a sales tax, environmental fee, or other fee. (Michigan is one of the states in which the sales tax is applicable to motor fuels.) In addition, Michigan is unusual in that the tax rate on diesel fuel is less than the tax rate on gasoline. In 2010, twenty-five states and the District of Columbia imposed the same tax on diesel fuel and gasoline, and sixteen states and the federal government imposed a higher tax on diesel. Among the nine states with a lower tax on diesel fuel, the difference between the gasoline tax rate and the diesel-fuel tax rate was greatest in Michigan. Only Alaska, Oklahoma, and Wyoming states had a lower excise tax on diesel fuel than Michigan.[26] Higher taxes on motor fuels would raise additional revenue, and they may also have environmental advantages. A strong case can be made for raising the tax rates on both gasoline and diesel fuel and raising the diesel tax rate far enough to be at least equal to the gasoline tax rate.

Earlier, I made the case for converting the taxes on beer, wine, and tobacco products from a unit basis to a percentage basis. It is more difficult to make the same argument for the motor-fuels taxes because of the high volatility of prices for gasoline and diesel fuel. Although I strongly suggest that we raise the rates of fuel tax, I do not believe it is necessary to convert them to a percentage.

Climate change caused by emissions of greenhouse gases is an increasingly important problem. Since it is a global problem, it would be good if we could address the problem at a global level. However, to date, the world's leaders have not been very successful at crafting agreements that would address climate change in a serious way. One way to reduce the amount of carbon dioxide emitted into the atmosphere would be to increase the price of carbon emissions, through taxes or other mechanisms such as a "cap and trade" plan.[27] Proposals along these lines are being debated in Congress, but it is unclear whether they will be passed into law. If Michigan desires to be a real leader on environmental issues, Michigan could go ahead with substantially higher taxes on gasoline, diesel, and other causes of carbon emissions. A very reasonable objection to such a policy is that it would be regressive (i.e., it would be paid disproportionately by low- and middle-income residents). However, an increase in environmentally motivated taxes could be accompanied by reductions in other taxes such as the income tax or the sales tax.[28] An increase in the gasoline tax could be coupled with a refundable credit in the income tax to offset the regressivity. The Canadian province of British Columbia has instituted just such a policy.

One more thing needs to be said before we leave the subject of taxes on motor fuels. Today, most people (including me) drive a gasoline-powered car. However, as the years go by, automakers are producing cars that get more and more miles per gallon. In addition, electric-powered and hybrid vehicles are likely to become more popular over time. It is possible that gasoline consumption may decline very substantially in the coming years. This will be good for the environment, but it will also mean that gasoline taxes will raise less revenue. *Now* is the time to start thinking about sources of revenue to replace the gasoline tax.

The Effects of the Michigan Tax System on Different Income Classes

In the case of a "proportional" tax, people with different incomes pay the same percentage of their incomes in tax. If a tax is "progressive," an increase in income leads to an increase in the percentage paid in tax. If a tax is "regressive," a movement up the income scale leads to a *decrease* in the percentage paid in tax. Thus a progressive tax takes relatively more from the people with the highest incomes, while a regressive tax takes relatively more from those with the lowest incomes.

As we have seen, the tax system in Michigan has many distinct components. In the next few pages, I will briefly discuss the distributional effects of several of these revenue sources.

The Distributional Effects of the Individual Income Tax

In Michigan in 2009, the income tax provided an exemption of $3,600 per person. Senior citizens get an extra exemption of $2,300, and children ages eighteen and under get an extra exemption of $600. Thus for a Michigan family with two adults and two children, the personal exemption would shield $15,600 from income taxes. The personal exemptions mean that Michigan families who are below the poverty line pay very little in state income tax. As a result of these exemptions, the individual income tax in Michigan is progressive at low- and mid-level incomes.

However, the Michigan income tax is not as progressive as the income taxes in many other states because the income tax in Michigan does not have graduated rates. (There are two main ways to generate progressivity in an income tax. Exemptions can create progressivity at the bottom of the income scale, and graduated rates can continue to impart progressivity at higher levels of income. Most states use both of these features and so does the federal government, but Michigan only uses exemptions.) As we move up the income scale, the exemptions are a smaller and smaller percentage of income. Therefore, the Michigan income tax becomes less and less progressive when we consider taxpayers with higher incomes.

For example, consider a Michigan family with two adults and two children with income (before exemptions) of $1,015,600. After the exemptions of $15,600, this family's taxable income is exactly $1 million. Based on a flat income-tax rate of 4.35 percent, the family will pay $43,500 in Michigan income tax. When we compare this amount of tax to the family's income (before exemptions), their effective average tax rate is about 4.29 percent. For another family with $2 million of taxable income, the average effective tax rate is only barely higher at about 4.32 percent. Thus personal exemptions can generate some progressivity to a flat-rate income tax at low income levels, but the tax is essentially proportional at high incomes.

State and local income-tax payments are deductible from the federal individual income tax. This alters the distributional effects of the Michigan income tax for those who itemize deductions on their federal income-tax returns. We will discuss the effects of federal deductibility in a later section of this chapter. As we shall see, interactions between the Michigan income tax and the federal income tax eliminate even the tiny amount of progressivity in the high-income ranges that we saw in the preceding paragraph.

The Distributional Effects of Other Taxes

Whereas the income tax is somewhat progressive (at least over a part of the income range), the general retail sales tax is somewhat regressive. This is because the sales tax only applies when people spend their money (i.e., the sales tax does not apply when people save). Since higher-income individuals tend to save a larger percentage of their money than lower-income individuals, the nontaxation of savings makes the sales tax somewhat regressive. As we have seen, Michigan's sales tax also does not apply to most services. The nontaxation of services affects different income groups in different ways, depending on their patterns of spending. I am not aware of a comprehensive study of this, but it should be noted that many of the untaxed services are consumed mostly by high-income people. For example, I am a season subscriber to the concerts of the Lansing Symphony Orchestra, and my concert tickets are not taxed. When I look around at the crowd that attends the concerts, it certainly appears to be an affluent group. Many entertainments are disproportionately consumed by high-income people, and the same goes for legal services, accounting services, and many other untaxed services. Thus it is possible that Michigan's sales tax is even more regressive than a uniform sales tax would be.

The cigarette tax is also regressive because smoking is more prevalent among those with lower incomes.[29] On the other hand, the taxes on alcoholic beverages are close to proportional. This is because expenditure on alcohol accounts for about the same percentage of income for most levels of income.

The state-run lotteries impose an implicit tax on gamblers because the lotteries return only a fraction of their gross revenues in prizes. In *Michigan at the Millennium*, Lawrence Martin calculates that the implicit tax rate in the Michigan lotteries is about 60 percent or ten times as high as the tax rate for general retail sales.[30] As we move up the income scale, there is very little increase if any in the amount spent on lottery tickets. Therefore, the *percentage* of income devoted to lottery tickets is highest for those with the lowest incomes. As a result, lotteries are the most regressive source of government revenue.[31]

There is controversy about the effects of property taxes on the distribution of income. If the residential property tax is viewed as a tax on housing, it would be somewhat regressive because housing accounts for a larger share of income for those with low incomes. If we view the property tax as a tax on capital, it would be somewhat progressive because high-income taxpayers receive relatively more of their income in the form of capital income, rather than wages and salaries. I tend to view the property tax as a tax on capital, so in my opinion, property taxes are a progressive element of the tax system.

The Michigan Business Tax (MBT) presents special challenges for anyone who would like to determine its effect on different income classes. For one thing, the MBT has a large exemption for small businesses. Thus the ultimate effects of the MBT depend partly on whether there are differences in the percentage of purchases that low-income and high-income consumers make from small businesses and large businesses. This is a subject about which we have very little information. The distributional effects of the MBT also depend on a number of other factors such as the degree of competitiveness of labor markets and goods markets.

If we put all of these pieces together, the tax system in Michigan is probably somewhat regressive over most of the income range. A study by Carl Davis and others provides comparisons of the distributional effects of the tax systems in the fifty states in 2007.[32] This study found that all state and local taxes in Michigan accounted for 8.9 percent of income for households with incomes below $15,000. This average effective tax rate rises to 9.9 percent for those between $15,000 and $32,000. Thus this study suggests that the Michigan tax system is slightly progressive over this range of incomes. However, at higher incomes the effective rates decrease, which means that the tax system becomes regressive. For those with incomes in excess of $365,000, state and local taxes in Michigan were only 6.4 percent of income. When we include the itemized deductions that these high-income folks take on their federal tax returns, their net effective tax rate drops to 5.3 percent.

In 2003, this group published a very similar study using data for the fifty states from 2002.[33] In this study, they found that Michigan was one of the ten most regressive states in the United States. However, in the new study with data for 2007, Michigan is *not* one of the most regressive states. Michigan's state and local tax system was regressive over most of the income range in both 2002 and 2007, but it became less regressive by 2007. A major reason for the change was the adoption of the Earned Income Tax Credit, which reduced the income taxes of low-income Michigan residents.

The Case for a Graduated Income Tax in Michigan

As mentioned in earlier chapters, the distribution of income has become much more unequal in recent decades. The theory of optimal income taxation shows that taxes should be more progressive when the underlying distribution of income is more unequal.[34] However, in spite of the large increase in inequality, tax policy in Michigan has been inconsistent. In the last twenty years, when the gap between residents with high incomes and those with low incomes has widened, some tax-policy changes have made the tax system more progressive, but others have made it more regressive.

Of course, income distribution is not the only consideration that should be taken into account when we decide on tax policy. Sound tax policy is based on many considerations, including economic efficiency and ease of administration, as well as fairness. There are tradeoffs among the various objectives. For example, even though the cigarette tax is regressive, I am strongly in favor of substantial taxes on cigarettes. Despite its regressivity, the cigarette tax can help to reduce one of the greatest challenges to the health of the American public. Nevertheless, I believe that a move toward increased progressivity would be a step in the right direction. In order to achieve the goal of increased progressivity, it would make sense for the income tax to play a more important role since the income tax is progressive over a large range of incomes.

In particular, I believe that the people of Michigan should institute a graduated income tax. My beliefs in this regard are stronger than they were ten or twenty years ago because of the ongoing surge in income inequality. The case for a graduated income tax in Michigan is stronger now than ever before.

One of my friends says that a graduated income tax is a "jobs killer." The idea behind this statement is that the disincentive effects of a graduated income tax are so large that they would outweigh any advantages. I acknowledge that we *do* have to worry about the disincentive effects of taxes. That's one of the reasons why President John F. Kennedy proposed to reduce federal income-tax rates. When Kennedy came to office in 1961, the top rate in the federal income tax was an astonishing 91 percent. (Today, the top federal rate is 35 percent.) *No one* today is saying that we should have rates anywhere near as high as we had in Kennedy's time.

However, just because we need to be concerned about the disincentive effects of the income tax, it does *not* necessarily follow that those effects are as huge as some folks suggest. The top rate in Michigan's income tax is lower than the top rate is thirty-nine other states.[35] Michigan has had a long period of sluggish economic growth despite having one of the lowest income-tax rates in the country. Those facts should make it clear that the income tax is not as powerful as some say it is: if the income tax were really so powerful, then

Michigan's economy should have been growing rapidly because of Michigan's low income-tax rate.

The opponents of a graduated income tax like to point to Texas and Florida. Neither of these states has an income tax, and each has had a good record of economic growth. However, Georgia, North Carolina, and Virginia have also had strong economic growth, and they all have a graduated income tax. In fact, North Carolina has a top tax rate of 7.75 percent, and it has still put together a very impressive record of economic growth.

The Michigan League for Human Services (MLHS) advocates a three-bracket system. The bottom bracket of 3.9 percent is less than the current flat rate of 4.35 percent. The middle bracket in the MLHS proposal is 4.35 percent. The top bracket, which applies to married couples with incomes greater than $120,000 per year, is 6.9 percent. It is estimated that this proposal would raise an additional $600 million per year to finance public services, even though it would give a tax cut to 90 percent of Michigan taxpayers.[36]

It is ironic that the most vocal opposition to this proposal comes from folks who often clamor for tax cuts. In other words, these "tax cutters" are opposed to a proposal that would provide a tax cut for 90 percent of Michigan's people! To me, it appears that the "tax cutters" aren't really interested in tax cuts as such. They are interested in tax cuts for high-income folks, but they are happy to keep taxes high for low- and middle-income Michigan residents. In other words, it seems to me that the main difference between me and the "tax cutters" doesn't have much to do with the economic effects of taxes; it has to do with the fact that the huge increase in income inequality is very troublesome to me, while it is less troublesome (or not troublesome at all) to the "tax cutters." (Even if we were to enact the MLHS proposal for a graduated income tax, the after-tax distribution of income in Michigan would still be *far* more unequal than it was a generation ago.)

I believe that the MLHS proposal or one like it would be a step in the right direction for Michigan. I say this even though I, personally, would pay more. I won't reveal my income here, although it is a matter of public record, so you can look it up if you wish. Suffice it to say that PhD economists have done very well in the last generation. Thus I am in the 10 percent of Michigan residents who would pay more under the MLHS proposal for a graduated income tax. In other words, I am in favor of a graduated income tax for Michigan even though it doesn't appear to be in my narrow self interest. That's because as a citizen of this state, I think of my interests more broadly. I believe the graduated income tax would be better for Michigan. I believe that a citizen sometimes needs to advocate things that are good for the entire population instead of merely looking to line his or her own pocket.

Public-opinion surveys have consistently shown that a strong majority of the Michigan public are in favor of graduated rates. For example, in 2008, Michigan State University's State of the State Survey found that 57 percent of respondents were in favor of moving away from Michigan's flat income tax.[37] A poll conducted by EPIC-MRA in 2010 found that 65 percent favored a graduated income tax. However, there is no guarantee that Michigan will get a graduated income tax, even though a substantial majority of Michigan residents are in favor of it. A graduated income tax would require an amendment to the Michigan Constitution. Thus it would first be necessary for a proposal for a graduated income tax to make it to the ballot. And if it does make it to the ballot, the proposal would have to withstand a negative advertising campaign by the moneyed interests that are so strongly opposed to progressive taxation.

If it is not possible politically to introduce graduated rates in the Michigan income tax, I would still advocate other changes. One possibility is to raise the flat income-tax rate, while keeping the exemption unchanged. For example, we could raise the income-tax rate from its current value of 4.35 percent to the 5 percent used in Utah. (I like to use Utah as an example since it is not known as a hotbed of left-wing radicalism.) If we were to do this, income-tax revenues for the State of Michigan would increase by about $1 billion per year. In addition to providing more resources for schools, roads, and other public services, this would increase the progressivity of the Michigan income tax over a part of the income range.

Another possibility is to increase the personal exemption. This would also increase progressivity, especially at low incomes. However, an increase in the personal exemption would reduce the revenues from the tax unless offsetting changes were made. In order to avoid exacerbating the budgetary difficulties faced by governments in Michigan, it would probably be best to couple the increase in the exemption with some other changes that would offset the revenue losses. Because the personal exemption has a negative effect on tax revenues, it is probably not a good idea to increase it by a very large amount.

The Estate Tax

An estate tax is levied on the value of the estate that is left when someone dies. Estate taxes, like graduated income taxes, are motivated partly by distributional concerns—one of the traditional goals of estate taxation has been to reduce the concentration of wealth. As a result, estate taxes usually have very large exemptions. Because of this, the vast majority of estates are not taxed at all, and estate tax revenue is only collected from a small number of very large estates.

There is controversy about the efficiency effects of estate taxes. In fact, some have argued that estate taxes actually improve economic efficiency (whereas most taxes have negative efficiency effects). For example, in his book *Gospel of Wealth* (written in 1900), the wealthy industrialist Andrew Carnegie argued that parents who leave enormous wealth to their children would deaden their talents and energies. Regarding estate taxes, Carnegie said, "Of all forms of taxation this seems the wisest." For a detailed discussion of the economic effects of estate taxes, see James R. Hines Jr., Joel Slemrod, and William Gale's *Rethinking Estate and Gift Taxation*.[38]

Michigan used to have an estate tax. In fiscal year 2000, Michigan collected $185.5 million in estate tax revenues. Michigan and other states used to receive a portion of the federal estate tax called a "pick-up" tax. However, between 2001 and 2005, Congress phased out the state share, eliminating the pick-up tax completely in 2005. A number of states have "decoupled" from the federal estate tax, so that they can continue to collect estate taxes. But Michigan has not done so. Thus Michigan no longer collects any estate tax revenue.

It would be relatively simple for Michigan to reinstate its estate tax. Depending on the details of the new estate tax law, we could reasonably expect an estate tax to bring in between $150 million and $250 million per year.[39]

Tax Exporting

"Tax exporting" occurs when the government of one jurisdiction collects tax revenues that are actually paid by residents of a different jurisdiction. For example, when an Ohio family takes a vacation in Michigan, they will pay some Michigan sales taxes. These sales-tax revenues will go to the State of

Michigan even though Ohio residents actually foot the bill. In this case, Michigan has "exported" some of its taxes to the residents of another state.

Tax exporting can take a variety of forms. In addition to exporting sales taxes through taxes on tourists, some states export income taxes by levying taxes on out-of-state commuters. However, the largest amounts of tax exporting occur because state and local income taxes and property taxes are deductible from the federal individual income tax. For example, consider a Michigan family who itemize their deductions in the federal income tax. For every dollar of income tax or property tax paid to a government in Michigan, the family gets to reduce their federal taxable income by one dollar. This reduces their federal tax liability. The amount of reduction in federal taxes will depend on their tax rate in the federal income tax. If the Michigan family is in the 25-percent federal tax bracket, their federal taxes are reduced by twenty-five cents for every dollar of state and local income taxes and property taxes. Governments in Michigan get a dollar, but the net cost to the Michigan taxpayer is only seventy-five cents![40]

The other twenty-five cents are effectively exported to taxpayers in the entire country. There are several ways in which the federal government might respond to the loss of federal tax revenue that stems from deductions of Michigan taxes. For example, the federal government might raise other taxes. If so, however, the additional taxes would be paid by people all across the country and not just by Michigan residents. Alternatively, the federal government might cut services. Once again, however, the cuts would be felt throughout the United States and not just in Michigan. Finally, the federal government might go further into debt. This would impose a burden on future generations of taxpayers in all fifty states, and not just in Michigan. Thus although the details will differ depending on the federal government's policies, deductibility means that some Michigan taxes are shifted from Michigan residents to the residents of other states.

Until 1986, the federal income tax offered a deduction for state and local income taxes, property taxes, and *sales taxes*. However, the deduction for state and local sales taxes was removed by the federal Tax Reform Act of 1986.[41] This gave states an incentive to *decrease* their reliance on sales taxes, since sales taxes were no longer deductible. It also gave states an incentive to *increase* their reliance on income taxes and property taxes, since those taxes were (and still are) deductible. However, Michigan did exactly the opposite.

When Proposal A was passed in 1994, the voters were given a choice between two packages of policies. Both of the packages would reduce property taxes. In one case, much of the lost revenue would be restored by income taxes (which were deductible in the federal income tax). In the other case, much of the lost revenue would be restored by sales taxes (which were *not* deductible from the federal income tax). Michigan's voters chose the sales-tax option. By decreasing income taxes and property taxes and increasing sales taxes, Michigan chose to "leave money on the table." It would have been possible for Michigan governments to raise the same amount of tax revenue in Michigan while sending fewer dollars to the federal government in Washington. But we have chosen not to do so.

The financial effects of this choice are very substantial. According to an estimate by the Office of Revenue and Tax Analysis, Michigan residents paid about $900 million more in federal taxes in 2003 than they would have paid if Proposal A had not been enacted.[42] It is likely that Michigan residents have now paid a total of more than $10 billion in additional federal taxes since the passage of Proposal A, because of our choice to rely more on sales taxes rather than on income taxes.

Why Do We Do So Little Tax Exporting?

On the basis of the analysis in the last few paragraphs, it is reasonable to ask why Michigan has been so reluctant to take advantage of tax exporting. Why have we chosen to leave billions of dollars on the table? Why have we said "no" to such a large federal subsidy? One possibility is that the issue of tax exporting has simply fallen under the radar screen of the public discussion. It certainly appears that tax exporting has played only a very minor role in tax-policy debates in Michigan. Another possibility is that the lack of tax exporting is connected to the regressivity of the tax system. Those who desire a more regressive tax system have achieved greater political power in the last few decades. They are willing to leave money on the table, if that is what it takes to achieve the goal of greater regressivity. Thus the amount of money left on the table provides us with a measure of the intensity of the desire to shift more of the tax burden in Michigan onto the shoulders of low-income residents.

I do not want to overstate the case for tax exporting. It is *not* clear that tax exporting through deductibility is a good policy for the nation as a whole.

On the other hand, if the federal government offers Michigan the opportunity to export taxes through deductibility, it is remarkable that we refuse to take greater advantage of the subsidy.

Tax Exporting and the Rate Structure of Michigan's Income Tax

We have discussed the large increase in income inequality over the last thirty-five years, and we have also discussed the chronic fiscal crises of governments in Michigan. An increase in Michigan's individual income tax would address both of these problems. An increase in the income tax would raise revenue for cash-strapped governments in Michigan, and it would also reduce the share of taxes borne by low- and middle-income residents.

However, income-tax revenues in Michigan can be increased in a variety of ways, and these different methods have very different implications for tax exporting. This is because only about one-third of taxpayers itemize deductions on their federal tax returns, and most itemizers have relatively high incomes. Therefore, if Michigan's income tax rates were increased, the amount of additional tax exporting would be greater if relatively more of the increase were applied to high-income residents of Michigan. The most effective way to do this would be to introduce graduated rates. If Michigan were to adopt a graduated income tax, we could increase the amount of tax exporting by several hundred million dollars per year.

Before concluding this section, I must again emphasize the fact that tax exporting through federal deductibility is only one consideration in the design of Michigan tax policy. Even if state and local income taxes were not deductible, I would still make the case for greater progressivity in the Michigan income tax, because of my concern about the widening gap between rich and poor.

Business Taxes

Over the years, there has been a great deal of discussion in Michigan of the effects of business taxes on the location of economic activity. It is widely asserted that the Single Business Tax (SBT) and its successor, the Michigan Business Tax (MBT) have been a deterrent to keeping businesses in Michigan.

Shortly, we will discuss the SBT and MBT in more detail. For the moment, however, it makes sense to think about whether the effects of business taxes are large or small.

The Effects of Business Taxes on the Location of Businesses

There is substantial literature on the effects of taxes on business location. Michigan residents Timothy Bartik of the Upjohn Institute and Leslie Papke of Michigan State University are major contributors to that literature. It is not easy to determine the effects of taxes on business location because it is necessary to factor in a wide variety of other influences. There is a lot of variation in the results that emerge from the studies. Some studies find that taxes do not have any effect. However, the consensus is probably that business taxes do have a modest effect, *all else equal*. In a recent paper, Bartik suggests that "a 10 percent decrease in overall state and local business taxes, *holding public services and other location factors constant*, increases the long-term level of economic activity in a state . . . by about 2 percent" (emphasis mine).[43]

Two things need to be said regarding this result about the effect of business taxes on the locations of businesses. First, this is a not a huge effect. It is large enough that we need to take it into consideration, but it isn't enormous. The effect is relatively small because taxes are only one of many things that go into businesses' decision about where to locate. Sometimes the advocates of lower business taxes make it sound as if business taxes are the only thing that matters, but that is simply not true. The number-one requirement for any successful business is to have the skilled workers who can do the work that needs to be done.

Second, when we say that business taxes have an effect, we are making an *all-else-equal* statement. Lower business taxes lead to a somewhat higher level of economic activity, *if* everything else (including the level of public services) remains the same. However, if business taxes in Michigan were reduced, not everything else would remain the same: other taxes would have to be increased or public services would have to be reduced. In recent years, the trend in Michigan has been toward cutting taxes, thus reducing the spending on public schools, higher education, transportation infrastructure, and just about everything else. But in Chapters 2 and 3 of this book, we emphasized the key role of education and roads in economic development. If the

MBT were eliminated and the resulting loss in tax revenue were to lead to further reductions in investments in Michigan's future, the state's long-term economic prospects would actually be harmed.

A concise summary of these ideas appears in a paper by Michigan State University's Leslie Papke and two of her coauthors:

> The economic effect of taxes tends both to be small and to be less important than other factors. Labor force availability and quality, for example, appear to be more important for explaining differences across locations in economic activity. How tax revenues are spent tends to be important enough that high relative taxes may not be a deterrent to economic growth if the revenues are used to finance services of value to business, such as education and transportation infrastructure. The studies do make clear that a policy of cutting taxes to induce economic growth is not likely to be efficient or cost-effective.[44]

Why Tax Businesses?

We have just seen that the economic effects of business taxes are probably not huge. However, it does not necessarily follow that taxes on business income are a sensible policy.[45] My next step is to examine why we have business taxes at all and whether business taxes are a good idea.

Some people suggest that Michigan "must" have a business tax. I disagree. There simply is not any rule that a state "has to" have some sort of business tax. Some of the political support for business taxes is based on the misguided impression that businesses are somehow separate from the rest of the economy and that businesses should pay their "fair share" of taxes. But businesses are an integral part of the economy—in a sense, they are *us*. Therefore, it is really not meaningful to speak of "business's share" of taxes. Ultimately, business taxes are borne by people, in the form of lower wages for workers, higher prices for consumers, or lower returns on investment for the owners of capital.

Based on my experience, some folks who believe that Michigan "must" have a business tax think that business taxes are borne by rich investors, and that these taxes are therefore progressive. It is certainly possible that a *portion* of business taxes is borne by rich investors. However, it is important to remember that many investors are not rich by any stretch of the imagination. Moreover, there are many ways in which business taxes can be "shifted," so that they are ultimately paid by someone who is not a business owner or an investor. In some cases, it may be possible for businesses to pass taxes on to consumers in the form of higher prices. In other cases, taxes may ultimately be paid by workers in terms of lower wages. In fact, economists believe that a large part of a tax like the MBT may ultimately be borne by workers.[46]

It appears that the public believes that business taxes are *not* ultimately paid by investors. In the late spring and early summer of 2008, MSU's State of the State Survey interviewed 1,008 Michigan adults and asked respondents about who bears the burden of business taxes.[47] Some 43.5 percent said they believe the tax is passed on to consumers, while 15.3 percent said the tax is borne by workers. Only 4.6 percent said the tax is borne by investors, and 36.5 percent said that business taxes are shared about equally by consumers, workers, and investors.

My overall conclusion is that the case for having a separate tax on business income is not very strong.

The Strange History of Business Taxation in Michigan

Now that we have discussed business taxes in general, the next step is to consider the MBT in more specific detail. I will begin by recapping some of the convoluted history of business taxation in Michigan. Michigan had a corporate income tax from 1968 to 1975. During those years, the state experienced huge fluctuations in corporate tax-revenue collections. Tax revenues from the Michigan corporate tax fell by about 40 percent between 1969 and 1971. Then corporate tax revenues doubled between 1971 and 1973 as the economy recovered from the recession of the early 1970s. But another recession came, and revenues fell by more than 40 percent between 1973 and 1975. Thus the corporate tax sent Michigan's fiscal system on a nauseating roller-coaster ride. This is not surprising, since corporate profits have bigger ups and downs than other types of income.

Large revenue fluctuations can create major problems for planning and delivering public services. One reason for the switch to the SBT in 1975 was a desire to get off the revenue roller coaster. In this regard, the SBT was a huge success. But the legislature could not resist the temptation to tinker with the SBT. Over the years, the SBT became riddled with more credits and special accounting rules, which in turn made it more complicated and less efficient.[48]

One problem with the SBT was that it was unique to Michigan; no other state imposed an SBT. Thus it is possible that the costs of complying with the tax may have kept some businesses away from Michigan. However, the compliance costs of the SBT were probably no greater than the compliance costs of the corporate taxes in most other states. But sometimes perception *is* reality. If businesses *believed* that the cost of complying with the SBT was high, they may have avoided doing business in Michigan even if the *actual* compliance costs were not unusually high. In fact, *many* of the problems of the SBT had more to do with false perceptions than realities. For example, one would often hear the objection that the SBT placed a heavy burden on small businesses. It was often erroneously called the "small business tax." In fact, however, the SBT contained a very generous exemption for small businesses, so that the overwhelming majority of SBT revenues were paid by large enterprises.[49]

Although the SBT was never as bad as its detractors said it was, it was eliminated in 2007. After much legislative wrangling, it was replaced by the MBT. In my judgment, the MBT is worse than the SBT. The Michigan Legislature managed to remove a so-so tax and replace it with a worse tax.

The Michigan Business Tax

The MBT has four main parts:

- *A business income tax.* This tax is based on federal taxable income, although it is subject to various adjustments. In the case of the business income tax, the MBT uses a "net" income concept. Roughly speaking, a business calculates its income by subtracting its expenses from its sales revenues. Expenses include things like the wages paid to workers, plus payments for electricity, materials, machinery, equipment, and so on.
- *A modified gross receipts tax.* A company's "gross receipts" are its sales revenues. Thus a gross receipts tax does not allow companies to take full deductions for all of their expenses. A pure gross receipts tax would not allow any deductions. Under a pure gross receipts tax, the farmer is taxed on the full value of the wheat, the miller is taxed on the full value of the flour, the baker is taxed on the full value of the bread sold to the grocery store, and the grocery store is taxed on the full value of the bread sold to its customers. This leads to "pyramiding" or "cascading," with taxes piled

atop taxes. A pure gross receipts tax is a disaster in terms of economic efficiency. It leads to an arbitrary and capricious pattern of effective tax rates, based on the number of times that intermediate goods are sold during the production process. When the MBT was being put together in 2007, legislators recognized that a pure gross receipts tax would be an extraordinarily bad idea. Thus the MBT offers deductions for some expenses such as inventory and capital expenditures. That's what makes it a "modified" gross receipts tax instead of a pure gross receipts tax. Without these deductions, the already-flawed MBT would be an absolute catastrophe from the perspective of economic efficiency. With these deductions, the MBT is merely really bad.[50]

- A *tax on insurance company premiums.* Insurance companies are not subject to the business income tax or the modified gross receipts tax.
- A *tax on the net capital stock of financial institutions.* Like insurance companies, financial institutions are not subject to the business income tax or the modified gross receipts tax.

After companies have calculated their basic MBT tax liability, they are then subject to a surcharge of 21.99 percent. But that is not the end of the story. The MBT also offers dozens of tax credits. Some of these apply to specific businesses, such as the Palace of Auburn Hills and Michigan International Speedway.

Business Tax Credits

One tax credit that has received a lot of attention is the film credit, which provides an incentive to make movies in Michigan. (The Clint Eastwood film *Gran Torino* is an example.) This section focuses specifically on my opinion of the film tax credit, although much of what I will say here is applicable to a wide variety of tax breaks.

The most important thing to remember is this: if we grant a special tax break to one business, then we must either increase taxes somewhere else in the economy or reduce expenditure on public services. That is why most economists are skeptical of tax policies that treat different sectors of the economy in different ways. These policies tend to be economically inefficient. Many business tax credits are inefficient and unfair (just like sales taxes that apply to most goods but few services).[51]

It is possible that the film tax credits aren't the worst tax credits given out by the State of Michigan. After all, many of the folks involved in the motion picture industry are talented and creative, and they use sophisticated technology. But just because other tax credits may be even worse than the film tax credits, it would be wrong to conclude that the film tax credits are a good idea.

The film tax credits have indeed convinced some movie projects to come to Michigan. (*Of course* we can get some film crews to come here, since the tax credit covers more than 40 percent of their operating expenses!) The real question is whether this makes economic sense. For example, if taxpayers were to provide enough of a subsidy, we could have a citrus-fruit industry in Michigan. Growers could build huge greenhouses in the Upper Peninsula, and they could use the tax credits to pay for the vast quantities of natural gas that would have to be burned to keep the greenhouses warm in the Michigan winter. With enough of a taxpayer-financed subsidy, we could grow oranges and grapefruit in Michigan. We *could* do it, but that doesn't mean we *should*.

I am not trying to say that every single tax credit is a bad idea. But most economists would agree that it is usually better to have a level playing field where all industries play by the same rules. One big problem is that until recently tax incentives have not been subjected to any systematic oversight or analysis. Fortunately, the Anderson Economic Group (AEG) has recently produced two careful studies of tax incentives in Michigan.[52] These studies show that business tax incentives have been used in a very haphazard manner in Michigan. The AEG studies suggest that there is very wide variation in the effectiveness of these programs. They find that some tax incentives (including the Industrial Property Tax Abatement) may be effective. However, many of the tax incentives are either ineffective, or they have small and mixed effects.

In my view, the system of business tax incentives in Michigan should be overhauled. We need a system of oversight and accountability. The business tax incentives need to have a "sunset" provision: If some of the programs can be shown to be effective, they can be renewed. Ineffective programs should be allowed to expire.

What Should We Do About the Michigan Business Tax?

Some have suggested that we eliminate the MBT surcharge and reduce other parts of the MBT. These proposals are a step in the right direction, *as long as we replace the revenues.* If we were to reduce the MBT and *not* replace the lost revenues, an extra shortfall would be added to the budget of the State of Michigan at a time when the state is already experiencing severe budget crises. Reducing the MBT without replacing the revenues would be fiscally irresponsible in the extreme. In fact, *as long as we replace the revenues,* I believe we should go even further than simply reducing the MBT. I believe the best option is to eliminate the MBT entirely. The MBT is an inefficient mess; if it were removed, it would be a strong signal of Michigan's desire for a more favorable business climate. No other tax-policy initiative has as much potential to improve Michigan's reputation as a haven for capital investment. Eliminating the MBT would not solve all of our problems, but it would be a step in the right direction. Once again, however, I want to emphasize that if the MBT is eliminated, *it is crucially important to replace the revenues.* If the legislature is unwilling to replace the revenues, then (regrettably) the MBT should be kept in place.

One advantage of completely eliminating the MBT is that it would take us a long way toward a level playing field in the taxation of business income. If there is no business income tax, then every business would pay the same amount of business income tax—none at all.

In the last few sections, I have written in favor of a graduated income tax, and I have also advocated the elimination of the MBT. The idea of a graduated income tax is more palatable to my "liberal" friends than to my "conservative" friends. Conversely, the idea of eliminating the MBT is easier to swallow for my conservative friends than for my liberal friends. In my view, sound policy does not necessarily always fit with one particular ideology.

The "Fair" Tax

In current policy discussions in Michigan, one sometimes hears the idea that we should increase the sales tax to replace not only the MBT but also the income tax and personal property tax. This is sometimes referred to as the "Fair" Tax.[53] One part of this proposal is consistent with the policy recommendations that I have put forth in this chapter: it would greatly broaden the base of the sales tax. However, one of the most important effects of the Fair Tax would be to shift even more taxes away from those with the highest incomes. If high-income folks end up paying less, then people who are lower on the income scale will have to pay more, or else we will have less money for schools, roads, Medicaid, and other public services. That is the main reason I am against the Fair Tax.[54]

Property Taxes

Prior to the enactment of Proposal A in 1994, property taxes in Michigan were based on "state equalized value" (SEV), which is equal to one-half of the assessed value of the property. Proposal A instituted the requirement that the taxable value of a property cannot increase in any one year by more than 5 percent or the rate of inflation (whichever is less). Thus even when the *true* value of a property increases by 8 percent in a year, the *taxable* value cannot increase by more than 5 percent, and the taxable value may increase by only a few percent when the overall rate of inflation is low. (Indeed, the inflation rate has been less than 5 percent per year throughout the entire period since the enactment of Proposal A.) However, when a property is sold, the taxable value reverts to the SEV, and the limitation on the increase of taxable value begins from a new baseline.

This "cap" on taxable value is associated with three important problems. First, the cap reduces the revenue-raising capacity of the property tax at a time when governments in Michigan are subject to chronic fiscal crises. The revenue losses are smaller than they used to be because of the recent decreases in property values. Still, the Michigan Treasury Department's latest "Executive Budget Appendix on Tax Credits, Deductions, and Exemptions" estimates that the revenue loss is $3.4 billion per year.[55]

The second problem with the taxable value cap is an issue of fairness. The cap means that two properties can have very different property-tax liabilities even if they have exactly the same true market value. It is easy to understand the political appeal of a provision like this: longtime residents tend to have more political power than those who have recently moved into a community. But the policy is still unfair.[56]

The third problem with the cap on taxable value has to do with economic efficiency. Because of the cap, the effective tax rate on some properties is lower than the effective tax rate on others. It would be more efficient to tax all properties at the same effective rate.

On the basis of these considerations, my conclusion is that the cap on property-tax assessments should be removed. However, this does not necessarily mean that total property-tax revenues must be increased. Michigan needs more tax revenues, but the additional revenues could come from a variety of sources other than the property tax. If it is desired to keep total property-tax payments relatively unchanged, we could couple the removal of the assessment cap with a reduction of overall property-tax millage rates. However, in these days of structural budget deficits, we should resist the temptation to enact any major *reductions* in property-tax revenues.

The Headlee Amendment and the Taxable Value Cap

In this chapter, we have devoted a great deal of discussion to Proposal A. However, Proposal A was not the first landmark change in property taxation in Michigan in the last few decades. The first was the Headlee Amendment of 1978. Whereas the assessment cap in Proposal A limits the taxes on *individual properties*, the Headlee Amendment limits the amount of property-tax revenue that can be raised by *jurisdictions*. If the total assessed value of property in a unit of local government increases faster than the consumer price index, there can be an automatic reduction in the property-tax millage rate. This type of tax-rate reduction is known as a "Headlee rollback."[57]

A large number of Headlee rollbacks occurred after the passage of the Headlee Amendment in 1978. However, the number of Headlee rollbacks decreased sharply after the passage of Proposal A in 1994. Both the Headlee Amendment and Proposal A involve limitations on property taxes; Proposal A made the Headlee limitations largely irrelevant. This is somewhat unfortunate. The Headlee Amendment provided a mechanism for limiting property-tax rates in a uniform manner across all properties in a jurisdiction. Proposal A effectively instituted a new system for limiting effective property-tax rates, but the Proposal A mechanism did not treat all properties in a jurisdiction uniformly. Instead, under Proposal A the taxable value cap reduced effective tax rates for existing homeowners, but not for new homebuyers.

Summary and Conclusion

In this chapter, I have described the tax systems of state and local governments in Michigan. In several respects, these tax systems are very much like their counterparts in most other states. As in most states, the revenue system is dominated by property taxes, individual income taxes, and general retail sales taxes. In some other respects, however, Michigan's tax system is unusual. When compared with the national average, the *state* government in Michigan collects a higher fraction of the total revenues, while the *local* governments collect less. Another unusual feature is that Michigan's income tax applies a single flat tax rate to all taxable income, instead of using a system of graduated marginal tax rates. Also, the Michigan Business Tax is unique among the fifty states.

The level of taxation in Michigan has fallen over the last few decades, and the decreases have been especially rapid in the last ten years. In the 1970s and 1980s, the percentage of personal income paid in state and local taxes was slightly higher in Michigan than the national average. However, in recent years, state and local tax revenues in Michigan have been below the national average (even though the national average had dropped substantially since the 1970s). Some of these reductions in tax revenues have been the result of explicit policy changes. However, most of the tax-revenue reductions have resulted from structural weaknesses in the tax system. For example, the sales tax does not apply to most services and entertainments. Over the years, services and entertainments have accounted for a steadily increasing fraction of the economy, which means that the revenue losses from nontaxation of services have continued to increase.

Michigan's tax system is regressive over most of the range of incomes, which means that a relatively large share of taxes in Michigan is borne by low-income residents. In recent years, however, the regressivity of the Michigan tax system was reduced by the Earned Income Tax Credit.

Michigan has increased its reliance on the sales tax, even though sales taxes are not deductible from the federal individual income tax. On the other hand, Michigan has reduced the rates of its income and property taxes, even though these taxes are deductible. This means that Michigan has reduced the extent to which it "exports" its taxes to the residents of other states. In fact, taxpayers in Michigan pay hundreds of millions of extra federal taxes every year as a result of the shift from deductible taxes to nondeductible taxes.

The Crucial Need to Reverse the Decline in Revenues

Any change in tax policy will face major political obstacles. Nevertheless, it is imperative to think anew about taxes in Michigan. The current tax system has serious structural problems, which we ignore at our peril. If nothing is done to address these problems, the Michigan tax system will become more inefficient, and it will become increasingly unable to finance an appropriate level of public services. Thus based on the analysis in this chapter, I have identified a number of tax-policy changes that I believe deserve serious consideration. The first and foremost need is to reverse the huge decline of tax revenues in Michigan.

When you're in a hole, stop digging. In view of the tremendous reductions in tax revenues that have occurred in the last decade, governments in Michigan should not enact any further explicit tax cuts unless replacement revenues are clearly identified. Currently, the Michigan income tax is levied at a flat rate of 4.35 percent, but the rate is scheduled to decrease in the near future. Unless the law is changed, the rate will drop by one-tenth of a percentage point in 2011, another one-tenth of a percentage point in 2012, another in 2013, another in 2014, and another one-twentieth of a percentage point in 2015. If these changes are allowed to happen, they would cut the income tax rate to 3.9 percent. By 2015, the cumulative revenue losses from that series of tax cuts would amount to more than $3 billion. It would be grossly irresponsible to allow these tax cuts to take effect. They should be repealed.

In addition to avoiding explicit tax cuts, we should also take steps to deal with the structural deficiencies that reduce revenues day after day. It makes the most sense to do this in ways that also help to achieve other objectives for the tax system, such as economic efficiency and fairness. The following proposals would raise revenue while also improving the tax system in other ways:

- *Taxing services and entertainments.* The general retail sales tax in Michigan applies to a few services and entertainments, but most of the service economy is untaxed, even though services have been steadily increasing in relative importance for decades. If more services and entertainments are taxed, the revenue-raising capability of the tax system will be reinforced. In addition, more complete taxation of services and entertainments will make the sales tax more efficient and more equitable.
- *Introducing a graduated income tax.* Michigan is one of only a few states that have an income tax with only a single tax rate. Of the forty-three states with an income tax, thirty-six have a system of graduated marginal tax rates with higher rates on those with higher incomes. A graduated income tax would raise additional revenue, and it would also provide some help for low- and middle-income residents of Michigan, who have fared so

much worse than affluent residents. Moreover, some of these additional income taxes would actually be borne by the residents of other states as a result of the deductibility of state and local income taxes in the federal income tax. If it proves politically impossible to introduce graduated marginal tax rates in Michigan, we can still take a step in the right direction by increasing the single tax rate in the income tax.

- *Reducing income-tax privileges for the elderly.* The income tax in Michigan provides extraordinary tax breaks for elderly residents. As a result, very few senior citizens in Michigan pay any income tax. On net, Michigan seniors actually pay *negative* amounts of income tax, and receive refunds. The revenue losses associated with these tax breaks are expected to grow substantially as the baby-boom generation enters retirement. If the taxation of senior citizens were brought more into line with the taxation of the rest of the population, it would help to preserve the integrity of the tax system.

- *Reinstating the estate tax.* Until a few years ago, Michigan collected estate tax from the estates of wealthy individuals. When federal laws were changed in 2001, Michigan did not make the corresponding changes that would have allowed it to continue collecting estate taxes. As a result, Michigan no longer collects estate taxes, but it would be easy to reinstate an estate tax in Michigan.

- *Changing the taxation of beer, wine, and tobacco products.* Currently, these taxes are levied on a *per-unit* basis. When taxes operate in this manner, their revenue-raising capacity is eroded over time by inflation. The unit taxes on beer and wine in Michigan have remained the same for decades, even though inflation has pushed prices dramatically higher. Therefore the effective tax rates on beer and wine have decreased greatly. If these tax rates were raised and then converted to a percentage basis, it would help to increase the state's revenue, and it would also help to discourage irresponsible drinking. I also think it would also be a good idea to convert the taxes on tobacco products to a percentage basis.

- *Changing the taxes on motor fuels.* A strong case can be made for raising the taxes on both gasoline and diesel fuel, with a larger increase in the diesel tax. Michigan is unusual in that the tax on diesel fuel is lower than the gasoline tax. An increase in the tax rate on diesel fuel would raise additional revenue, and it would eliminate the inequitable treatment of drivers of different vehicle types. If the tax rates on gasoline, diesel, and other fossil fuels are raised substantially because of environmental concerns, then these increases could be combined with reductions in other taxes.

• *Removing the "assessment cap" in the property tax.* Since the passage of Proposal A, the *taxable* value of any individual property cannot increase in one year by more than the overall rate of inflation or 5 percent (whichever is less), even if the *market* value of the property increases by more. However, properties are reassessed at full value when sold. As a result, two adjacent properties can have very different property-tax bills, even if they have the exact same market value. If the assessment cap were removed, this inequity would be removed along with it, and additional revenue could be raised. The elimination of the cap could be phased in gradually, and it could be accompanied by an overall reduction in property-tax rates. However, such a rate reduction should not be too large, or it would merely exacerbate Michigan's budgetary problems.

Finally, policy makers in Michigan must decide what to do with the Michigan Business Tax. In my judgment, the best policy would be to eliminate the MBT entirely. However, if the MBT is to be eliminated, it must be replaced with *something.* (The best sources of revenues to replace the Michigan Business Tax are the individual income tax and the general retail sales tax. However, I hope this discussion has shown that we can draw from a wide variety of choices.) To eliminate the MBT and *not* replace it would be astonishingly fiscally irresponsible. If the legislature is unwilling to replace the lost revenues, then the MBT must be kept in place.

NOTES

1. See Charles L. Ballard, Paul N. Courant, Douglas C. Drake, Ronald C. Fisher, and Elisabeth R. Gerber, eds., *Michigan at the Millennium: A Benchmark and Analysis of Its Fiscal and Economic Structure* (East Lansing, MI: Michigan State University Press, 2003). Taxes take center stage in several of the chapters in *Michigan at the Millennium*. I wrote an overview of the state and local revenue system in Michigan (see "An Overview of Michigan's Revenue System"). Joel Slemrod of the University of Michigan wrote a chapter on the sales tax (see "Michigan's Sales and Use Taxes: Portrait and Analysis"). Paul Menchik of Michigan State University wrote a chapter about the income tax (see "Michigan's Personal Income Tax"). A chapter

on property taxes entitled "The Property Tax in Michigan," was written by Naomi Feldman (formerly of the University of Michigan, now with Ben-Gurion University of the Negev), Paul Courant of the University of Michigan, and Douglas Drake (formerly of Wayne State University, now with Public Policy Associates). James R. Hines Jr., of the University of Michigan wrote a chapter on business taxes (see "Michigan's Flirtation with the Single Business Tax"). Lawrence Martin of Michigan State University wrote a chapter on the lottery tax, taxes on alcohol and tobacco, and other revenue sources (see "Miscellaneous Taxes in Michigan: Sin, Death, and Recreation"). Susan Fino of Wayne State University wrote about the Headlee Amendment in her chapter, entitled "Tax Limitation in the Michigan Constitution: The Headlee Amendment." Kenneth Boyer of Michigan State University wrote on motor fuel taxes (see "Michigan's Transportation System and Transportation Policy"). All of these chapters are highly recommended for any reader who wants to study the Michigan tax system in greater detail.

2. The states with no income tax are Alaska, Florida, Nevada, South Dakota, Texas, Washington, and Wyoming.

3. Delaware, Montana, New Hampshire, and Oregon have no retail sales taxes.

4. See the U.S. Census Bureau, "State and Local Government Finances," http://www.census .gov/govs/estimate.

5. Data for the state governments are more readily available since there are only fifty state governments. However, to provide good quality data for local governments, the Census Bureau must acquire information from thousands of counties, cities, townships, school districts, and special districts. This takes time.

6. The Single Business Tax received its name because it replaced seven smaller business taxes. In addition to Michigan, the states without a corporate income tax are Nevada, Texas, Washington, and Wyoming. (Texas has the Franchise Tax, which is somewhat similar to a corporate income tax.)

7. As of January 1, 2010, the highest cigarette tax rate in the country was $3.46 per pack in Rhode Island. The tax rate was $3 per pack in Connecticut and $2.75 in New York. Michigan was one of five states with a tax rate of $2 per pack, which puts Michigan in a tie for the eleventh highest cigarette tax rate. The lowest rates were 36 cents per pack in Louisiana, 17 cents per pack in Missouri, and 7 cents per pack in South Carolina. See the Federation of Tax Administrators, "State Excise Tax Rates on Cigarettes," http://www.taxadmin.org/fta/ rate/cigarette.pdf.

8. In 1992, about 3.7 percent of the property taxes in Michigan were collected by the state government. By 2007, state property taxes accounted for about 16 percent of the property taxes collected in Michigan.

9. In addition to Michigan, the other states with a flat-rate income tax are Colorado, Illinois, Indiana, Massachusetts, Pennsylvania, and Utah. For details on the income-tax rates in the various states, see the Federation of Tax Administrators, "State Individual Income Rates," http://www.taxadmin.org/fta/rate/ind_inc.pdf.

10. The personal exemptions in the individual income tax also have an effect on the distribution of the tax burden among people of different income classes. As of January 1, 2007, some thirty-five states used a personal exemption. The personal exemption for a married couple was larger in Michigan than in twenty three of these states, smaller than in two of these states, and the same as in nine of these states. Eight states used a credit in lieu of a personal exemption. See Rob Reinhardt, "Informational Paper 4: Individual Income Tax Provisions in the States," Wisconsin Legislative Fiscal Bureau, http://www.legis.state.wi.us/lfb/Informationalpapers/4_individual%20income%20tax%20provisions%20in%20the%20states.pdf. The effects of the personal exemptions are discussed in greater detail, later in this chapter.

11. For annual data from 1992 onward, see the U.S. Census Bureau, "State and Local Government Finance," http://www.census.gov/govs/estimate. For 1972, 1977, 1982, and 1987, the data are taken from the Census of Governments, vol. 4, no. 5, "Compendium of Government Finances," Washington, D.C.: United States Government Printing Office. In constructing Figure 6.1, the years between 1972 and 1977, 1977 and 1982, 1982 and 1987, and 1987 and 1992 were interpolated. For more on calculations of this type, see my report "Michigan's Tax Climate: A Closer Look," prepared for the Michigan Chamber Foundation, April 2004. This report is available on request.

12. The exact amount by which School Aid Fund revenues have fallen depends on the price index that is used to adjust for inflation. If we use the overall rate of inflation, the decrease is about 13 percent from 2003 to 2009. If we use the Commerce Department's price deflator for state and local government expenditures, the inflation-adjusted decrease is about 20 percent over that same period. This is because a large portion of the money spent by local governments is spent on things with relatively high rates of price increase, such as health care. For the U.S. Commerce Department's price indexes, see the Bureau of Economic Analysis, "Table 1.1.4. Price Indexes for Gross Domestic Product," http://www.bea.gov/national/nipaweb/SelectTable.asp?Selected=N.) Regardless of which price index is used, further reductions are expected.

13. Figure 6.2 adjusts for inflation on the basis of the deflator for state and local government expenditures, provided by the Bureau of Economic Analysis of the U.S. Department of Commerce. See "Table 1.1.4, Price Indexes for Gross Domestic Product," http://www.bea.gov/national/nipaweb/SelectTable.asp?Selected=N .

14. Department of Technology, Management, and Budget, "Executive Budget: Fiscal Year 2011," State of Michigan, http://www.michigan.gov/documents/budget/2_310743_7.pdf.

15. Charles L. Ballard, "An Overview of Michigan's Revenue System," in *Michigan at the Millennium*.

16. "Michigan's Defining Moment: Report of the Emergency Financial Advisory Panel," February 2, 2007, http://www.michigan.gov/documents/gov/Emergency_Financial_Advisory _Panel_Report_185781_7.pdf.

17. Some anti-tax enthusiasts are fond of suggesting that reductions in tax rates will pay for themselves. (A leading proponent of this idea is Arthur B. Laffer, who illustrated it with his "Laffer Curve.") The idea is that a reduction in tax rates will lead to an enormous burst of economic activity. As a result, even though the tax *rate* has fallen, the tax *base* would increase by so much that tax *revenues* would actually increase. In reality, these "perverse revenue effects" are rare because the increase in economic activity is usually not even close to being large enough to lead to an increase in tax revenues. It is absolutely certain that the reductions of tax rates in Michigan led to reductions in tax revenues.

18. Federation of Tax Administrators, "Sales Taxation of Services: Updates," http://www.tax admin.org/fta/pub/services/services.html[0].

19. See the Department of Treasury, "Executive Budget Appendix on Tax Credits, Deductions, and Exemptions: Fiscal Year 2010," State of Michigan, http://www.michigan.gov/docu-ments/treasury/ExecBudgAppenTaxCreditsDedExemptsFY10_302899_7.pdf. These tax breaks are sometimes called "tax expenditures." A tax expenditure is the number of dollars by which potential tax revenues are decreased as a result of some provision of the tax code. The phrase "tax expenditure" highlights the fact that a tax reduction has the same effect on the budget deficit as an explicit government expenditure.

20. Several of the services that *are* taxed in Michigan are business services. Thus Michigan's sales tax manages to tax some things that should not be taxed, while failing to tax a very large number of items that could be taxed in a way that would enhance the efficiency of the tax system.

21. See the Department of Treasury, "Michigan's Sales and Use Taxes: 2008," http://www .michigan.gov/documents/treasury/Sales__Use_Tax_Report_December_2009 _305451_7.pdf. For economic analysis of the effects of not taxing Internet sales, see my paper (coauthored with Jaimin Lee), "Internet Purchases, Cross-Border Shopping, and Sales Taxes," *National Tax Journal* 60 (2007): 711–25.

22. See Paul Menchik, "Michigan's Personal Income Tax" in *Michigan at the Millennium*. As pointed out in his chapter, the inflation-adjusted value of the personal exemption is now only about half as large as it was when the Michigan income tax was established in the late 1960s.

23. The tax on cigarettes in Michigan was three cents per pack in 1947. It was raised on several occasions, reaching twenty-five cents per pack in 1987. It was subsequently raised from seventy-five cents per pack to $1.25 per pack in 2002 and then to $2.00 per pack in 2004.

24. This calculation is based on the Implicit Price Deflator for Personal Consumption Expenditures. See the U.S. Department of Commerce Bureau of Economic Analysis, "Table 1.1.4. Price Indexes for Gross Domestic Product," http://www.bea.gov/national/nipaweb/Select Table.asp?Selected=N. If we use the Consumer Price Index, the increase of the price level from 1966 to 2009 is even steeper, at more than 560 percent. For technical reasons, I prefer to use the Personal Consumption Expenditures deflator. However, either of these inflation measures makes it clear that the price level has risen a great deal in the last forty-plus years. Thus if we adjust for inflation, the beer tax is only a shadow of its former self.

25. Of course, taxes on alcoholic beverages are not a very precise method of discouraging excessive drinking, since the tax on the casual drinker is levied at the same rate as the tax on the binge drinker. It is important to enforce drunk-driving laws, regardless of the tax rate on alcoholic beverages. There is evidence that the optimal fine for a drunk-driving arrest should be very high. See Steven Levitt and Jack Porter, "How Dangerous are Drinking Drivers?" *Journal of Political Economy* 109 (2001): 1198–1237.

26. Federation of Tax Administrators, "State Motor Fuel Tax Rates," http://www.taxadmin.org/fta/rate/mf.pdf.

27. Under a "cap and trade" system, there would be a "cap" on the total amount of emissions. The cap would be operated through a system of licenses. In order to emit a ton of carbon, a company would need a permit. The "trade" part of the term comes from the fact that the permits could be traded among companies. Thus, if a company's technology allows it to clean up cheaply, it would want to sell its permits, while a company with a more expensive pollution-abatement technology would need to buy permits. This system would be efficient, in that it would minimize the total cost of pollution abatement. It would also give companies a financial incentive to find new pollution-abatement technologies. If a company can find a cheaper way to clean up, it will not need to buy as many pollution permits. This type of system was part of the Clean Air Act Amendments of 1990, and it has done a very good job of reducing sulfur dioxide emissions.

28. I have written two research papers on environmentally motivated taxes. See Charles Ballard and Steven Medema, "The Marginal Efficiency Effects of Taxes and Subsidies in the Presence of Externalities: A Computational General Equilibrium Approach," *Journal of Public Economics* 52 (1993): 199–216; and Charles L. Ballard, John H. Goddeeris, and Sang-Kyum Kim, "Non-Homothetic Preferences and the Non-Environmental Effects of Environmental Taxes," *International Tax and Public Finance* 12 (2005): 115–30.

29. See Lawrence Martin, "Miscellaneous Taxes in Michigan: Sin, Death, and Recreation" in *Michigan at the Millennium* for an extensive discussion of the effects of the cigarette tax on the distribution of income. The economist Jonathan Gruber has advanced a novel argument suggesting that the cigarette tax is not regressive, but his perspective is still controversial. In this discussion, I will maintain the traditional view that cigarette taxes are regressive.

30. Lawrence W. Martin, "Miscellaneous Taxes in Michigan: Sin, Death, and Recreation," in *Michigan at the Millennium.*

31. Charles Clotfelter and Philip Cook provide an overview of the economic issues associated with lotteries in "On the Economics of State Lotteries," *Journal of Economic Perspectives* 4 (1990): 105–19.

32. Carl Davis, Kelly Davis, Matthew Gardner, Robert McIntyre, Jeff McLynch, and Alla Sapozhnikova, "Who Pays? A Distributional Analysis of the Tax Systems in All Fifty States," 3rd ed. (Washington, DC: Institute on Taxation and Economic Policy, 2009). The report is available at http://www.itepnet.org/whopays3.pdf.

33. Robert S. McIntyre, Robert Denk, Norton Francis, Matthew Gardner, Will Gomaa, Fiona Hsu, and Richard Sims, "Who Pays? A Distributional Analysis of Tax Systems in All Fifty States," 2nd ed. (Washington, D.C.: Institute on Taxation and Economic Policy, 2003). The report is available at http://www.itepnet.org/pdf/wp2003.pdf.

34. Roughly speaking, the idea is that if everyone had the same income, there would be no reason to use the income tax to achieve greater income equality. Using the income tax to achieve greater equality is more applicable when there is a lot of inequality. Much of the economics profession's thinking about redistributive taxation was developed in the 1970s. For example, see Nicholas Stern, "On the Specification of Models of Optimum Income Taxation," *Journal of Public Economics* 6 (1976): 123–62.

35. Here are the states in which the top income-tax rate is higher than the rate in Michigan: Alabama, Arizona, Arkansas, California, Colorado, Connecticut, Delaware, Georgia, Hawaii, Idaho, Iowa, Kansas, Kentucky, Louisiana, Maine, Maryland, Massachusetts, Minnesota, Mississippi, Missouri, Montana, Nebraska, New Hampshire, New Jersey, New Mexico, New York, North Carolina, North Dakota, Ohio, Oklahoma, Oregon, Rhode Island, South Carolina, Tennessee, Utah, Vermont, Virginia, West Virginia, and Wisconsin.

36. For the details of the MLHS proposal for a graduated income tax, see the Michigan League for Human Services, "Income Tax: It's Time for the Flat Tax to Go," http://www.milhs.org/Media/EDocs/GraduatedIncomeTaxWEB.doc.

37. This survey result is from Round 47 of the State of the State Survey. The codebook, methodological report, and data set for the survey are available at http://ippsr.msu.edu/SOSS/SOSSdata.htm.

38. James R. Hines Jr., Joel Slemrod, and William Gale, eds., *Rethinking Estate and Gift Taxation* (Washington, DC: The Brookings Institution, 2001).

39. For a good discussion of the prospects for an estate tax in Michigan, see the Michigan League for Human Services, "Estate Taxes: Michigan Stands to Gain Revenue," http://www.milhs.org/Media/EDocs/FederalEstateTaxFM.pdf.

40. Earlier in this chapter, we discussed the effect of the Michigan income tax on the distribution of income. The income tax is somewhat progressive at low incomes because of the personal exemptions. For middle incomes, the tax is approximately proportional because it has only a single flat rate. However, because of deductibility, the net effect of the Michigan income tax is actually somewhat regressive at high incomes. For example, consider a married couple with $70,000 of federal taxable income in 2009. This family would have been in the 25 percent federal tax bracket. When the couple paid a dollar of Michigan income tax, they would save twenty-five cents of federal tax, so their net payment would be seventy-five cents. On the other hand, a couple with $400,000 of federal taxable would have been in the 35 percent federal bracket. When this couple paid a dollar of Michigan income tax, their net payment would be only 65 cents.

One other complication should also be noted. The federal income tax includes an Alternative Minimum Tax (AMT). When it was instituted in 1969, the AMT was targeted at a very small number of taxpayers with very high incomes, who had taken advantage of special provisions of the tax code to avoid paying any federal income tax. The AMT is not adjusted for inflation, and the AMT rules have not been adjusted to keep pace with other tax-policy changes. Hence, unless the law is changed, the number of taxpayers affected by the AMT will skyrocket in the next few years. The AMT is relevant to tax exporting because AMT liability can be triggered by deductions for state and local taxes. If the deductions cause "too much" of a reduction in a taxpayer's regular federal income-tax liability, the taxpayer may have to pay AMT. Thus one effect of the AMT is to create a backdoor method of reducing the deduction for state and local taxes. Effectively, the AMT reduces tax exporting, but it does not eliminate it. The best policy for the federal government would be to eliminate the AMT entirely, and to make up the lost revenues from other sources. This would make the federal income tax more transparent, and it would reduce the cost of complying with the tax. For the last several years, however, Congress has settled for tweaking the AMT every year, so as to avoid an unpopular explosion in AMT liabilities.

41. In 2007, the deduction for state and local sales taxes was partly reinstated. Taxpayers can now deduct either their state and local income taxes or their sales taxes, but not both. As a practical matter, this will not have any effect on most Michigan taxpayers. Its greatest effect will be for taxpayers in states like Florida and Texas, which do not have an income tax.

42. See the Department of the Treasury, "School Finance Reform in Michigan: Proposal A: Retrospective," State of Michigan, http://www.michigan.gov/documents/propa_3172_7.pdf.

43. See Timothy Bartik, "Michigan's Business Taxes and Economic Development: Possible Reforms," Upjohn Institute, http://www.upjohninst.org/TJB_testimony_2-17-06.pdf.

44. See Stephen T. Mark, Therese J. McGuire, and Leslie E. Papke, "What Do We Know about the Effect of Taxes on Economic Development? Lessons from the Literature for the District of Columbia," *State Tax Notes*, August 25, 1997: 493-510.

45. For administrative reasons, most taxes are *remitted* by businesses. For example, most payroll taxes and income taxes are withheld by employers, and the sales tax is handled by retailers. However, even though businesses are involved in the collection process, these taxes are not usually thought of as business taxes. When I use the phrase "business taxes" in this chapter, I am referring primarily to corporation income taxes, the Single Business Tax, or the Michigan Business Tax.

46. If retail markets are very competitive, it may be difficult for sellers to pass along much of the business tax to consumers. Also, if capital is mobile across state boundaries, then it may be difficult to pin much of the business tax on business owners, since they can move their operations to other states. If consumers don't pay the business tax and if business owners don't pay the tax, then workers are the only ones left to bear the burden of the tax.

47. This survey result is from Round 48 of the State of the State Survey. The codebook, methodological report, and data set for the survey are available at http://ippsr.msu.edu/SOSS/SOSSdata.htm.

48. For a detailed description of the complicated history of the SBT, see James R. Hines, "Michigan's Flirtation with the Single Business Tax," in *Michigan at the Millennium*.

49. The SBT was also sometimes criticized because companies had to pay SBT even if they were not turning a profit. Once again, this is not a very strong argument. Businesses are required to pay the payroll taxes for their employees' Social Security, Medicare, disability insurance, and unemployment insurance, regardless of whether they are making a profit. The taxes are just like any other cost of doing business. Retailers are not allowed to skim off a portion of the sales taxes they collect just because they are not making a profit.

50. I wrote my earlier book about the Michigan economy at a time when the SBT was still in place. At that time, there was much discussion about the possibility of repealing the SBT and about what might replace it. I devoted several paragraphs to a discussion of the possibilities for replacing the SBT. I did not include a gross receipts tax, because I did not believe we would be so foolish as to even consider adopting a gross receipts tax. I was wrong.

51. Another example is the federal corporation income tax, which applies to the income of corporations, but not to partnerships or to most income from agriculture or real estate.

By taxing some forms of capital income but not others, the corporate tax creates economic inefficiency. This has been studied in a number of classic research papers, including Arnold Harberger, "Efficiency Effects of Taxes on Income from Capital," in *Effects of the Corporation Income Tax*, ed. Marion Krzyzaniak (Detroit: Wayne State University Press, 1966); and John Shoven, "The Incidence and Efficiency Effects of Taxes on Income from Capital," *Journal of Political Economy* 84 (1976): 1261–83.

52. Both of these studies were commissioned by the Michigan Education Association and the National Education Association. See Patrick Anderson, Alex Rosaen, and Hilary Doe (May 2009), "Michigan's Business Tax Incentives," Anderson Economic Group, http://www.andersoneconomicgroup.com/Portals/0/upload/MEA_TaxAbatements_Public.pdf; and Anderson, Rosaen, and Theodore Bolema (March 2010), "Effectiveness of Michigan's Key Business Tax Incentives," http://www.andersoneconomicgroup.com/Portals/0/upload/MEA_Evaluating_TaxAbatements_Public.pdf.

53. I put "Fair" in quotation marks. From the standpoint of public relations, the proponents of this proposal are clever to refer to it as the Fair Tax. After all, who could object to something that is called "fair?" But just because the proposal's advocates refer to it as "fair," does not necessarily make it so. After a third of a century of unprecedented increases in inequality, I certainly do not consider it fair to increase taxes on middle-income Michigan residents, while reducing taxes on those at the top.

54. Also, proponents of this type of tax change often drastically understate the tax rates that would be needed to replace the revenue coming from the taxes that are to be eliminated. See William G. Gale and Janet Holtzblatt, "The Role of Administrative Issues in Tax Reform: Simplicity, Compliance, and Administration," in *United States Tax Reform in the Twenty-First Century*, eds. George R. Zodrow and Peter Mieszkowski (Cambridge: Cambridge University Press, 2002).

55. See "Executive Budget Appendix on Tax Credits, Deductions, and Exemptions, Fiscal Year 2010," http://www.michigan.gov/documents/treasury/ExecBudgAppenTaxCredits DedExemptsFY10_302899_7.pdf. As long as taxable value is less than state equalized value, taxable value is allowed by law to increase by the rate of inflation, even when state equalized value is declining. Thus in the last few years, many Michigan homeowners have experienced the odd combination of falling home values and rising property-tax bills. In the public discussion leading up to Proposal A, little or no attention was focused on the possibility that home values could potentially see a widespread decline. Recently, the combination of falling property values and rising tax payments has been the cause of much public outcry, despite the fact that many of the affected homeowners have received substantial tax reductions from the taxable value cap over the years.

56. Mark Skidmore is a colleague of mine at Michigan State University. Skidmore and I, along with a graduate student named Timothy Hodge, have written a research paper on the taxable value cap in Michigan, "Property Value Assessment Growth Limits and Redistribution of Property Tax Payments: Evidence from Michigan," *National Tax Journal* 63 (2010): 509-38." We find that, on balance, the taxable value cap makes the property tax more regressive than it would otherwise be.

57. Under certain circumstances, a community can avoid being constrained by the Headlee limitations. For example, new construction is excluded from the Headlee calculations. Thus, all else equal, it will be easier for a rapidly growing community to avoid a Headlee Rollback than it would be for a community that is not experiencing much growth.

■ 7

What Will Michigan's Economy Be Like in 2030?

O n December 1, 1862, in the midst of the greatest crisis in American
history, Abraham Lincoln sent his second annual message to Congress. He wrote, "The dogmas of the quiet past are inadequate to the
stormy present. The occasion is piled high with difficulty, and we must rise
with the occasion. As our case is new, so we must think anew, and act anew.
We must disenthrall ourselves, and then we shall save our country."

The difficulties facing the people of Michigan today are not nearly as profound as the difficulties faced by Lincoln and his fellow citizens during the Civil
War. Nevertheless, Michigan is at a critical moment in its history. We too face
an occasion that is piled high with difficulty, and we too must rise to the occasion. We in Michigan in 2010 would do well to heed Lincoln's words: yesterday's
dogmas are inadequate for today. If Michigan's economy is to reverse the long,
slow slide of the last several decades, we will need *new attitudes* and *new policies*. In
this book, I have discussed attitudes and policies that will lead toward a brighter
future for Michigan, in terms of the economy and in other ways.

In this final chapter, I ask what Michigan will be like in the year 2030
(rather than 2011, 2012, or 2013). Although we cannot ignore what happens in
the next few years, I frame this question in terms of a twenty-year time line

because Michigan faces *long-term* economic problems. These problems will not be fixed in the next year or two, or even in the next four years. However, if the people of Michigan have the wisdom and courage to do something about it, we can make some major improvements over the longer term.

Much of this chapter is devoted to a summary and synthesis of the policy analyses from earlier chapters. However, before I get to that summary and synthesis, I want to say more about the *values* that have formed the basis of the policy recommendations in this book. People with different values can look at the same set of facts and reach different policy conclusions. Thus the policy recommendations discussed here are not merely the result of my economic analysis; they are also the result of my values.

Values Regarding Future Generations of Michigan Residents

As I see it, the people of today have a moral obligation to pave the way to a decent future for the people of tomorrow. Unfortunately, many of the decisions being made today in Michigan and across the country are doing a disservice to the people of future generations. For example, the private savings rate in the United States has been declining for decades. And except for the brief period from 1997 to 2000, the federal government has run large budget deficits for the past forty years. Consequently, Americans have now borrowed *trillions* of dollars from other countries. Americans are spending like there's no tomorrow, rather than saving and investing to prepare for the future. Here in Michigan, we are cutting our investments in education. At this crucial moment, we in Michigan are eating our seed corn, with little regard for future generations.

I believe these trends are taking us in the wrong direction. The problem with behaving like there's no tomorrow is that tomorrow will inevitably come, regardless of whether we prepare for it. To use the jargon of economists, I believe that we should not "discount" the future very greatly. Those who discount the future very heavily may look at today's situation and say that everything is fine. Many of my recommendations will not make much sense to those who place far more weight on today than tomorrow. Maybe I'm wrong. Maybe we should consume as much as we want to consume now and leave future generations to fend for themselves. But I don't think so.

Values Regarding Middle-Income and Low-Income Michigan Residents

The second set of values that must be mentioned are those concerning the distribution of income. I am troubled by the increasing inequality of income and wealth in Michigan and throughout the United States. Those with the most education and skill have done very well in the last few decades. CEOs have done amazingly well in Michigan and across the country. But many of the rest of Michigan's people have lost ground. As I said in an earlier chapter, some inequality is necessary to give people an incentive to work hard and get an education. However, the trend toward greater inequality has increased rapidly in the last few decades, and in my view, it has gone too far.

Once again, not everyone shares my values in this regard. Many of the recommendations in this book probably will not make much sense to those who have relatively little concern for the people on the lower rungs of the economic ladder. Many of my recommendations will not make sense to those who are comfortable with a wider gap between rich and middle class and a wider gap between middle class and poor. I have recommended that Michigan should devote more resources to K–12 education. From the perspective of the affluent few who can easily afford private-school tuition, this may not seem very reasonable. I have also recommended that we ensure that all schoolchildren in Michigan are educated in adequate facilities, including those children who live in poor communities. Again, from the perspective of some affluent folks, this may not make sense. I have also recommended greater state support for public colleges and universities, but this may seem strange to those who can afford to send their sons and daughters to expensive private colleges. I have recommended that we repair the frayed social safety net in Michigan, but we know that not everyone shares those values. I have recommended that the income tax in Michigan should be made more progressive. But some affluent Michigan residents may ask, Why shouldn't we do as much as possible to put the tax burden on the shoulders of the middle-income and low-income people of Michigan, thus reducing the tax burden for the most affluent?

It is commonplace to say that Michigan's economy is not performing well. I have said this on several occasions in this book. But we need to keep in mind that this is a statement about the Michigan economy *as a whole*. For the most affluent folks in Michigan, the economy has performed astonishingly well. The incomes of the top 20 percent have skyrocketed. At the same time,

Michigan has a regressive tax system. All of these policies are consistent with a philosophy that has relatively little concern for the people in the bottom 80 percent of the income distribution in Michigan.

These are not merely economic issues. They are moral issues. Like many of Michigan's people, I grew up in a Christian tradition. I am a firm believer in the separation of church and state, and it is not my purpose to proselytize. However, people of many faiths turn to sacred texts for comfort, illumination, and inspiration. One of my favorite passages is from the Gospel according to St. Mark: "Jesus sat down opposite the place where the offerings were put and watched the crowd putting their money into the temple treasury. Many rich people threw in large amounts. But a poor widow came and put in two very small copper coins, worth only a fraction of a penny. Calling his disciples to him, Jesus said, 'I tell you the truth, this poor widow has put more into the treasury than all the others. They all gave out of their wealth; but she, out of her poverty.'"[1]

This is only one of dozens of Biblical passages that speak much more favorably of the poor than of the fortunate few. When I speak for those at the bottom and middle of the economic ladder, I feel I am on firm moral ground.

Of course, very few people will outwardly admit that they want the rich to get richer and the poor to get poorer. And few will admit that they don't care very much about the people of future generations. But actions speak louder than words. If one looks at Michigan's economic policies of the last few decades, one sees a pattern that fits with values that are very different from the values I have espoused here. The pattern of recent economic policy in Michigan is consistent with a set of values that places relatively little emphasis on the needs of the people of future generations or the people in the bottom 80 percent of the income distribution.

Key Features of the Economic Situation in Michigan

This book covers a very wide range of economic issues facing the people of Michigan. However, four aspects of Michigan's economic situation are of central importance.

Manufacturing has been in long-term decline. As a percentage of the economy, manufacturing has been shrinking for decades, both in Michigan and in the rest of the country. In Chapter 1 we saw that manufacturing accounts for a significantly larger share of the economy in Michigan than in the United States as a whole. Thus the transition out of manufacturing has been more difficult for Michigan than for most other parts of the country. Many of Michigan's economic difficulties can be traced, directly or indirectly, to the heavy reliance on manufacturing and the auto industry in particular.

Manufacturing was the foundation of Michigan's tremendous economic success in the middle of the twentieth century. Although manufacturing will remain important to the Michigan economy for many years to come, there is no reason to believe that it will return to the dominant position that it enjoyed fifty years ago. The old days are gone, and they aren't coming back. Thus we must look to a future that will be different from the past.

The future belongs to people with skill, but Michigan's education system has fallen short of what is needed. The evolving global economy is centered on highly skilled, highly educated, creative people. Unfortunately, as discussed in Chapter 2, Michigan's educational system is not delivering enough workers who can take advantage of the new economic realities. Achievement scores for elementary and secondary students are close to the national average, but the national average is pitiful.

The proportion of Michigan's adult population with a college degree has lagged substantially below the national average for many years. This may have made sense in the heyday of manufacturing, when a young person with only a high school diploma had a good chance of getting a highly paid factory job. These economic realities of yesteryear are long gone, but unfortunately some of the old attitudes linger on. Thus too many of Michigan's people are inadequately prepared for the high-tech, high-skill jobs of the future. And yet the budget for higher education has been slashed dramatically.

Incomes have become dramatically more unequal. As mentioned above, Michigan lags behind the national average in the portion of its adult population with a college degree. However, those who *do* have a college education have fared extraordinarily well in the last thirty-five years. After adjusting for inflation, the labor-market earnings of Michigan workers with a college degree have soared. The earnings of people with a high school diploma have fallen slightly, and the earnings of those with less than a high school education have plummeted. As a result, the income gap has widened significantly. In Michigan and in the rest of the United States, the degree of inequality has now climbed to levels not seen since the early part of the twentieth century, if ever.

Tax revenues have plummeted. At one time, taxes in Michigan were slightly above the national average, but this is no longer true. As a proportion of personal income, state and local tax revenues in Michigan have declined fairly steadily for more than thirty years, and at an especially rapid pace in the last ten years. If state and local taxes in Michigan were at the average level of the last generation (as a percentage of the economy), they would bring in about $10 billion more per year.

Some of the reductions in tax revenues have been caused by explicit cuts in tax rates. However, most of the revenue losses are caused by structural weaknesses in the tax system. As discussed in Chapter 6, these weaknesses can be found in the income tax; property tax; sales tax; and the excise taxes on beer, wine, and tobacco products. In other words, *every important revenue source for state and local governments in Michigan has serious structural problems.* As a result, the taxed portion of the economy has diminished substantially over the years. The tax system's ability to raise revenues has been seriously eroded, and the state and local governments in Michigan are in a state of chronic fiscal crisis.

Of course, the four trends discussed in the preceding paragraphs are not the only things going on with Michigan's economy. In my opinion, however, these four interrelated trends are the most important forces shaping the economy. If the people of Michigan understand these trends clearly, they will have taken an important step toward a brighter economic future.

On the basis of the analysis of these and other trends, I have included a number of policy suggestions in this book. In the next few pages, I include a brief review of these ideas for improving economic policy in Michigan.

K–12 Education Policies

Michigan is underinvested in every single part of the educational system from preschool to PhD. If the people of Michigan are going to make long-term economic improvements, their top priority should be to increase the skill level of the population. I developed several recommendations for Michigan's K–12 educational system in Chapter 2 of this book:

- *Provide stable and adequate funding for operating expenses for every school district, while allowing individual school districts to provide limited additional amounts.* Proposal A, passed in 1994, led to very substantial increases in funding for the lowest-spending school districts in Michigan. This was a great achievement, and it has led to improvements in educational outcomes. However, funding has been reduced substantially in the last decade, and this threatens to wipe out the gains of the past. The state government should reverse the trend of budget cuts, to ensure that the funding for the lowest-spending school districts is maintained at a strong level.

- *Provide additional state funding for capital expenditures for public schools.* Since the passage of Proposal A, the funding for *operating* expenses for the public schools has been liberated from its earlier dependence on local property taxes. However, *capital* expenditures still rely almost exclusively on local property taxes. Consequently the poorest school districts in Michigan are unable to provide adequate physical facilities for their students, even though many of them have high property-tax rates. The state government should assume a much larger share of the financial responsibility for capital expenditures, with the near-term goal of ensuring that every student in Michigan goes to school in a physical environment that is safe, modern, and educationally sound.

- *Shift more of the financial responsibility for pensions and medical care for retired teachers to the state government.* Currently, the individual school districts in Michigan are responsible for retired teachers' pensions and health care. These costs have been rising rapidly, and they are expected to increase even more rapidly in the coming years. These escalating costs have already forced many school districts to make painful cuts in services. If nothing is done, the school districts will have to make even more severe cuts in the near future. The state government should take on some of the burden that is now faced by school districts, but teachers should also pay a substantially larger fraction of the cost of their fringe benefits.

- *Increase the amount of instruction.* Cognitive, social, and emotional development begins very early in life, and we need to do more in the area of early-childhood education. The cutoff age for compulsory school attendance has been increased, and that is a step in the right direction. However, today's school calendar with a three-month summer break is better suited to the economic needs of one-hundred years ago than to the needs of today. We should lengthen the school year, perhaps to 190 or 200 days. If this is done, it would be important not to offset the change by increasing the number of "half days." It would also be good to require (or at least encourage) school districts to use full-day kindergarten programs. All of these changes will cost money. The state government should require schools to make these changes, and the state government should provide the financial means to carry them out.

Higher Education Policies

In addition to the discussion about K–12 education, Chapter 2 also included a discussion about higher education. Some of the recommendations that emerged from this discussion are as follows:

- *Reverse the trend toward reduced state support for community colleges and universities.* In Chapter 2, we discussed the strong effects of postsecondary education on productivity and earnings. The wage premium for a college education has grown sharply in the last thirty-five years. Moreover, research universities provide other benefits for the state through a wide variety of channels, such as bringing in federal research dollars. Yet Michigan has been slashing its financial support for institutions of higher learning. This shortsighted strategy must be reversed.
- *Ensure access to higher education for students from middle-income and low-income Michigan families.* Young people from families of modest means are the least likely to attend college, often because of financial difficulties. Policies regarding tuition and financial aid should give strong consideration to financial need. Financial aid can come from both public sources and private sources such as the Kalamazoo Promise. Our goal should be to make sure that none of the talented young people in Michigan is prohibited from attending college because of cost.

Economic-Development Policies

If Michigan is to develop a successful economic-development strategy, it is very important to understand that some widely touted policies will *not* get us where we need to go. In the policy debate regarding economic development in Michigan, it is often suggested that taxes play a huge role and that business tax cuts can have almost magical effects. But in reality the decisions of businesses actually depend on many things other than taxes. In fact, business taxes are fairly far down on the list of criteria that businesses use when making decisions about location. Although businesses do pay attention to taxes, they also pay attention to the availability of skilled workers, and to transportation infrastructure, access to natural resources, the availability of cultural and recreational amenities, and many other factors.

I have suggested that Michigan should greatly reduce the Michigan Business Tax (MBT) or even repeal it. This may seem inconsistent with my statements about the modest effects of taxes. However, I really do believe that Michigan's economy will be improved if we were to replace the MBT. We should keep our expectations realistic about this. Repeal of the MBT will not lead to a dramatic transformation of the Michigan economy. The long-term structural problems of Michigan's economy are large enough that even a repeal of the MBT will only have a moderate effect. In other words, eliminating the MBT is not a cure-all silver bullet. Nevertheless, since eliminating the MBT will have a moderate positive effect, we should do it, *but only if the revenues are fully replaced.* Regardless of what happens to the MBT, we should be careful about using tax breaks as an economic development tool. Although some tax incentives may work, others may not. Michigan needs to establish a system of regular evaluation and oversight of tax breaks.

Michigan already has a very substantial economic-development program. In many ways, our economic-development efforts are solid. It is true that the overall performance of the Michigan economy has been mediocre, but this is primarily due to other factors and not to a lack of economic-development efforts. Still, these efforts could be improved. It would help to have greater consistency over time in economic-development policies, and it would help to undertake periodic outside reviews that assess the effectiveness of the existing programs and suggest new ones. We need to double our efforts to provide "one-stop shopping" for businesses, with integrated assistance for site location, infrastructure, and training.

Transportation Policies

In Chapter 3, we evaluated Michigan's physical resources, including transportation. Several recommendations came out of that discussion:

- *Don't turn down billions of dollars of federal road money.* Michigan is not a poor state, but we are not so very rich that we can afford to turn down huge amounts of money from the federal government. The fact that some Michigan politicians would even *consider* turning down billions in federal road money is insane.
- *Reallocate state highway funds.* The roads in Michigan are of poorer quality than the roads in neighboring states. The problems are especially severe in urban areas. One reason for this is that highway funds in Michigan are allocated on the basis of a formula that is biased in favor of sparsely populated rural counties. This formula should be changed, so as to increase the funding for roads in the urban areas that contain the vast majority of Michigan's people. This would be both more equitable and more efficient.
- *Consider stricter truck weight limits.* The weight limits for trucks are far higher in Michigan than in the rest of the country. There is a good possibility that ultraheavy trucks do an unusually large amount of damage to the roads. Thus Michigan should consider adopting weight limits that are more in line with those in the rest of the United States. More scientific research should be undertaken to improve our understanding of the damage done to roads by heavy trucks.
- *Increase the taxes on gasoline and diesel fuel, with a larger increase on diesel fuel.* Currently, Michigan is one of only a few states in which the tax rate on diesel fuel is lower than the tax rate on gasoline. The diesel tax should be increased so that it is at least equal to the gasoline tax.
- *Consider greater use of tolls.* Tolls can raise revenue for road construction and maintenance. Also, tolls can help to spread out the volume of traffic thus increasing the effective capacity of the existing roads. Michigan has never made substantial use of tolls, but they are proving increasingly effective in other states and other countries.

Land-Use Policies

If Michigan's economic-development policies are successful in attracting more businesses, there will be increased pressure to develop land for industrial, commercial, and residential uses. Even if the Michigan economy continues to grow slowly, land use will continue to be hotly contested. Much of the controversy involves the density of development. In recent decades, the population density of metropolitan areas has been decreasing in Michigan and in the rest of the United States. In Michigan, even though the total population of metropolitan areas has been increasing fairly slowly, the urbanized land area has grown rapidly. This low-density development brings many problems, including suburban congestion, loss of open space, and increased infrastructure costs.

One of the themes that has emerged in this book is the persistent tilt of economic policy toward rural areas and suburbs. The widening gap between rich and poor has favored affluent suburban residents over those who live in the cities, and Michigan's tax policies have exacerbated the trend. Also, local school districts must rely exclusively on local property taxes for their capital expenditures. Thus the poorest urban districts are unable to provide adequate facilities for their schoolchildren, even though they often have high property-tax rates. This accelerates the flight to the suburbs. The funding formula for highways is also strongly slanted in favor of lightly populated rural counties. And the Headlee Amendment restricts the ability of local jurisdictions to raise property-tax revenue, but it favors regions with new growth over older areas that are already urbanized. All of these policies contribute to a situation in which rural and suburban areas in Michigan are favored, and cities (especially older, poorer cities) are penalized. Michigan should treat older, developed areas on a more equal basis with undeveloped and newly developing areas.

Environmental Policies

Until the 1960s and early 1970s, neither Michigan nor the rest of the United States had much of an environmental policy. Since then, however, an increased environmental awareness has led to state and federal policy initiatives in many areas. Many sources of air pollution have been reduced, as has phosphorus pollution in the Great Lakes. Michigan is one of the nation's leaders with its deposit and return system for bottles and cans. The trend toward destruction of wetlands has slowed down. Nevertheless, a number of challenges remain for environmental policy.

Climate change from greenhouse gas emissions will only be solved through policies that are coordinated internationally, but that does not mean that Michigan can't take a leadership role. One think-outside-the-box possibility would be for Michigan to institute substantially higher taxes on fossil fuels and rebate the revenue to households to avoid harming low-income residents.

Other environmental problems will continue to be addressed at the state and local levels, as well as at the federal and international levels. One of these problems is the contamination of groundwater and sediments. The key to success in this area does not come so much in the form of a particular policy. Instead, the key is to recognize that complete elimination of contaminants is prohibitively expensive. Rather than engaging in a doomed effort to eliminate contamination completely, the best policy is to identify the sites that pose the greatest risk to the public health and find cost-effective methods of dealing with those sites.

Corrections Policies

In the 1980s and 1990s, prisons were the fastest-growing sector of the Michigan economy. It is possible that the people of Michigan are safer with more prisoners behind bars. Nevertheless, our incarceration policies are very expensive. Thus I recommend that we make greater use of probation, halfway houses, and electronic monitoring as alternatives to incarceration.

Partly as a result of long prison sentences, the incarceration rate is substantially higher in Michigan than in neighboring states. If the incarceration rate were the same in Michigan as in other states in the region, Michigan's prison spending would be reduced by several hundred million dollars per year. It is not clear that the high rate of imprisonment is worth it. I am not suggesting that we change our policies toward the most violent criminal offenders. However, for some offenders, alternative methods of punishment have the potential to provide security for the public at a considerably lower cost.

Health-Care and Health-Insurance Policies

We discussed health care and health insurance in Chapter 5. For health-care policy and health-insurance policy, perhaps the most important thing is for the public to understand the situation. New medical technologies have led to large reductions in death rates, but these advances have not come cheaply. The trend toward higher health-care expenses is expected to continue for many years to come. This is partly because the population is aging and partly because medical research is expected to continue to produce new medicines, new techniques, and new devices. These new developments will save lives, but they will be expensive. If we are to take advantage of the new developments, *someone* will have to pay for them. Hard choices will have to be made. The financing problems are worsened by the fact that America's health-care system is very wasteful. Hundreds of billions of dollars are spent annually on treatments that do not actually improve health. The federal health-care reform legislation of 2010 will eventually increase access to health care, but it does not do very much to address the cost issues.

The current trajectory of health-care spending is simply not sustainable. Therefore, the federal government will eventually have to take serious steps to rein in costs. Important choices will also be made by individuals and policymakers in Michigan. Individuals make choices every day about diet, exercise, smoking, and other factors that affect health. For policymakers in Michigan, one of the biggest issues will be how to handle the burgeoning Medicaid program (assuming that the current division of Medicaid responsibility between the states and the federal government is maintained). It will be necessary to raise taxes, cut other areas of spending, reduce the number of people eligible for Medicaid, or reduce the expenditures per Medicaid recipient.

Antipoverty Policies

The best antipoverty policies have nothing to do with public-assistance programs. In the long run, by far the most important antipoverty policies have to do with education, which provides the foundation for good jobs. The Earned Income Tax Credit that was recently instituted in Michigan is a major victory for low-income families. Nevertheless, about 1.3 million Michigan residents were in poverty in 2008, according to the official poverty definition used by the federal government. Alleviation of poverty is one of the major goals of public-assistance policies and other policies for low-income families, which were discussed in Chapter 5.

Beyond education and the Earned Income Tax Credit, the following are among the policies that have the potential to help those residents who are in or near poverty:

- Improved public transportation
- Streamlined procedures for assessment and referral for those with mental-health or substance-abuse problems
- Community service jobs
- Greater use of supported-work situations in which enhanced supervision is provided for those who have difficulty in making the transition to work

Tax Policies

We have discussed taxation in several chapters in this book. However, most of the discussion of taxes was concentrated in Chapter 6. Several recommendations came out of that discussion:

- *Extend the sales tax to a greater variety of services.* Michigan exempts most services from taxation. (In fact, Michigan exempts even more services than most states.) Services have grown rapidly in recent decades and account for an ever-growing portion of the economy. Thus the revenue losses from nontaxation of services have increased over the years. If the sales tax in Michigan is broadened to include more services, it will be possible to raise additional revenues while reducing the sales-tax rate from its current rate of 6 percent. A sales tax that applies to services is both fairer and more efficient than the current sales tax.
- *Make the income tax more progressive.* The Earned Income Tax Credit is one of the best policy changes of recent years because it provides some relief for low-income working families. Nevertheless, overall, the tax system in Michigan exacerbates the trend toward greater inequality by putting relatively more of the tax burden on the shoulders of middle-income and low-income people. The income tax can help to reverse this trend, because the income tax is the only tax that is levied on the basis of ability to pay. Michigan's income tax is unusual in that it has only a single flat tax rate on all taxable income. A graduated income tax is the best way to shift some of the tax burden away from those at the bottom of the income scale

(although this would require a constitutional amendment). Another way to make the income tax more progressive without instituting graduated rates would involve increasing both the personal exemption and the single tax rate. If Michigan were to raise more revenue from the income tax, a substantial part of the additional tax revenue would actually be paid by residents of other states, because state and local income taxes are deductible from the federal income tax.

- *Remove the assessment cap in the property tax.* Since 1994, Michigan has limited the amount by which the taxable value of a property can increase from year to year. However, properties are reassessed to their full value when they are sold. The "assessment cap" erodes the revenue-raising capability of the property tax. It also creates an inequity, because a property that has been sold recently will pay higher taxes than a comparable property that has been held by the same owner for many years. Removal of the assessment cap would fix these problems. If there is a desire to keep the overall amount of property-tax revenue from increasing, removal of the cap could be coupled with a reduction in property-tax rates.

- *Convert the excise taxes on beer, wine, and tobacco products to a percentage of the sales price.* Most tax revenues come from taxes that are levied as a percentage of a dollar value. However, the selective excise taxes are "unit taxes." For example, the cigarette tax is levied as a number of dollars per pack, and the wine tax is on a per-gallon basis. Over time, inflation will erode the real revenue-raising capability of a unit tax unless the tax rate is raised explicitly. The tax rate on cigarettes has been raised substantially, so the only need for the cigarette tax is to convert to a percentage basis. The taxes on beer and wine have stayed at the same nominal level for decades. Thus for beer and wine, the tax rates should be increased very substantially to make up for the erosion of the past, and the taxes should also be converted to a percentage basis.

- *Reinstate the estate tax.* Michigan used to tax the estates of wealthy decedents and could decide to do so again. An exemption of a few million dollars would guarantee that only a small fraction of estates would be subject to tax.

- *Establish regular review and oversight for the many tax breaks that are currently on the books in Michigan.* Tax breaks should be subject to "sunset provisions." If a tax break can be shown to be effective then it can stay. Otherwise, it should be eliminated.

- *Repeal the MBT, but only if the revenues are replaced fully.* In 2007, the Single Business Tax (SBT) was eliminated and replaced by the MBT. The SBT wasn't perfect, but the MBT is even worse. We should repeal the MBT, but only if the revenues are replaced. To repeal the MBT without replacing the revenues would be extraordinarily fiscally irresponsible. If the legislature only has the will to replace a portion of the MBT revenues, then the gross-receipts portion of the MBT should be eliminated.

Policies to Strengthen Michigan's Democracy

The main purpose of this book has been to suggest ways to improve Michigan's economic policies. However, regardless of how much analysis is offered by me and by other economists, Michigan's policies can only be changed through the political process. In my view, the political system in Michigan is not *completely* broken, but it certainly does not function very well. Before closing, I offer some thoughts about how to improve the political system.

Relax term limits. I became a member of the faculty at Michigan State University in 1983. By the time I had been on the job for six years, I had published a book and some articles, and I had improved my teaching techniques. I was off to a decent start, but I was still not nearly as effective as I would be after gaining more years of experience. In any complex job, it takes time to learn how to do things better. (That is why workers with a lot of experience typically earn so much more than inexperienced workers. In fact, the typical wage premium for experienced workers has increased sharply in the last few decades.) Yet because of term limits, members of the Michigan House of Representatives are forced to move on after only six years on the job, and members of the Michigan Senate have to leave after only eight years. This means that many of the people making vital decisions about Michigan are remarkably inexperienced, and they lack the factual knowledge that is necessary to serve effectively. Nowhere else in our society is so much responsibility given to people with so little experience. Moreover, since members of the legislature can only serve for a relatively short time, their incentive to work on difficult, long-term issues is reduced.

I must make clear that I *do* believe in term limits for members of the Michigan legislature (and for members of Congress as well). With no term limits, a legislator can serve for decades on end. It is easy for such a legislator to become stale and corrupt or to lose touch with his or her constituents. Also, as I have watched ancient U.S. senators such as Strom Thurmond (R–South Carolina), who was the only senator to serve at the age of one hundred, and Robert Byrd (D–West Virginia), who was still in the Senate at age 92, I have become more convinced that some sort of term limits are a good thing. But it is possible to have too much of a good thing. Therefore, I believe that the current legislative term limits in Michigan should be relaxed but not eliminated. My preference for the maximum length of service in the legislature would be something like twenty-four or thirty years. However, I am not deeply invested in any particular number. In today's legislature, *any* increase in term limits, no matter how small, would be a step in the right direction.

As the director of MSU's State of the State Survey, I have analyzed the public's response to survey questions about legislative term limits. When asked a generic question about the basic idea of term limits, the responses are very strongly in favor of the concept, with more than 70 percent approving term limits.[2] On the basis of these responses, I believe it would be a waste of time, energy, and money to try to repeal term limits entirely.

However, when asked about reforms of term limits (short of outright repeal), the public is much more open to reform. For example, the current rules allow for six years in the House and eight years in the Senate. Since six plus eight is fourteen, one possibility would be to have a limit of fourteen years but to allow an individual to serve all fourteen years in the House or all fourteen in the Senate (or any combination that adds up to fourteen years). This would not solve all the problems caused by term limits, but it would mean that each house of the legislature would be more likely to have at least a few folks with a bit more institutional memory. In round fifty-two of the 2009 State of the State Survey, respondents favored this reform by a margin of 54 percent to 42 percent.[3] Another possibility would be to require individuals to leave the legislature at the end of their fourteen years, but then to allow them to run again after being out office for a period of four years or more. Respondents favored this reform by a margin of 62 percent to 36 percent.

I am in favor of some combination of these proposals. I believe that Michigan's people would be well served if the total number of years in the legislature is increased beyond the current limit of fourteen, and I also believe that there should not be separate limits on service in the House and service in the Senate. However, if reforms like these are to take place, they will need to be put on the ballot, and the voters will need to approve the ballot proposal. That will take *leadership*.

I believe that some of the public's support for term limits is a mile wide but an inch deep. There is a gut feeling of suspicion toward elected officials and a desire to "throw the bums out." But many Michigan citizens have not had time to think about the issue, and it hasn't been explained to them very clearly. Many haven't considered all the problems caused by an ill-informed and inexperienced legislature. Thus we need *leaders* to explain the issue to the public and keep hammering away at the issue. Many members of the legislature are very reluctant to take on a leadership role in this regard, because they are afraid of being seen as self-serving. I do hope that senators and representatives will find the courage to overcome their reluctance. But the governor of Michigan has the greatest power to shape the public debate. In 2010, the people of Michigan will elect a new governor. I hope that the new governor will have the wisdom and courage to press hard for term-limits reform.[4]

Relaxing term limits will not solve all of our problems. The U.S. Congress has no term limits, and I am often disappointed with the way Congress does its job. And even if we were to relax the term-limits rules tomorrow, it would take years before the Michigan legislature would have many people with much experience. Nevertheless, the current system of term limits is so restrictive that I am very confident that relaxing them will be good for Michigan.

Before leaving the subject of term limits, there is one other issue that requires attention. When term limits were instituted in the 1990s, they were put in place all at once. As a result, every eight years almost the entire Senate is turned out of office. The 2010 elections will decide all thirty-eight seats in the Senate, and it appears that at least thirty of the thirty-eight winners will be people who have never served in the Senate before. This problem could be reduced by staggering the Senate terms, so that half of the Senate seats are elected every two years.[5]

End gerrymandering of legislative districts. Term limits are an important issue. However, the way legislative district boundaries are drawn is just as important. The practice of drawing district boundaries to benefit one political party is called "gerrymandering."[6] In recent years, computers have made it possible for politicians to engage in gerrymandering with unprecedented precision.

In a gerrymandering scheme, the party that controls the state government will strategically draw the district boundaries to its own advantage.

This usually involves herding most voters into uncompetitive districts. Gerrymandering has two poisonous side effects. First, a gerrymandered legislature may be fairly unrepresentative. In the extreme case, the party that controls the legislature at the time of redistricting may be able to maintain its grip on power, even if it does not have the support of a majority of voters. This occurred in Michigan in 2006. In the elections for the Michigan Senate in that year, Democrats received about 54 percent of the votes and Republicans received about 45 percent. (The other 1 percent went to an assortment of smaller parties and write-in candidates.) That's nearly a landslide in favor of the Democrats. Yet because of gerrymandering, Republicans retained majority control of the senate. (In pointing out this undemocratic result, I don't want to sound like I am only bothered by Republican gerrymandering. Gerrymandering by Democrats would be just as bad. It's just that Republicans were in charge in Michigan at the time of the most recent redistricting after the 2000 Census.)

The second side effect of gerrymandering may be just as bad or even worse. Gerrymandering works by concentrating voters into relatively uncompetitive districts, even when it would be possible to have more competitive districts. In the Michigan legislature, as in the U.S. House of Representatives, gerrymandering means that most voters are either in safe Republican districts or safe Democratic districts. In safe, uncompetitive districts, politicians from the dominant party have little reason to appeal to moderate voters, because they can rely on the overwhelming power of those who are faithful to their party. In fact, any attempt to appeal to moderate voters may be harmful to the career of a politician in an uncompetitive district, because it might incur the wrath of the extreme elements of his or her party. Thus uncompetitive districts are more likely to elect representatives from the extremes of the political spectrum. Consequently, the governing body has relatively few voices from the middle, even though most voters actually reside fairly close to the center of the political spectrum. Moderate voters are underrepresented, while the more extreme elements are overrepresented.

One solution to the gerrymandering problem is to remove politicians from the redistricting process. We could place redistricting in the hands of an independent, nonpartisan panel, with explicit instructions to avoid favoring one political party over another. If Michigan were to adopt this kind of system, we would have many more meaningful, competitive races than we have now. The legislature would be more truly representative of the people of Michigan.

Earlier, I mentioned the 2009 State of the State Survey in which voters expressed majority approval for some reforms of term limits. In that same survey, we asked a question about having an independent, nonpartisan commission to draw the legislative district lines. In this case, an overwhelming majority of respondents were in favor. The proposal for a nonpartisan commission was favored by 82 percent of respondents and opposed by only 17 percent. If a proposal to eliminate gerrymandering gets on the ballot, it is very likely to pass, especially if the next governor exerts some leadership on the issue.[7]

Reduce partisan and ideological bitterness. In the preceding section, I have argued that gerrymandering contributes to partisan and ideological division. Regardless of whether anything is done about gerrymandering, partisan rancor serves us very badly. A story will help to illustrate my point. A couple of years ago, I had the privilege to attend a dinner where the guests included two distinguished former members of the Michigan legislature: Fred Dillingham, a Republican from Livingston County, and David Hollister, a Democrat from Lansing. The two openly acknowledge that they disagree on many issues of public policy. But they are also proud to be personal friends, and proud to have been able to listen to each other and work together. One of their finest accomplishments was hospice-care legislation.[8] Four members of the current legislature were also at the event—a Democrat and a Republican from the House, and a Democrat and a Republican from the Senate. But I won't write down their names. They made it clear that they did not want it known that they were attending. At a formal committee hearing, they are allowed to rub elbows with members of the other political party. But they said that if the legislative leadership knew that they were in this informal setting with members of the other party, they feared they would be stripped of privileges.

Fortunately, some members of the legislature are trying to break the stranglehold of partisanship in the legislature. The Freshman Bipartisan Caucus is to be commended for their efforts. Still, we have a long way to go. Too many members of today's legislature behave as if they are party members first and Michigan citizens second.

In my view, the partisan and ideological divisions in Michigan are fueled by a national trend toward ugly partisanship. We saw an example of this recently when a member of the U.S. House of Representatives loudly called the president of the United States a liar during the president's speech to a joint session of Congress. This kind of disrespectful behavior ought to have no place in our politics.

America has been suffering through a period of decreased civility in public life.[9] The increasing coarseness of our public discourse is pushed along by cable news programs where shouted insults seem to be prized over thoughtful debate. On May 1, 2010, President Obama addressed the graduating class of the University of Michigan in Ann Arbor. He called for a "basic level of civility in our public discourse."[10] Americans from all parties and ideologies would do well to heed his words. If we want to learn from the example of a Michigan leader who could be both strong and decent, we would do well to recall former Governor Bill Milliken, whose life and career are chronicled in Dave Dempsey's book *William G. Milliken: Michigan's Passionate Moderate.*[11]

Although I am hopeful that the pragmatic, moderate center of the Michigan political spectrum will be strengthened in the future, I do believe that some fairly extreme folks are currently feeling very energized. That's one of the reasons why I am not in favor of a constitutional convention at this time. The November 2010 ballot will ask Michigan voters whether they want a constitutional convention, and I will vote no. My fear is that, if a convention is called, too many of the delegates would be from the fringes of the political spectrum. One reason for my fear is that the delegates would be elected on the basis of today's legislative districts. These are the same grotesque and unrepresentative districts that I discussed a few paragraphs ago. As long as the legislative districts are gerrymandered, I will be against a constitutional convention. Moreover, in today's budget climate, I am not enthusiastic about spending tens of millions of dollars on a constitutional convention when there are so many other pressing needs.

Let's consider a unicameral legislature. Michigan is one of forty-nine states with a bicameral legislature (a legislature with two houses). Nebraska has a unicameral legislature, with only a single house. The historical roots of today's bicameral legislatures go back to Great Britain's Parliament, which has two houses, with membership in the two houses based on class. The idea was that the House of Lords would represent the aristocracy, while the House of Commons would represent more ordinary people. (These days, most important decisions are made by the House of Commons, although the House of Lords once had great strength.) The men who wrote the U.S. Constitution had formerly been British subjects, and so they were very familiar with the idea of a bicameral legislature. In fact, some of the founding fathers wanted to imitate the British system by having houses based on social and economic class.

Ultimately, the U.S. Constitution did continue with the idea of a bicameral legislature, although the U.S. Senate was designed to represent states, rather than the aristocracy. The bicameral U.S. Congress was the result of a crucial compromise between large states and small states.

Every state except for Nebraska has imitated the bicameral idea. This is a bit strange, since the reasons for a bicameral legislature mentioned in the preceding paragraph do not apply in the case of the states. Michigan certainly has no need for one house to represent the aristocracy, nor does it have a need for a bicameral legislature as an ingredient in a political compromise. It isn't at all clear that Nebraska has suffered from having a unicameral legislature. (In fact, Table 1.3 showed that per capita income in Nebraska was about 12 percent higher than per capita income in Michigan in 2008.)

I believe the time has come to have a serious discussion of whether Michigan should go to a unicameral legislature. As with so many of the ideas discussed in this book, the unicameral legislature is not a magical solution to our problems. However, it might streamline the workings of the legislature. As such, it is worthy of careful consideration.[12]

Reform the campaign finance laws. Even if we relax term limits and eliminate gerrymandering, effective policymaking in Michigan will still face an uphill battle because of our system of campaign finance. A few months ago, I received a phone call from a young man who wants to run for a seat in the legislature. He wanted to discuss economic policy with me, because he felt he had an inadequate knowledge of some of the economic issues facing Michigan. But his lack of knowledge was not the result of a lack of interest or a lack of intelligence; he is obviously a very smart fellow. The problem was that he had to spend every spare moment fundraising. By his own admission, if he wins, he will be in an awkward position when it comes time to say "no" to some of the folks who gave money for his campaign.

Like many other states and the federal government, Michigan has a system of campaign finance that is in serious need of reform. Honestly, it would be best if we had an effective system of public financing for campaigns, to limit the amount of special-interest money flowing into the system. But I don't see that happening any time soon. For now, the biggest need is for greater transparency. If the spigot of special-interest money is wide open, at least the public has a right to know where the money is coming from.

One of the real unsung heroes of Michigan is Rich Robinson, executive director of the Michigan Campaign Finance Network (MCFN). Robinson and his organization are engaged in an often-thankless effort to clean up the mess that is campaign financing in Michigan. The special interests that provide so much of the money for political campaigns don't want the public to know what's going on. And so it's very difficult to get any reforms through the legislature. (This is another place where it is hoped that the next governor will have the wisdom and courage to exert some leadership.)

Anyone who wants to know what is really going on in Michigan politics should visit the Web site of the MCFN at http://www.mcfn.org. The MCFN's *2008 Citizen's Guide to Michigan Campaign Finance* is available at http://www .mcfn.org/pdfs/reports/MCFNCitGuide08.pdf. The *Citizen's Guide* provides an excellent description of the problems in our broken system of campaign-finance laws, along with possible remedies. Here is a very brief synopsis of some of the most important problems and possible solutions:

- *Inadequate disclosure.* Under Michigan law, the sources of funds for a political advertisement do not have to be disclosed, unless the advertisement *explicitly* encourages voters to vote for or against a candidate. If an advertisement merely comments on a candidate's record, character, or qualifications, then the ad does not have to be disclosed in a campaign finance report, and the sources of funds do not have to be reported. The remedy to this is awfully simple. *All* advertising should be regulated. *All* spending should be reported. *All* contributors should be disclosed.
- *Infrequent reporting.* In a year that is not an election year, officeholders only have to file one campaign finance report for the entire year, despite the fact that they may be raising huge war chests of money. Political action committees file only three campaign finance reports each year, and there is a six-month gap between two of the reports each year. Because of the infrequent reports, it is difficult for voters to exercise enough oversight. I agree with the MCFN recommendation that all political committees should have to report at least quarterly.
- *Lack of contribution limits.* Under Michigan law, there is a limit on the amount a contributor can give *directly* to a candidate for office. However, contributions to political action committees or political parties are unlimited. It is easy for big contributors to state political campaigns to circumvent the candidate contribution limits by giving an unlimited amount to a political action committee or party committee, and having the political action committee or party spend an unlimited amount as an independent

expenditure. Once again, I agree with the MCFN recommendation: in order to limit the influence that can be exercised by any one contributor, Michigan should establish reasonable limits on contributions to political action committees and political party committees, as well as an aggregate individual contribution limit.

Within the last few sections, I have called for many reforms of our political system. I believe our government will work better if we relax term limits, eliminate gerrymandering, reduce poisonous partisanship, and reform our campaign finance laws. However, even if we do all of those things, our elected officials still need to *do their jobs*. Regardless of the institutional structure, individual people will need to step up. If you have seen the movie *The Wizard of Oz*, you know the three key characteristics that are needed (but often lacking) in our elected leaders—they need a heart, a brain, and courage. Two out of the three are not good enough; an effective leader needs all three. And of the three, I believe courage is the most important.

Will Michigan Have a Brighter Future?

There is plenty of reason for concern about the Michigan economy, which recently has not performed as well as the economy of the United States as a whole. However, there is also plenty of reason for hope. One reason for hope is that economic policy is getting a lot of attention in Michigan. If you are reading these words, you are interested in the Michigan economy. Even though the public still has a very incomplete understanding of the situation, I sense an increase in public awareness that the dogmas of the past are not working. Many fine people are working passionately to turn things around. Some groups that I think are really fighting the good fight are A Better Michigan Future,[13] The Center for Michigan,[14] the Citizens Research Council of Michigan,[15] Michigan Future Inc.,[16] and the Michigan League for Human Services.[17] Public policies in Michigan still have a long way to go, but an increasing number of Michigan's people are looking to the future in a smart and serious way.

I believe Michigan will have a better future, both economically and in other ways. The main purpose of this book has been to describe policies that will help. But a better future is not just about policies. It's also about the way we feel about ourselves. The last few decades have unquestionably been difficult for many of Michigan's people, and it is easy to become discouraged. Thus while we work on policies that will lay the foundation for a better future, we also need to keep our heads up. Different people use different methods to keep going during difficult times, and I want to mention a couple of these.

I have already quoted scripture once in this chapter, and I'll do it again. Around 55 AD, the apostle Paul wrote his second letter to the Corinthians. In the fourth chapter, he wrote, "We are hard pressed on every side, but not crushed; perplexed, but not in despair; persecuted, but not abandoned; struck down, but not destroyed."[18] Regardless of your religious faith, I hope you can see the relevance of these words for Michigan's people today. We *have* been hard pressed. But we have weathered tough times before. In fact, we have weathered much tougher times than these. The people of Michigan have come through the Civil War, the Great Depression, and the Second World War, and I have faith that we will come through this, too, stronger than ever.

Singing is another way to keep going through difficult times, and thus I have made it my mission to get Michigan to sing more. I grew up mainly in Texas, and in fourth grade, we learned the state song for the State of Texas: "Texas our Texas, all hail the mighty state! Texas our Texas, so wonderful, so great! Largest and grandest. . . ."[19] A few years ago, it dawned on me that I had no idea what the state song for the State of Michigan might be. I asked several friends, and they did not know, either. As it turns out, there is some controversy about our state song. My favorite is the unofficial 1902 version of "Michigan, My Michigan." There's even controversy about this particular song, because it can be sung to more than one tune. I prefer the tune that is most familiar, which is "O Christmas Tree." Here is the first verse of "Michigan, My Michigan:"

A song to thee, fair state of mine, Michigan, my Michigan,
But greater song than this is thine, Michigan, my Michigan:
The whisper of the forest tree, the thunder of the inland sea,
Unite in one grand symphony of Michigan, my Michigan.

I invite you to sing our state song every chance you get.

Some of the policy proposals in this book are probably familiar to many people who have followed the policy debate in Michigan. But I imagine that some of the proposals are new to many, and I recognize that it usually takes time for new ideas to gain wide acceptance. But I remain hopeful that even the newest ideas described here will flourish. After all, it was once considered radical to say that women or blacks should be allowed to vote, but now the idea of universal suffrage is no longer radical at all.

I began this chapter with words written by Abraham Lincoln during the Civil War. I end it with words written by the great British economist John Maynard Keynes during another severe crisis, the Great Depression. Keynes laid much of the foundation for modern macroeconomics in his 1935 book *The General Theory of Employment, Interest, and Money.* Toward the end of the book, Keynes wrote of his hope that his ideas would eventually have an influence on economic policy. My contribution here is small compared with that of Keynes, but I cannot refrain from recalling Keynes's words: "If the ideas are correct . . . it would be a mistake, I predict, to dispute their potency over a period of time . . . The ideas of economists and philosophers, both when they are right and when they are wrong, are more powerful than is commonly understood . . . I am sure that the power of vested interests is vastly exaggerated compared with the gradual encroachment of ideas."[20]

NOTES

1. Mark 12: 41–44 (New International Version).
2. For details, see the Institute for Public Policy and Social Research, "State of the State Survey," http://www.ippsr.msu.edu/SOSS/SOSSdata.htm. Questions on legislative term limits were asked in rounds thirty-three, thirty-five, forty-one, forty-seven, and fifty-two of this survey. In round fifty-two, survey respondents were asked about the actual length of the term limits that are currently in effect. Those who had a response were all over the map, and 32 percent answered that they did not know. Thus the public appears to have strong opinions about term limits, even though there is limited knowledge of the actual details of Michigan's term-limits laws.
3. The codebook, methodological report, and data set for this survey can be found at the website of the State of the State Survey, http://ippsr.msu.edu/SOSS/SOSSdata.htm.
4. The governor is also subject to term limits. The governor can serve only two four-year terms, for a total of eight years. My preference is that this be relaxed to three terms, for a total of twelve years. (John Engler served as governor for twelve years, from 1991 to 2003, because the voters elected him on three occasions. If the gubernatorial term limit were relaxed, it would once again be possible for a governor to serve as long as Engler served.)

5. District boundaries are redrawn every ten years. This is not a problem for the House of Representatives, since the House has two-year terms, and ten years is evenly divisible by two years. However, it is a problem for the Senate, since the Senate has four-year terms and ten is not evenly divisible by four. Fortunately, there is a solution to this technical problem. In each decade, each Senate district could have two four-year terms and one two-year term, adding up to a total of ten years. In order to stagger the elections in the Senate, half the districts would need to be on a two-four-four schedule, and the other half on a four-four-two schedule.

6. Elbridge Gerry was governor of Massachusetts in 1812, at the time of a redistricting scheme that favored the Republican Party over the Federalist Party. A cartoonist drew one of the oddly shaped legislative districts to look like a salamander. The phrase "Gerrymandering" was born from "Gerry" and "salamander." If you want to see the results of gerrymandering in action, take a look at the map of Michigan's Senate districts, at http://senate.michigan.gov/2003/senatedistricts.pdf. Senate district four in Detroit is a grotesque contribution to modern abstract art. The text description of district four runs to three pages! Senate district seventeen, which includes Monroe County but then snakes across parts of Washtenaw and Jackson Counties, will probably strike most people as amusing or horrifying or both.

7. Putting a nonpartisan panel in charge of the redistricting process is not the only way to deal with gerrymandering. A second possible reform involves a system of proportional representation. We are accustomed to the idea of a legislature in which every member has exactly one vote. However, it is perfectly possible to have a different system, under which different members of the legislature would have different numbers of votes. In each district, the two candidates with the most votes in the general election would both win a seat in the legislature. For example, consider a district where the Republican candidate receives 53 percent of the vote and the Democratic candidate receives 47 percent. Each of the candidates would go to the legislature. The Republican would be able to cast 0.53 votes in the legislature, and the Democrat would be able to cast 0.47 votes. Under our current system, elections to the legislature are "winner-take-all." When the winner takes all, the drawing of district boundaries can make a huge difference. Under the proposed system of proportional representation, however, the district boundaries would not be nearly as important. At this time, my judgment is that an independent, nonpartisan panel is more likely to occur, although proportional representation is definitely worth thinking about.

8. Dillingham and Hollister said that they worked on the hospice-care legislation for eight years. Clearly this was in the days before term limits. Today if a member of the legislature believes it might take that long to get a bill passed, there is little incentive even to try.

9. I had an interesting encounter with the coarseness of public discourse in October 2009, when I received an e-mail message from a Lansing man. It appears that the writer did not agree with a study I had done earlier in that year about the retrenchment of the state government workforce in Michigan. He wrote, in part, "You are certainly lucky 'economists' have no ethical standards to abide by, or you would be heading to prison for this WORTH-LESS study!!! Out of curiosity, how do you manage to sleep at night? . . . By the way, your graduate student will fail in life if this is the quality of education you are bestowing upon GRADUATE students!!! However, it does make me appreciate I couldn't afford MSU and be fed GARBAGE data!!!! Thanks again." (For the record, I think he may not have been completely genuine when he said "Thanks again.")

10. For coverage of the President's speech, see Helene Cooper, "At a Graduation, Obama Urges Openness and Defends Government," *New York Times*, May 1, 2010, http://www.nytimes.com/2010/05/02/us/politics/02obama.html.

11. Dave Dempsey, *William G. Milliken: Michigan's Passionate Moderate* (Ann Arbor: University of Michigan Press, 2006).

12. If Michigan were to adopt a unicameral legislature, some of the issues discussed in the section on term limits would go away.

13. For more information about A Better Michigan Future, see http://www.abettermichiganfuture.org.

14. For more information about the Center for Michigan, see http://www.thecenterformichigan.net.

15. For more information about the Citizens Research Council, see http://www.crcmich.org.

16. For more information about Michigan Future Inc., see http://www.michiganfuture.org.

17. For more information about the Michigan League for Human Services, see http://www.milhs.org.

18. 2 Corinthians 4: 8–9 (New International Version).

19. I learned "Texas Our Texas" in the early 1960s. By that time, Alaska had been admitted to the Union, and so Texas was not in fact the largest state. Thus it seemed strange to me that the state song would include the word "largest." This must have bothered some other folks, too. As I understand it, "largest" was eventually changed to "boldest." In any event, the bombastic words of the song make clear that Texans are a proud bunch. I want the people of Michigan to be just as proud.

20. John Maynard Keynes, *The General Theory of Employment, Interest, and Money* (New York: Harcourt, Brace, & World, 1964), 383–84.

Index

Note: The italicized *f* and *t* following page numbers refer to figures and tables respectively.

M

mail-order sales, tax evasion on, 185–86

manufacturing, 3, 3t; decline, 4–7, 5f, 228–29; and politics, 6; transitions, 9–10

Martin, Lawrence, 193

Medicaid, 154

medical care, state funding, 231

men and college attainment, 71–73, 72f

Menchik, Paul, 28, 51

Mexico trade, 133

Michigan at the Millennium (Ballard, et al.), xiii, 48, 49, 50, 52, 104, 108, 110, 111, 114, 115, 143n4, 151, 154, 158,168n1, 180, 193, 214–15n1

Michigan Business Tax (MBT), 205–6, 207–8, 233; repeal, 240

Michigan Campaign Finance Network (MCFN), 246–47

Michigan Chamber of Commerce, 107

Michigan Department of Community Health, 147

Michigan Department of Corrections, 162-63

Michigan Department of Environmental Quality, 116

Michigan Department of Transportation, 105

Michigan Department of Treasury, 186

Michigan Environmental Protection Act, 114

Michigan Future Inc., 248

Michigan Land Use Leadership Council, 111

Michigan League for Human Services (MLHS), 196, 248

Michigan Public Employees Retirement System (MPSERS), 83

Michigan's Economic Future: Challenges and Opportunities (Ballard), xiii

"Michigan's Land, Michigan's Future," 111

Michigan State University, xiii, xx, 11, 13, 68, 69, 70, 85, 86

Michigan State University Press, 136

Michigan Technological University, xvi

Milliken, Bill, 6, 181, 245

minimum wage, 155–56, 167

mining, 3t, 4

minorities: labor force, 50–51; population in Detroit, 48f

modified gross receipts tax, 205–6

motor fuels tax, 107, 190–91, 213, 234

N

National Assessment of Educational Progress (NAEP), 56, 57t

National Bureau of Economic Research, xxiiin2

National Superconducting Cyclotron Laboratory, 11

net capital stock tax, 206

Northern Michigan University, xvi, 68

O

Oakland County, 35

Oakland University, xvi

Obama, Barack, 11, 30–31, 49, 91, 154, 245

obesity rates, 169n9

Olds, R. E., xiv

open space, xxii, 111–12, 120, 235

P

Papke, Leslie, 79, 202–3

parks, 112

partisan politics, 244–45

About the Author

C harles Ballard's Michigan roots go back to the nineteenth century, when his ancestors moved to the southeastern Lower Peninsula. His grandparents grew up in Ypsilanti and Detroit, and his mother was raised in Detroit. His parents were married in Detroit in 1950. His father, a chemist, worked for Ford Motor Company and then for Dow Chemical Company. Ballard attended kindergarten in the public schools in Midland, Michigan (where Dow's home offices are located) and spent most of his childhood on the Texas Gulf Coast, where his father worked at Dow's facilities in Freeport, Texas.

Professor Ballard has been a part of the Economics faculty at Michigan State University since 1983, when he received his PhD from Stanford University. In 2007, he became the director of the State of the State Survey for MSU's Institute for Public Policy and Social Research. Also in 2007, he won the Outstanding Teacher Award in MSU's College of Social Science. He has served as a consultant with the U.S. Departments of Agriculture, Health and Human Services, and Treasury, and with research institutes in Australia, Denmark, and Finland.

Ballard was one of the editors of *Michigan at the Millennium*, published in 2003 by the Michigan State University Press. In 2006, he wrote *Michigan's Economic Future: Challenges and Opportunities*, which was also published by the MSU Press.

In addition to his research on the Michigan economy, Ballard has written extensively on education policy, tax policy, and government budgeting. His research papers have appeared in the *American Economic Review*, the *Journal of Public Economics*, the *National Tax Journal*, *International Tax and Public Finance*, the *Journal of Asian Economics*, the *Journal of Economic Education*, *Feminist Economics*, and many other publications.

Since the publication of *Michigan's Economic Future: Challenges and Opportunities*, Professor Ballard has given more than 160 speeches and presentations regarding the Michigan economy, and he has given nearly 1,000 interviews with newspapers, radio, television, and online media. Most of these interviews have been with Michigan media outlets, although Ballard has also been on national and international news programs, including *The News Hour with Jim Lehrer*, BBC Radio, RTE Irish Television, and La Sette Italian Television. Professor Ballard's print interviews include *The Economist*, the *Los Angeles Times*, the *New York Times*, the *Toronto National Post*, the *Wall Street Journal*, the *Washington Post*, and the *Yomiuri Shimbun* (Japan's largest newspaper).